Early Modern Constructions of Europe

Between the medieval conception of Christendom and the political visions of modernity, ideas of Europe underwent a transformative and catalytic period that saw a cultural process of renewed self-definition or self-Europeanization. The contributors to this volume address this process, analysing how Europe was imagined between 1450 and 1750. By whom, in which contexts, and for what purposes was Europe made into a subject of discourse? Which forms did early modern 'Europes' take, and what functions did they serve? This book examines the role of factors such as religion, history, space and geography, ethnicity and alterity, patronage and dynasty, migration and education, language, translation, and narration for the ways in which Europe turned into an 'imagined community.' The thematic range of the volume comprises early modern texts in Arabic, English, French, German, Greek, Italian, Latin, and Spanish, including plays, poems, and narrative fiction, as well as cartography, historiography, iconography, travelogues, periodicals, and political polemics. Literary negotiations in particular foreground the creative potential, versatility, and agency that inhere in the process of Europeanization, as well as a specifically early modern attitude toward the past and tradition emblematized in the poetics of the period. There is a clear continuity between the collection's approach to European identities and the focus of cultural and postcolonial studies on the constructed nature of collective identities at large: the chapters build on the insights produced by these fields over the past decades and apply them, from various angles, to a subject that has so far largely eluded critical attention. This volume examines what existing and well-established work on identity and alterity, hybridity, and margins has to contribute to an understanding of the largely unexamined and undertheorized 'preformative' period of European identity.

Florian Kläger is Assistant Professor of British Studies at the University of Münster, Germany.

Gerd Bayer is Reader in the English Department at Erlangen University, Germany.

Routledge Studies in Renaissance Literature and Culture

Early Modern Constructions of Europe

Literature, Culture, History

Edited by Florian Kläger
and Gerd Bayer

 Routledge
Taylor & Francis Group

LONDON AND NEW YORK

First published 2016
by Routledge

2 Park Square, Milton Park, Abingdon, Oxfordshire OX14 4RN
52 Vanderbilt Avenue, New York, NY 10017

Routledge is an imprint of the Taylor & Francis Group, an informa business

First issued in paperback 2018

Library of Congress Cataloging-in-Publication Data

Names: Kläger, Florian, editor. | Bayer, Gerd, editor.
Title: Early modern constructions of Europe: literature, culture, history /
edited by Florian Kläger and Gerd Bayer.
Description: New York, NY; Milton Park, Abingdon, Oxon: Routledge,
2016. | Series: Routledge studies in Renaissance literature and culture |
Includes bibliographical references and index.
Identifiers: LCCN 2015041379
Subjects: LCSH: Renaissance. | Europe—Civilization. | European
literature—History and criticism.
Classification: LCC CB361 .E17 2016 | DDC 940.2/1—dc23
LC record available at http://lccn.loc.gov/2015041379

ISBN: 978-1-138-93159-6 (hbk)
ISBN: 978-0-367-17574-0 (pbk)

Typeset in Sabon
by codeMantra

Contents

PART III
Values

List of Figures

Introduction
Early Modern Constructions of Europe

Florian Kläger and Gerd Bayer

Over a decade ago, J. G. A. Pocock cautioned against the tendency in cultural history of viewing everything as 'invented' or 'constructed' (2002). He did so with particular reference to the idea of Europe, admitting that the cultures and histories that make up the complex we blissfully call Europe today were indeed constructed at some point, but stressing that in the specific contexts in which these inventions and constructions occurred, "the process of construction becomes a kind of reality and cannot just be reduced to a limited number of constructions and inventions waiting for us to come and deconstruct them" (56). It is very much in this spirit that this volume approaches what we call 'early modern constructions of Europe' in literature and culture: we ask for their specific historical forms and functions because these are no less relevant than nonconstructed versions of Europe (if those in fact exist). Peter Burke's famous question, "Did Europe exist before 1700?" (Burke 1980), provides the point of departure for this volume. To posit that Europe was 'constructed' in the early modern period is neither to claim that it did not exist before nor to maintain that it sprang, Athena-like, ready-made from the heads of early modern inventors. Instead, what informs the chapters collected here is the fundamental observation that there are genuinely 'early modern' ideas of Europe to be encountered in the period of c. 1500–1700 that, on the one hand, differ significantly from earlier conceptions (out of which they may nonetheless have developed), and that, on the other hand, are recognisably *early* modern and thus differ in important ways from present-day ideas of Europe. Like antiquity and the Middle Ages, the early modern period invented its own versions of Europe, and to study these versions is to trace the discursive roots of present-day Europe as much as those precursors that were abandoned along the way.

In a sense, it goes without saying that Europe, or particular versions of Europe, were invented in early modernity: clearly, there is no one perennial Europe but a multiplicity of historical versions of it. Hence, there was always a time 'before' any given version. As with other discursive formations, then, it makes sense to ask for the particular demands that prompted the development of new ideas of Europe, and to inquire into the genesis or transformations of these demands as compared to earlier periods. The various historical forms that Europe has assumed can tell us something about the communities that produced them, and about the particular historical entity that Europe is today. Further, it can highlight what it has meant and can mean for Europe to 'be' anything at all. When, we may ask, and under what precise circumstances did ideas of Europe enter into discourse at all? What characterizes the discourse on Europe? What are the distinguishing marks that create the early modern discourse in the first place, marking it off from earlier and later discourses on Europe? It is questions such as these, in brief, that this collection intends to open up for discussion. It does so through a number of case studies from a range of disciplines, showing how Europe features (often by another, or no name at all) in a number of early modern signifying practices all marked, to a greater or lesser degree, by their representational character. In an Aristotelian or, perhaps, neo-Aristotelian sense not entirely alien to the period in question, one might suggest that versions of Europe emerge from mimetic acts that represent not what is, but what could be, contrasting 'brazen' reality with the 'golden' potential of Europe (Sidney 1965, 100). That such utopian views of Europe *by Europeans* were by no means self-evident is illustrated especially in their juxtaposition with perspectives from 'outside,' some of which are also discussed in the following. What is more, a number of contributions also explore where Europe is *not* to be encountered in early modernity, in spite of the modern observer's expectations.

* * *

In one sense, Europe was invented in antiquity: the myth of Europa tells of the daughter of a Phoenician king (or merchant), abducted by Zeus (or Greek traders) to the West that was to bear her name (see Hay 1968, 1). In the Christian tradition, the three continents of Europe, Asia, and Africa were identified with the descendants of Noah's sons Japheth, Sem, and Ham, providing a biblical rationale for the ideology of European superiority based on Gen. 9:27, which proclaims that "God shall enlarge Japheth, and he shall dwell in the tents of Shem; and Canaan [Ham] shall be his servant." The High Middle Ages saw a formative phase in the 'Europeanization of Europe' during which there was "a dramatic change in what was shared and how widely" throughout the continent, as Robert Bartlett argued so compellingly in *The Making of Europe* (1993, 269). The humanists' politicocultural idea of a shared origin in Greco-Roman civilization and Christian religion that united European peoples across national and regional divides was powerfully articulated in the fifteenth century. They also introduced an emphasis on freedom as a distinctly European value, looking back to the antagonism between Athens and Persian despotism that would be so frequently reiterated in early modern descriptions of the Turks. Around the beginning of the period in question here, then, 'Europe' had already acquired a number of discursive meanings that rendered it more than a merely geographical term.

There are also good reasons for arguing that Europe had become fully 'invented' at the end of the period covered by this volume: hence, many historians claim that the modern idea of Europe can be found fully fledged in the eighteenth century's revolutions in thought and politics (cf. Delanty 2013, 147–168). It is the period of transformation between the Middle Ages and modernity that the present work undertakes to study, as ideas of Europe and Europeanness developed on the threshold of modernity out of a number of older discourses and towards a more recognizably contemporary version of Europe. It might not be wrong to suggest that between 1500 and 1700 no coherent idea of Europe existed, and this might be truer of this period than of others. To put it in a grossly but perhaps usefully reductive way: in the Middle Ages, 'Europe' was rather unproblematically identified with the *communitas Christiana*; and since the Enlightenment, 'Europe' has come to stand for a number of political ideals and narratives that were simply assumed to constitute fundamental forces of history, notwithstanding the troubled legacy of the Enlightenment in recent criticism (see Chakrabarty 2008). From today's perspective, the period between these received, if not 'easy,' identifications is a fascinating topic for historical study for a number of reasons. Among the discourses that fed into early modern conceptions of Europe are many that are still recognizable in the early twenty-first century, and a number of older ones that over time have disappeared or declined in importance. Factors that were germane to this period include the external threat by the Ottoman empire, which created a sense of unity; the perceived difference between the 'Old' world and the newly discovered Americas, which sharpened a sense of what is familiar; humanist ideas of a shared faith and canon of literature, which merged in the idea of a *res publica literaria*; and dynastic and religious strife on the continent, which contributed to the desire for peace and balance among the growing, and increasingly literate, populations in Europe.[1]

The diversity of these discursive formations brings with it various risks when studying the historical traces of what would eventually congeal into a rather stable notion of Europe. The topic of this volume accordingly foregrounds a fundamental problem for the cultural historian, a problem relating to the question of how we know what to look for as we sift the archives: what *was* early modern Europe, and what do we hope to find as we study it? The first choice scholars who study these aspects need to make is to decide whether they take a nominalist or a realist stance towards 'Europe.' Nominalism would suggest that no essential, universal, or ideal Europe existed behind the abstract term, which requires us to examine the sundry meanings that were ascribed to it in various historical contexts. Realism would assume that there was, indeed, some universal *je-ne-sais-quoi* behind the term 'Europe,' and that it is possible to study this concept even where the word does not occur in the historical sources. Both strategies offer certain advantages; both bring with them particular risks and pitfalls.

As far as practical solutions for critical studies are concerned, this twofold conceptual approach translates either into looking for the uses of the term 'Europe' in various textual sources and determining what meanings and connotations they attach to it; or into trying to find out whether early modern authors were thinking about some universal Europe without necessarily using the actual term itself. In that latter sense, one would assume that "[t]he inhabitants of the European continent *thought* and *acted* as Europeans long before they *spoke* of themselves as Europeans" (Bohrer 2012, 587). Following the first approach, one might consider the case of Charlemagne's stylization as *rex*, *pater*, and *apex Europae* by contemporary encomiasts (see Quast [forthcoming]). These authors of the eighth and ninth centuries already used the European frame of reference because it was politically less problematic than other terms, such as *imperium Romanorum* or *regnum Francorum*, and because it helped integrate those writing from the margins into a wider whole that transcended classical precedents (Schneidmüller 1997, 9). Thus, the term 'Europe' was used precisely by virtue of its neutrality. The same effect can still be observed in the seventeenth century, when in tracts such as *Europe a Slave unless England break her Chains* (1677), English Protestant pamphleteers were urging an attack on the Catholic French. Since "the French king was officially styled 'the most Christian King' and the Catholic Church in its official utterances still spoke in the name of *respublica christiana*," 'Europe' offered a less value-laden frame of reference than 'Christendom' (Schmidt 1966, 173). In both instances, 'Europe' is a signifier that is used precisely by virtue of its emptiness, and where it is offered as an alternative to religious, geographical, national, partisan, or other conceptions, usage of the term speaks eloquently about the dynamics of these collective identities in the respective contexts.

Pursuing the 'realist' approach, the question arises of how to tell when early modern authors were talking about Europe in the first place. Surely, we can only find, recognize, and study in the past what we look for and know in the present. Following this path, modern historians would be looking for their own conceptions of Europe in historical texts and would have to ask: what sense of 'Europe' is employed here, and what makes a statement 'about Europe' meaningful to the modern observer? Early modern constructions of Europe are constructions of Europe in this sense if they stand in a relationship to our present concept of Europe that illuminates it in a productive manner. As all history is present history, we look for roots of 'our' Europe, and we are interested in finding out about its genealogy in the sense that we trace its crucial constituents back until we arrive at their putative sources. We consider, as it were, the building blocks of each construction (cf. Molho 2007, 8). The universal Europe we look for behind the name is the Europe we now know—whatever that means: the student of past Europeans must hence rationalize what constitutes their contemporary Europe, a difficult enough task. Consulting, for lack of a better source, the Lisbon Treaty on European Union, we find emphasis in its preamble on "the cultural, religious and humanist inheritance of Europe" as well as on its explicitly political, geographical, legal, and social dimensions (Treaty of Lisbon, 2007, 10–11). With its explicit reference to an inheritance from the past, this contemporary construction expresses a shared sense of entitlement as well as obligation that characterizes the Europe of today. This unspecific, cultural aspect is nonetheless frequently translated into concrete political consequences. For instance, the present-day rhetoric against admitting Turkey to the European Union will usually appeal to the Christian heritage of Europe. Reiteration of such claims for an essential 'Europeanness'—irrespective of their truth—can create discursive 'facts.' This process of historical construction, which has found its way into the Treaty, is the subject of this book.

Historians have specified what the *je-ne-sais-quoi* of Europe behind the name may have been in the early modern period. Among the best-discussed candidates are: a foggy geographical notion; the *communitas Christiana* that finds its identity in the antagonism with the Ottoman empire but is continually embarrassed by the alterity of the Greek and Russian orthodoxies, let alone the Muslim and Jewish "others" of Europe; and the shared inheritance of Greek and Roman antiquity, sometimes supplied with the element of Germanic folk culture. More specifically, Heinz Duchhardt has identified eight "common denominators" that constituted early modern Europe as a "community of values and experiences" of greater coherence than Asia and Africa. Some of these square with the features of Europe set down in the Lisbon Treaty's contemporary definition, such as the normative character of law on the basis of a fusion of Roman law and Christian natural law, offering a body of shared conceptions of what was right. Between the legal and political domains sits the development of a body of self-evident rights of the individual that first reached a culmination point in the French Revolution's declaration of human rights. They converge in the relatively strong development in Europe of the idea of political participation of subjects and the importance of reaching political consensus. Next to these dimensions, Duchhardt also identifies features of a more widely conceived cultural sense: the cohesive effects of various *linguae francae*; Christianity and its moral and religious norms; the tight social network created by marital unions between the continent's various noble houses; the distinctive feeling of superiority with which Europeans encountered other cultures and states; and finally the extreme degree of internal competition concerning space and resources, as well as the question after the right path in terms of faith, government, and trade. This competition, according to Duchhardt, generated a specifically 'European' emphasis on knowledge and communication (1997).

We do not have to agree with Duchhardt's claims for European exceptionality in each particular, but from this "bundle of factors" (1997, 195), as he calls it, we do believe that a rather distinctive Wittgensteinian family resemblance emerges that—and this is crucial—describes some of the historical aspects of the Treaty's Europe even into the twenty-first century. It characterizes one contemporary consensus (there are others, of course) on what we look for when we look for the roots of contemporary Europe. Hence, we might study the diachronic or synchronic expressions of any of these ideas and thus contribute to a genealogy of the idea of Europe that transcends a nominalist approach that focuses solely on uses of the name 'Europe.' However, to do so would run the risks not only of contributing to a teleological master narrative of European identity, but also of perpetuating blind spots. We risk overlooking concepts or ideas that were attached to 'Europeanness' in early modernity if they are not covered by this matrix, simply because we have set our sights too closely on the well-known features of contemporary Europe. As Jeroen Duindam has suggested, early modern conceptions of Europe would be more centrally concerned with "patterns of representation, ritual, redistribution, patronage, brokerage, and elites" than with the more recent and "self-referential" categories "such as democracy, civil society, public sphere, rule of law, impersonal bureaucracy" (2010, 609). Hence, we operate from foregone conclusions if we only examine those roots of Europe that still attach to the trunk today; and we risk overlooking those strands that may have been severed and the reasons for this process of severing. It is in this context that historians have contemplated whether the very concept of 'early modernity' in the received sense even means anything at all outside of the European context (see Delanty 2013, 160–168).

If, on the other hand, critics are interested in seemingly abandoned, discarded, or withered meanings of Europe, they might focus not on the forms of Europe (either in name or in features) but on the function of such constructions; asking not what Europe was at any particular point in time, but what its purpose was. In a nutshell, this is to ask the classic hermeneutical question at the basis of conceptual history: if Europe was the answer, what was the question? Clearly, in the case of Charlemagne's stylization as "*pater Europae*," 'Europe' here answered a very pressing and highly specific demand, *viz.* how to define a present balance of power in such a way as to shift it in one's favour. Ultimately, Europe was invoked in this context as a rhetorical figure that bestowed symbolic capital on Charlemagne, thus benefiting both the receiver and the inventors. This is a function in which the idea of Europe is 'exported' from one group to another in an appeal to convince the recipients of their shared membership in a collective with the givers. In a word, it serves an integrative function by positing a collective that transcends the nation but is not as all-comprehensive as 'humankind.' However, within these tiers of collective identities, the term could also be employed with a self-reflexive bent towards a single collective.

The standard account of this function tells us that Europe has long been the contrast foil against which emerging conceptions of national identity could be negotiated. Since the crucial difference between medieval *nationes* and the modern nation was the requirement that, in the modern nation, all nationals actually perceived themselves as such (Ehlers 1999, 1036), it became essential that alternative options for collective identification be negotiated vis-à-vis each other. While the strong reliance on distinctions between Europe, Asia, and Africa has remained a dominant force in how these cultural spheres have defined themselves in opposition to one another, points of contact and cross-pollination have only relatively recently captured sustained scholarly attention. For instance, the manner in which Hellenistic culture has been taken as an essential mainstay in determining the uniquely European approach to culture and civilization points to a desire, on the side of its self-declared heirs, to remove from this narrative the contributions that classical Greece had graciously accepted from their neighbours in Africa and Asia. The removal of such an un-European episode in the early stages of forming a continent, to follow Martin Bernal in *Black Athena*, only occurred at a much later point, when proto-nationalist Romantics abhorred the idea that the European purity of ancient Greece was "the result of the mixture of native Europeans and colonizing Africans and Semites" (1991, 2). This late eighteenth-century development reveals how the idea of Europe, in at least one significant respect, follows trajectories similar to those that have been described for the formation of national identities.

Drawing on Ernest Renan's famous late nineteenth-century essay, Ernest Gellner has emphasized that "[m]ost persisting groups are based on a mixture of loyalty and identification (on *willed* adherence), and of extraneous incentives, positive or negative, on hopes and fears" (1983, 53). Even though his main aim here is to define the rise of nationalism, his definition also provides insight into how a supranational form of identification, as found in the case of Europe, relies on a more or less conscious autopoetic will: the kind of "social and textual affiliation" (Bhabha 1990, 292) that frequently convinces people of the actual reality of a particular phenomenon such as the nation or a continental collective. What E. J. Hobsbawm has set out as the temporal logic of nations—"Nations do not make states and nationalisms but the other way round" (1990, 10)—thus also translates to the formative stage of a European identity. Clearly, ideas of Europe form an extreme case of what Benedict Anderson (2003) has famously described as "imagined communities," and like Anderson's nationalisms, they rely on discursive practices, on particular narratives that provide the kind of 'evidence' on which such a belief system depends. It would be naïve, of course, to assume that throughout early modernity this narrative was never challenged or did not experience changes and developments. Rather, what marks the history of any idea of Europe are the opposing narrative strategies that Homi Bhabha, in writing about the tension within national narratives, has defined as pedagogical and performative, as the two attitudes towards cultural groups that, respectively, either emphasize their unchanging continuity or instead acknowledge the range of differences within them. What Bhabha celebrates as the "pluralism of the national sign" (1990, 305) also affects the way Europe has been represented, and these representations can now be used to reconstruct the meaning of that sign—witness the prolixity of the term in the eighth and seventeenth centuries discussed above. In the same way that the institution of literature has been shown to be closely related to the formation of nationalism (see During 1990), literary and visual texts can also provide answers to questions about the formation of a European sense of identity.

Clearly, analyses of this kind are most immediately relevant in the history of regions whose membership in Europe has been debatable. We can observe it very much in effect even today, as Euro-scepticism generates reflections about national specificities and the relative importance of collective identities. Consider the case of Britain: given its perpetually close involvement with the continent on the one hand, and its insular position on the other, the history of relations between the two provides a particularly fruitful instance of cultural exchange. In the early modern period, with the development of English national consciousness and the waning of influence on the continent, that relationship became increasingly problematic. Concerning the geographical scope of Europe, John Speed's survey of Europe, published in 1631 and reprinted several times, is quite clear: Britain is not part of Europe but sits on its margins, ruling the seas if not much else. Speed rehearses Strabo's classical description according to which Europe comprises, from West to East:

1   *Spain*
2   *France*
3   *Belgia*
4   *Germany*
5   *Italie*
6   *Denmarke*
7   *Hungarie*
8   *Polonie*
9   *Slavonia*
10   *Greece*
11   *Dacia*
12   *Norwegia*
13   *Suevia*
14   *Muscouia*

(Speed 1631, 7)

Other historiographers emphasized other differences. For instance, in Holinshed's *Chronicles* we find agreement with the popular climate theory that has led to constitutional differences between Britain and the continent:

Howbeit, as those which are bred in sundrie places of the maine, doo come behind vs in constitution of bodie, so I grant, that in pregnancie of wit, nimblenesse of limmes, and politike inuentions, they generallie exceed vs: notwithstanding that otherwise these gifts of theirs doo often degenerate into méere subtiltie, instabilitie, vnfaithfulnesse, & crueltie.
(Holinshed 1587, 1:114)

British identity is constructed, at least in part, through reference to a 'continental' (i.e., geographical) other without mentioning the term 'Europe.'

Alterity is constructed on the basis of geography, but that geography is also, and in a genuinely early modern way, entwined with anthropology and morality to produce national stereotypes. In this way, the early modern genesis and negotiation of ideas of Europe are connected to ideas of nationhood, in the positive and negative sense: Europe can serve as the contrast foil against which the nation is defined but also as the reference frame within which the nation becomes 'thinkable' in the first place.

Whether nominalist or realist approaches to the study of early modern constructions of Europe will yield more fruitful results is moot; both approaches must supplement each other, and they do so in the chapters that follow. A nexus between the two is to be found in a dimension on which literary scholars are particularly qualified to comment: in the formal shape that negotiations of Europe take. As one widely held view has it, Europe was frequently invoked from the Middle Ages until 1800 and beyond as a means of distinguishing between 'us' and 'them'. Gerard Delanty has rightly observed that Europe's external 'others' have been far too variable, its internal rivalries too numerous, and Europe at large far too intimately tied into cosmopolitan networks for this model to hold exclusive explanatory power (2013). Although alterity is thus perhaps less central than it has sometimes been taken to be, its opposite, 'the European self,' has certainly always been an issue. It is in this self-reflexive sense that historians have considered not "the *content* of European traditions but their *form*" (Delanty 2003, 485).

Paul Ricoeur has described the self-criticism of cultural identities as the "unique" feature and the "only specificity of Europe." He claimed that "the kind of universality that Europe represents contains within itself a plurality of cultures, which have been merged and intertwined, and which provide a certain fragility, and ability to disclaim and question itself" (in Kearney 1992, 117, 119). Similarly, Anthony Pagden has observed that the "sense that it might be possible to belong to something larger than the family, the tribe, the community or the nation yet smaller and more culturally specific than 'humanity'" may indeed be a distinctly European conception (2002, 53). Rémi Brague agrees and puts it in even stronger terms: a European, for him, "is one who is conscious of belonging to a whole" that is distinct from the entirety of the human species (2009, 5). That whole extends not only in space but also in time, and to be European means, for Brague, to place oneself consciously and willingly in a tradition through a process of what he calls "inverse adoption":

> Those who came later chose their ancestors for themselves. The European heritage is the object of a vast usurpation of a legacy. The Europeans are the heirs of antiquity in nothing. At the very least, they are not, if it is necessary as in most cases to understand by "heir" someone who has not only taken "the trouble to be born," and who has received from the cradle all material and cultural goods, which his parents have left him. They are heirs, on the other hand, if one

conceives of the fact of being an heir as nothing more than an activity of appropriation. (2009, 131)

As self-appointed heir to a shifting array of historical cultures, Europe is marked by the *awareness* of its own cultural secondarity. There is nothing specifically European except the interpretative appropriation of something other, which Brague calls "Europeanization":

> Europe, I say, is nothing other than a constant movement of self-Europeanization. Europeanization is a movement internal to Europe; and moreover, it is the movement that constitutes Europe as such. Europe does not pre-exist Europeanization; Europe is the result of Europeanization, and not its cause. (2009, 147)

As Gerard Delanty sees it (2003, 486), this focus on form rather than content helps Brague avoid essentialist claims. Identity is replaced by identification, specifically: by identification that is based on a fundamental awareness of its own procedural and secondary nature, which integrates a self-reflexive distance from both self and other.

What this focus on forms and their functions foregrounds is the place of literature and culture in the process of constructing Europe. As Peter Burke argued not long ago, Europe could be seen as a Bakhtinian chronotope, "a space-time package" insofar as "any attempt to divide Europe into cultural areas needs to be situated in time." Burke explains that, for instance, "an early modern historian might usefully ask whether there were more or fewer Europes in 1750 than there had been in 1450" (Burke 2006, 236). Burke's highly apt simile suggests the close connection between chronotopes and literature—Bakhtin developed the concept of the chronotope as he was discussing the novel, and indeed, he deems chronotopes "the organizing centers for the fundamental narrative events of the novel." A novel's chronotope is its space–time continuum, that is, its coherent world:

> In the literary chronotope, spatial and temporal indicators are fused into one carefully thought-out, concrete whole. Time, as it were, thickens, takes on flesh, becomes artistically visible; likewise, space becomes charged and responsive to the movements of time, plot and history. This intersection of axes and fusion of indicators characterizes the artistic chronotope. (1937/1981, 84–85)

If Burke's suggestion is taken seriously, a programme for scholarly research opens up that examines the chronotopes of Europe in specific discourses. To do so is to study how chronotopes, as the product of mimetic practices, create 'European' meanings, to in turn create 'Europes' that function as referents and sources of signification. Since the chronotope's function is to 'fuse' time and space, it can be seen as the active attempt to create a meaningful and coherent whole from powerful forces that, outside of literary and other forms of representations, are beyond any individual's control.[2] This predicament, of course, very closely matches the utopian project of forging a European identity. In other words, the analysis of the chronotopes of Europe offers a window on processes of sense-making that resist contingency to imagine meaningful wholes, but it also highlights the very contingency of any such effort.

* * *

Shakespeare provides a convenient starting point for rehearsing a fusion of the 'nominalist' and the 'realist' approaches. In his plays, he uses the term 'Europe' 10 times. Nine of these references are comparative and function as mere hyperbole to describe the relative values of things and people. For example, in the first part of *King Henry IV* Falstaff speaks of "the dearest chandler in Europe," when he might have said 'the most expensive chandler anywhere' (Shakespeare 1998, *H4.1*, 3.3); and imprisoned Paulina in *The Winter's Tale* mourns that "No court in Europe is too good" for her (*WT*, 2.2). In these and the other canonical instances of geographical hyperbole, the term 'Europe' substitutes the expression 'all the world,' but with a small and important qualification: Europe is the frame of reference that is understood to instil all these comparisons with meaning. The Duke of Orleans's horse in *Henry V* is not really "the best horse of Europe" (*H5*, 3.7); rather, it is the best in all the known, and hence relevant, world. Europe *is* the world here, for all practical purposes. It is the chronotope that shapes the narrative's meaning, as Bakhtin puts it (1937/1981, 250). This recalls the familiar poststructuralist point that a text's omissions can be more eloquent than its preoccupations: the idea that the rest of the world does not even matter for the evaluation processes at hand here bespeaks a sense of European myopia and arrogance. However, it also attests to the characteristically early modern awareness that one's own frame of reference is, indeed, limited to a familiar environment that is, in turn, surrounded by *terrae incognitae* that potentially hold such riches that they might dwarf all 'domestic' frames of evaluative reference. This awareness is latent in the one Shakespearean usage of the term that breaks the pattern of geographical hyperbole, and it is telling that it occurs in a play that is set outside of Europe or at least on its fringe. In *The Tempest*, Sebastian laments that Alonso, the king of Naples, married his daughter Claribel to the king of Tunis and "would not bless our Europe with your daughter, / But rather lose her to an African" (*T*, 2.1). As soon as an external frame of reference is introduced, European scales of evaluation are disturbed. That Shakespeare should put this speech into the mouth of Sebastian suggests that he is aware of the (racialist) narrowmindedness that characterizes Eurocentric thought. The chronotope of Europe that is created in the Shakespearean canon, then, is that of a self-contained historical and geographical entity that is highly self-referential, preoccupied with relative evaluation, and wilfully blind to its surroundings.

Near the end of the period covered by this volume, Jonathan Swift has his hapless traveller beyond the confines of the old world regularly use Europe as a frame of reference. In his conversations with foreign princes, but also with the reader, Gulliver frequently speaks of Europe and Europeans. His very first reference suggests an awareness of the same wilful moral blindness Shakespeare suggests in *The Tempest*: Gulliver suspects in the letter to Captain Sympson that "that infernal habit of lying, shuffling, deceiving, and equivocating" which is "so deeply rooted in the very souls of all my species" is particularly prominent among Europeans (Swift 2001, 8). Other references to Europe tend to fulfil a similar function to those references in Shakespeare in that they offer comparisons to a frame of reference that is already familiar to the reader: the waiters in Lilliput serve Gulliver through a pulley system "in a very ingenious manner, by certain cords, as we draw the bucket up a well in Europe" (Swift 2001, 61). As he is sold in Brobdingnag, his former master demands

> a thousand pieces of gold, which were ordered him on the spot, each piece being about the bigness of eight hundred moidores; but allowing for the proportion of all things between that country and Europe, and the high price of gold among them, was hardly so great a sum as a thousand guineas would be in England. (95)

This passage indicates a characteristic shift in *Gulliver's Travels* at large: Europe is the larger frame of reference, but Gulliver will *always* talk about Britain when he needs to be more accurate. The price he fetches is small compared to the European gold price, and more specifically, it is below a thousand English guineas. This pattern is repeated in Gulliver's conversations with the king of Brobdingnag, who asks him to talk about "the manners, religion, laws, government, and learning of Europe." The guest's response is to talk about "my own beloved country, of our trade and wars by sea and land, of our schisms in religion, and parties in the state." He never questions that England is representative of Europe at large; indeed, it is "the mistress of arts and arms, the scourge of France, the arbitress of Europe, the seat of virtue, piety, honour, and truth, the pride and envy of the world" (100). Swift's cultural relativism is much developed by comparison with that found in *The Tempest*, which enables him to make Europe and England the object of his satire through the comparison with the extra-European (as Montaigne had famously done in 'Of Cannibals'). However, *Gulliver's Travels* asserts the national paradigm within the European framework much more strongly than in Shakespeare.

While Swift thus playfully alluded to the idea that nations within Europe cannot really claim for themselves a pure genealogy, his contemporaries frequently forgot such knowledge and even repressed it. When a young

Dutchman named William of Orange ascended to the English throne in 1689, many of his new subjects felt uncomfortable about his ostensible un-Englishness. The supposed purity of English bloodlines, both royal and pedestrian, appeared severely at risk under such foreign monarchical rule. Yet, late seventeenth-century Englishmen were also able to reflect critically on their own cultural commitment to stereotyping ethnic others, as is visible in numerous travel fictions published at the time (see Bayer 2012). In such transnational rhetorical gestures, a more 'European' sense of identity can be seen to replace orthodox national frames of reference. Wolfram Schmidgen describes Daniel Defoe as "[t]he most aggressive and visible contender for England's discontinuous national history and its mixed racial heritage in the early eighteenth century" (Schmidgen 2013, 6). Defoe's "The True-Born Englishman" (1701), written in support of foreign King William, famously presents a bitterly sarcastic survey of all the various historical waves of immigration and moments when the Isles were conquered by ethnic and cultural others. Defoe employs the phrase that gave the poem its title as some sort of returning chorus. Arguing that England's glory stems largely from its multinational history, Defoe presents such national impurity as typically European. He argues in his "Explanatory Preface" that if he were to "examine all the Nations of *Europe*," he could show "[t]hat those Nations which are most mix'd, are the best, and have least of Barbarism and Brutality among them" (23). England is clearly presented as essentially European; and this Europe exists predominantly in contradistinction to barbarians, belabouring a trope that goes back at least to the Greek etymology of the word "barbarian" and its focus on linguistic and cultural difference. When Defoe reminds his English readers that "we are really all Foreigners our selves" (25), he silently reduces the level of foreignness to a European realm. This illustrates the self-reflexive form of negotiations of 'Europeanness' while also foregrounding the importance that concepts such as 'civility' played for the self-conscious definition of an other that had been historically transcended in the 'civilizing process' towards modernity (Elias 1978).

In the ironic survey of the devilish national characteristics of England's European neighbours that complements his self-deprecating comments on Englishness, Defoe heavily draws on national clichés. And he reserves the strongest descriptors for non-European others such as the Chinese (lost in "Wit") or Persians (dismissed as "Effeminate"); or marks them off as excessively different owing to their non-Christian religious beliefs. His mention of "*Turks* and *Moors*" belittles them as being lost in their attachment to "*Mah'met*" (35). The abject nature of England as the recipient of all these tainted arrivals gives occasion to hyperbolic excess: "We have been *Europe*'s Sink, *the Jakes* where she / Voids all her Offal Out-cast Progeny" (39). The Europeanness that he praises as the new king's most precious gift to England is thus also scatologically attached to a genealogy about which one had best remain silent. Yet the final mention of "Europe" reinstates a history of greatness, implicitly contrasting it once again with the barbarian others

who—during this early stage of imperial colonialism that had already witnessed the acquisition of Bombay in 1661—were thus effectively silenced.
England's glory, the readers are told, remains unchallenged as a result of
its military might, and nobody would dare challenge the telling of such a
history: "Stories which *Europe*'s Volumes largely swell" (65). The masculine
pride taken in the erection of such a voluminous history eventually returns
England to the top of the European league and firmly establishes Europe as a
literary and historical entity that endows its constituent nations with moral
gravitas. In the flattering light of such European grandeur and discursive
legitimacy, Defoe reduces any allusion to national identity to the status of a
purely rhetorical gesture, allowing him to deride any claim to pure national
heritage. Any such attempt deserves utter contempt, which Defoe describes
as "In Speech an Irony, in Fact a Fiction" (43). In the end, the only cultural formation that provides value and stability appears to be Europe. With
Defoe's poem, then, Englishness is reduced to a variety of Europeanness, and
so is every other national collective of any reputation. The 'secondarity' that
Brague (2009) identifies as a distinctly European feature—the freedom to
choose one's ancestors and to put oneself in a certain tradition—is evident
once again as a formal feature of this construction of Europe.

   What, then, does it mean to study early modern forms and functions
of the idea of Europe? If we are interested in the functions of the idea of
Europe, it makes sense to assess these functions in a clearly defined and
study-able domain for which more or less reliable accounts of its constitution as a subject of ethnogenesis and academic study exist. In this spirit, the
present volume collects contributions located within and beyond various
national literatures across Europe. All contributors examine the forms and
functions assumed by constructions of Europe and 'Europeanness' in early
modernity, not only in the encounter with extra-European others but also
within the cultural formation that would today be called Europe.

* * *

The following chapters are arranged under three headings addressing three
separate approaches to thinking about Europeanization in early modernity.
While all three categories—others, genres, and values—form central concerns in reflections about what it means, at any historical moment, to be
European and as such feature in almost each individual chapter, the group-
ing nevertheless points to a more concerted focus in particular chapters.

   Surely, the most frequently studied early modern arena for negotiating
ideas of Europe is the contact with the non-European other. It is a truism
that Europeans realized their own Europeanness in encounters with peoples
they perceived as being so radically different as to render negligible all
difference with their nearer neighbours. They saw a common denominator
between Europeans, but not with others, from which an idea of Europe
developed. To pursue the metaphor, the precise value of that denominator is

an unknown in each specific equation produced by an encounter with others. This is especially true, and especially difficult to solve, for those fringe areas where hybridity between Europeans and non-Europeans was the norm rather than the exception. Research on early modern Europeans' perceptions of others has focused largely on their dealings with Islamic peoples to the East and South—a focus that is also reflected in this collection. This is not to say, however, that there was no alterity to be found among the Christians of the North and East, with whom there were close commercial, dynastic, and political ties but also differences in terms of religion, legal systems, and culture. As Anita Gilman Sherman has recently argued, the multinational Commonwealth of Poland–Lithuania (incorporating much of present-day Ukraine, where the identity and compass of Europe have been so tragically contested) was perceived in sixteenth- and seventeenth-century England as no different "from other European countries," in spite of its "formidable constitutional experiments" including elective monarchy, religious tolera- tion, and a federated structure (2015, 76). Here as elsewhere, the perplexing religious multifariousness of the *oriens Christianus* troubled all notions of a 'Christian' Europe pitted against non-Christian others.

By way of introduction to the first section on "Others," in Chapter 1 David Blanks traces lines of development between some of the most influ- ential grand narratives of the idea of Europe in the mirror of its others. In his critical review of the historiography of 'Europe' in the Middle Ages and early modernity, Blanks addresses the institutional contexts that generated histories of the 'construction' of Europe in past decades. Discussing key con- tributions by Norman Daniel, Edward Said, Gerard Delanty, and Charles Taylor, Blanks considers the shift of focus away from cultural alterity towards diversity, cosmopolitanism, and conviviality, reflecting on how such concepts tend to introduce their own teleologies in place of older, discarded ones. How, Blanks asks, did a European mentality—*avant la lettre*—come into being during an early modernity that was, indeed, linked to the very concept of modernity itself? Drawing attention to a range of natural, economic, and dynastic factors, which he cautions must not be neglected, Blanks presents, at the heart of his argument, the idea of critical reason as a determinant of European modernity—a modernity that is both deeply secular and obsessed with questions of identity and alterity. Blanks's explorations, personal and committed both in the experience they draw from and in the conclusions they present, historicize the academic discourse on early modern Europe and remind us that the Europes we construct in retrospect are chronotopes no less than the ones we undertake to study.

In a sense, in Chapter 2 Nabil Matar studies a similar topic from another perspective: he inquires how "Europe" was, or rather was not, conceptual- ized and perceived as a unit by Arabic-speaking peoples from the Middle Ages into the eighteenth century. Although Europeans so often objectified these peoples as the other by which they defined their self, neither Arabs not Turks seem to have perceived a shared 'Europeanness' during the period in question. While there is an Arabic word, *Ürubba*, treacherously attractive to the reader of early modern texts, it was not pre-eminently used and was often mistranslated even at the time. Where European travellers to Arabic-speaking areas presented themselves as Christians, their hosts responded with a similar religious self-definition. Hence, it is not surprising that the identification of Europe with Christendom, so common within Europe, was also effective in Arabic sources, where *Ürubba* was used to describe the lands of the Christians. While sometimes following this identification of landmasses with religious affiliations, Arabic geographers also thought in alternative units, focusing on political centres such as Byzantium and Rome. Still, accounts of journeys to Europe were not frequent because scholars, traders, and pilgrims looked to the East instead. Maps drawn up for economic and political purposes identified ports, cities, linguistic, and national units, and acknowledged their religious community or, from the Reformation onwards, division. Matar's study of Arabic sources impressively documents that, if early modern Europeans developed a sense of their own homogeneity that set them apart from those non-Europeans with whom they most frequently and most closely interacted, they failed to present this homogeneity to their other convincingly.

One key literary factor for creating a sense of homogeneity was myth: Troy and the *Iliad* provide a classical reference for the national geneses of many early modern European nations, and as such they clearly constitute part of a collective identity based in their shared reception. In Chapter 3 Ladan Niayesh examines how the myth of Troy is utilized in Robert Greene's debut play, *Alphonsus, King of Aragon* (c. 1587), to 'Europeanize' a collective usually perceived as non-European: the Ottoman Turks. Niayesh shows that Greene refutes the Scythian origins of the Turks articulated in such influential accounts as Richard Knolles's *General History of the Turks* (1603). Instead, the play reiterates their Trojan roots and hence, their 'familiarity.' Trojanized Turks are integrated into a familiar—European—system of values and the *translatio imperii* scheme; their appropriation acts as a mode of ideological wish-fulfilment that sees the enemy renounce their false religion in favour of the superior power of the Christian God. Niayesh examines how the narrative conventions of romance enable the overcoming of otherness that was, outside of fiction, enacted in economic and military associations between England and the Ottoman empire. By means of narration, the self-defining other is reined in; its foreignness is reduced to a (much inferior) version of the self in an early modern premonition of those mechanisms Edward Said has described for eighteenth- and nineteenth-century orientalism (1978).

The second section of the present volume, titled "Genres," picks up the cue from Niayesh's explorations of 'work on myth' and asks what role literary forms played in allowing authors to reflect on and shape the discourse on Europe. How, our contributors ask, did literary forms channel the discourse on Europe, and how did the circulation of specific forms create a reception community that was defined as much by reading as by writing? Genres offer frameworks for speaking and thinking; they enable discourse at the same time as they constrain it; and they can bestow authority on utterances and ideas that, outside of their generic form, might be highly contentious. Thus, genre can ensure the survival of ancient concepts as much as it can serve to introduce and negotiate new ideas by integrating them into traditional forms. Generic transformation can signal changes in the cultural outlook, dissatisfaction with traditions, and the perceived need for new ways of conceptualizing the world. Opening this section, in Chapter 4 Clara Pascual-Argente analyses how the romance of antiquity, also known as *roman antique*, presented readers with a place of origin for European identity. She considers the fate of this far-reaching tradition during the fifteenth century, when potentially competing models for the European relationship to the classical past, principally in the form of vernacular humanisms, gained a solid foothold across the continent. The chapter focuses on three *roman antique* narratives in fifteenth-century Castile. It first discusses an instance of clear opposition between vernacular humanism and *roman antique* by considering the use of an old Alexander romance by writer Gutierre Díaz de Games in his *Victorial*. It next follows the European travels of the *Sumas de historia troyana* from Castile to the Burgundian ducal court, through the conduit of a noted contributor to vernacular humanism, Mosén Diego de Valera. The final section explores the Apollonius of Tyre narrative through *Vida e historia del rey Apolonio*, a printed and illustrated volume with close connections to Southern German books and their printers that highlights the European network of commercial relationships during the incunabula period. In all of these forms, medieval antiquity lives on through transformations, not only as a marker of European elite culture and diplomatic interactions, but also as part of new printed genres with the potential to reach audiences far beyond the courtly milieus where the *roman antique* first appeared.

Turning from Romance languages to a Germanic context, Nicolas Detering in Chapter 5 also discusses the way in which generic traditions drew on and contributed to the discourse about Europe. The late seventeenth century, Detering shows, saw a proliferation of both literary and nonliterary texts in Germany that made prominent use of the term 'Europe' in their titles. Especially the German gallant novel evinced the European fashion around 1700, when titles such as Eberhard Werner Happel's *The European Toroan* (1676), Johann Beer's *The European in Love* (1682), August Bohse's *The Lovely European Constantine* (1698), or Christian Friedrich Hunold's popular *Love- and Heroic Stories from European Courts* (1705) were published. These popular novels all combine entertaining love stories between princes and princesses from a range of 'European' countries with didactic digressions that provide factual information on these countries, including their geography, their politics, or their culture. The chapter demonstrates how, during the Thirty Years' War, there emerged a new form of periodical writing that used the term 'Europe' to denote the political history of the time in contrast to the universal and teleological historiography that was common in earlier periods. Therefore, the term became closely linked to contemporary politics and its public reporting, to transnational wars, the world of courtly tactics and of power struggles. These periodical records of contemporary politics soon merged with fiction and were popularized in the form of love and adventure stories, which contributed significantly to the German historiography of Europe in the late seventeenth century, shaped as it was by a particular focus on contemporaneity that itself was inherited from journalistic media.

Closing the section on genres, in Chapter 6 Goran Stanivukovic explores how boundaries between the Christian West and the Islamic East define Europe in Renaissance maps and prose romances set in the Mediterranean. The purpose of his comparative assessment is to analyse how in the representation of the Mediterranean in both maps and romances, the West and the East compete for the symbolical claim of the sea and its surrounding territories, and to show the extent to which Europe was enmeshed in the wider Mediterranean world of the early modern period. Focusing on maps by the Italian cartographer Jacopo Russi and by Pierre Desceliers, Stanivukovic traces how actual and fictional territories mix with symbolic representations of landscape, making these cartographic spaces at once sources of real geographical knowledge and narratives of a fictional geography that defines the Mediterranean. The maps, therefore, construct the East and West not as divided but as joint spaces, in turn making of Europe not an independent entity but a constituent territory of the East. The chapter compares these visual strategies with narrative patterns in Richard Johnson's (1506–1597) *The Seven Champions of Christendom*. Like the maps of the Mediterranean, this romance mixes fictional with real geographical places, creating a discourse about Europe and the East as one continuous space whose margins remain necessarily contested.

In the closing section, on "Values," early modern Europe is analysed through tropes that connect to moral and ethical discourses. Nina Berman, in Chapter 7, asks what happens when we read Luther's treatises about the Ottoman invasions in the early sixteenth century alongside a text that is considered to be the first critique of imperial genocide, namely, Bartolomé de Las Casas's "Account, Much Abbreviated, of the Destruction of the Indies" (1552). This textual confrontation raises a number of questions that relate to the manner in which early modern European self-perceptions as a community of values emerged in opposition to ethnic and cultural others. Building on these ideas, Berman asks how the critique of the violence inflicted on the indigenous populations of the newly discovered Americas resonates with the condemnation of the Ottoman treatment of conquered European peoples. The chapter shows how these two related discourses germinated a self-critical discussion about what it meant to be European, when opportunistic interests in political partnerships with Ottoman powers and popular discourses about the violent other clearly jarred. Berman suggests that in this early modern moment of imperial expansion, the parameters of state-condoned violence against cultural and religious others come into full focus. In addressing this violence at the core of the early modern engagements of Europe with its colonized others, Berman questions the conventional narrative about Europe's 'Enlightened' origins.

In his account from another 'margin' of Europe, Willy Maley in Chapter 8 examines John Milton's *History of Britain* (1670) for its debunking of origin myths as part of a radical critique of Britain's national genesis: the *History* rejects the significance of a (recent) descent from continental peoples and instead directs the reader's attention to the biblical and classical origins of Europe. In his search for the origins of English liberty, Milton found that—in contrast to what 'Saxonist' and antiquarian contemporaries claimed—national history did not yield the desired evidence: he saw the post-Roman Britons as misguided in inviting their future slavers; the Saxons appeared to him as superstitious barbarians, and their king Arthur as a myth; and the later Danish and Norman invaders were no better. Foreign yoke follows on foreign yoke, with no pristine national liberty to uncover in the past. Instead, in his quest for a positive value to identify with, Milton looks to classical Rome as a source of civilisation, admiring its humanist heirs. Their 'foreign books' are his proposed remedy to misgovernment by the (monarchical) state, which is to be countered by a civilized self-government of the individual. Britain is to thrive, not on its native tradition, but on a European civility that, Maley argues, remains relevant today.

In Chapter 9, devoted to John Dee's *General and Rare Memorials Pertayning to the Perfect Arte of Navigation* (1577), Eliza Richter considers the uses of imagery and iconography of Europe. The frontispiece to Dee's work, which calls for the improvement of the English navy, shows Elizabeth at the helm of a ship enticingly named not 'England' but 'Europe.' This curious transformation of the familiar 'ship of state' trope is the more surprising since Dee nowhere addresses the European dimension in the text of his book. The frontispiece thus suggests a European frame, by that name, which appears difficult or inopportune to explicate in writing. Richter traces the symbolic, allegorical, and iconographic implications of this imagery, highlighting the classical, hermetic, and political traditions that inform both woodcut and text. As in Maley's chapter, we can see a British author lament that his compatriots are thinking in national, not European, terms. In a climate of patriotism, Dee argues that England's glory is relative to a European frame. The Europe that emerges, mostly implicitly but nonetheless clearly, is that of a struggle for domination: it is a power system defined by the competitors and the means of competition (in this case, sea power, but also the codes in which it is negotiated, of the Judaeo-Christian and Graeco-Roman traditions).

Chapter 10, the concluding chapter by Paul Michael Lützeler, provides an outlook from early modernity into the more recent past, as he traces the ways in which Europe has served as a utopian site in the discourse on peace since the fourteenth century. Lützeler describes how Europe came to function as a social imaginary in the sense described by Castoriadis, which, in its opposition to ideological dogmatization and reduction, works to expand the boundaries of collective identities rather than buttress them. In contradistinction to theories of the formation of European identity such as Rémi Brague's and Edgar Morin's, Lützeler prefers to examine the functions of the discourse on peace in negotiating between European identity on the one hand and competing collective identities on the other. This discourse, which revolves around Europe as a factor for the pacification, not only of Europe itself, but also of the world at large, is thus particularly suited to the promotion of European identity as part of a subsidiary collective identity ranging from the local to the global. What is striking about the discourse on peace, Lützeler argues, is that it has been conducted almost exclusively by writers and intellectuals thinking 'outside the box' of political discourse, claiming a particular liberty of thought unfettered by dogma. In what Lützeler demonstrates to be a strong tradition of reflections on Europe, these authors imagine or construct versions of Europe that are to ensure peaceful cohabitation.

The chapters collected in *Early Modern Constructions of Europe* resemble, in a sense, that *unity in diversity* that is also the motto of Europe's current political union. The volume aims to stimulate debate not only about their specific subjects, but also about their shared interest in early modern 'versions' of Europe. We believe that valuable insight into the prehistories of some ideas or versions of Europe that remain with us today, and about a number of those that have fallen by the roadside, is to be gained from the study of the forms and functions of early modern discourses on this enigmatic entity. To think about Europe as a spatiotemporal 'sense-making framework' of the kind described by Bakhtin under the rubric of the chronotope, to think about it as a social imaginary in Castoriadis's sense or as a reception community in the sense proposed by Benedict Anderson, to turn one's gaze upon it in a kind of reverse orientalism and to assess from without its efforts at self-definition—these approaches might assist us in understanding better what the idea of Europe was, is, and can be, and how it has contributed to getting us where we are today.

Notes

1. All of these factors, their early modern specificity notwithstanding, continue to influence contemporary perceptions of Europe. Witness, for instance, Samuel S. Huntington's grim reiteration that "Europe ends where Western Christianity ends and Islam and Orthodoxy begin" (2011, 158).

2. The concept of the chronotope might also prove useful for describing the spatiotemporal frameworks that inform, are produced by, and make sense of such historiographical 'versions' of Europe as Chabod's (1961), Fèbvre's (1999), or more recently, Burke's (1998) and Davies's (1997), but also of works of criticism such as Curtius (1953) and Auerbach (2003). Molho (2007) and Ramada Curto (2007) offer a number of pertinent reflections on the historiographical method which, we believe, might usefully be combined with the view of Europe as a chronotope.

Works Cited

Anderson, Benedict. 2003. *Imagined Communities: Reflections on the Origin and Spread of Nationalism*. Rev. ed. London: Verso.

Auerbach, Erich. 2003. *Mimesis: The Representation of Reality in Western Literature* [1946]. Translated by Willard R. Trask. 50th anniversary ed. Princeton, NJ: Princeton University Press.

Bakhtin, Mijail Mijaïlovich. 1937/1981. "Forms of Time and of the Chronotope in the Novel: Notes toward a Historical Poetics." *The Dialogic Imagination: Four Essays*, edited by Michael Holquist, translated by Caryl Emerson and Michael Holquist, 84–258. Austin: University of Texas Press.

Bartlett, Robert J. 1993. *The Making of Europe: Conquest, Colonization and Cultural Change, 950–1350*. London: Penguin.

Bayer, Gerd. 2012. "Negotiating Ethnic Difference in Restoration Travel Fiction." *Arcadia* 47 (1): 34–53.

Bernal, Martin. 1991. *Black Athena: The Afroasiatic Roots of Classical Civilization*. Vol. 1. London: Vintage.

Bhabha, Homi K. 1990. "DissemiNation: Time, Narrative, and the Margins of the Modern Nation." *Nation and Narration*, edited by Homi K. Bhabha, 291–322. London: Routledge.

Bohrer, Karl Heinz. 2012. "'Europe' as Utopia: Causes of Its Decline." *New Literary History* 43: 587–605.

Brague, Rémi. 2009. *Eccentric Culture: A Theory of Western Civilization*. South Bend, IN: St. Augustine's Press.

Burke, Peter. 1980. "Did Europe Exist before 1700?" *History of European Ideas* 1 (1): 21–29.

Burke, Peter. 1998. *The European Renaissance: Centres and Peripheries*. Oxford: Blackwell.

Burke, Peter. 2006. "How to Write a History of Europe: Europe, Europes, Eurasia." *European Review* 14 (2): 233–239.

Chabod, Federico. 1961. *Storia dell'idea d'Europa*. Bari: Laterza.

Chakrabarty, Dipesh. 2008. *Provincializing Europe: Postcolonial Thought and Historical Difference* [2000]. Princeton, NJ: Princeton University Press.

Curtius, Ernst R. 1953. *European Literature and the Latin Middle Ages* [1948]. Translated by Willard R. Trask. New York: Pantheon Books.

Davies, Norman. 1997. *Europe: A History*. London: Pimlico.

Defoe, Daniel. 1701/1927. "The True-Born Englishman." *The Shortest Way With the Dissenters, And Other Pamphlets*, 21–71. Oxford: Blackwell.

Delanty, Gerard. 2003. "Conceptions of Europe: A Review of Recent Trends." *European Journal of Social Theory* 6 (4): 471–488.

Delanty, Gerard. 2013. *Formations of European Modernity: A Historical and Political Sociology of Europe*. Basingstoke: Palgrave Macmillan.

Duchhardt, Heinz. 1997. "Was heißt und zu welchem Ende betreibt man—europäische Geschichte?" In: *"Europäische Geschichte" als historiographisches Problem*, edited by Heinz Duchhardt and Andreas Kunz, 191–202. Mainz: Zabern.

Duindam, Jeroen. 2010. "Early Modern Europe: Beyond the Strictures of Modernization and National Historiography." *European History Quarterly* 40 (4): 606–623.

During, Simon. 1990. "Literature—Nationalism's Other? The Case for a Revision." *Nation and Narration*, edited by Homi K. Bhabha, 138–153. London: Routledge.

Ehlers, Jürgen. 1999. "Natio, 2. N. (Nation) Methodisches." In: *Lexikon des Mittelalters*, 10 vols. (Stuttgart: Metzler, [1977]–1999), Vol. 6, cols. 1035–1036, in *Brepolis Medieval Encyclopaedias—Lexikon des Mittelalters Online*.

Elias, Norbert. 1978. *The Civilizing Process: The History of Manners*. New York: Urizen Books.

Fèbvre, Lucien. 1999. *L'Europe: Genèse d'une civilisation: Cours professé au Collège de France en 1944–1945*. Edited by Thérèse Charmasson and Brigitte Mazon. Paris: Perrin.

Gellner, Ernest. 1983. *Nations and Nationalism*. Ithaca, NY: Cornell University Press.

Hay, Denys. 1968. *Europe: The Emergence of an Idea*. Rev. ed. Edinburgh: Edinburgh University Press.

Hobsbawm, E. J. 1990. *Nations and Nationalism since 1780: Programme, Myth, Reality.*Cambridge: Cambridge University Press.

Holinshed, Raphael, ed. 1587. *The First and second volumes of Chronicles. Comprising 1 The description and historie of England, 2 The description and historie of Ireland, 3 The description and historie of Scotland. ...* London: Henry Denham.

Huntington, Samuel P. 2011. *The Clash of Civilizations and the Remaking of World Order*. New York: Simon & Schuster.

Kearney, Richard, ed. 1992. *Visions of Europe: Conversations on the Legacy and Future of Europe*. Dublin: Wolfhound Press.

Molho, Anthony. 2007. "A Harlequin's Dress: Reflections on Europe's Public Discourse." In: *Finding Europe: Discourses on Margins, Communities, Images ca. 13th–ca. 18th Centuries*, edited by Anthony Molho and Diogo Ramada Curto, 1–17. New York: Berghahn Books.

Pagden, Anthony. 2002. "Europe: Conceptualizing a Continent." In: *The Idea of Europe: From Antiquity to the European Union*, edited by Anthony Pagden, 33–54. Washington, DC: Woodrow Wilson Center Press.

Pocock, J. G. A. 2002. "Some Europes in Their History." In: *The Idea of Europe: From Antiquity to the European Union*, edited by Anthony Pagden, 55–71. Washington, DC: Woodrow Wilson Center Press.

Quast, Bruno. 2016. "Bedrohte Christenheit: Über Ikonologie im *Rolandslied* des Pfaffen Konrad." In: *Europa gibt es doch ... Krisendiskurse im Spiegel der Literatur*, edited by Florian Kläger and Martina Wagner-Egelhaaf, 29–41. Paderborn: Fink.

Ramada Curto, Diogo. 2007. "Rethinking the History of Europe: Old and New Approaches." In: *Finding Europe: Discourses on Margins, Communities, Images ca. 13th–ca. 18th Centuries*, edited by Anthony Molho and Diogo Ramada Curto, 19–35. New York: Berghahn Books.

Said, Edward. 1978. *Orientalism*. New York: Pantheon Books.

Schmidgen, Wolfram. 2013. *Exquisite Mixture: The Virtues of Impurity in Early Modern England*. Philadelphia: University of Pennsylvania Press.

Schmidt, H. D. 1966. "The Establishment of 'Europe' as a Political Expression." *Historical Journal* 9 (2): 172–178.

Schneidmüller, Bernd. 1997. "Die mittelalterlichen Konstruktionen Europas: Konvergenz und Differenzierung." In: *"Europäische Geschichte" als historiographisches Problem*, edited by Heinz Duchhardt and Andreas Kunz, 5–24. Mainz: Zabern.

Shakespeare, William. 1998. *Complete Works* (The Arden Shakespeare), edited by Richard Proudfoot, Ann Thompson, and David Scott Kastan. Walton-on-Thames, Surrey: Nelson.

Sherman, Anita Gilman. 2015. "Poland in the Cultural Imaginary of Early Modern England." *Journal for Early Modern Cultural Studies* 15 (1): 55–89.

Sidney, Philip. 1595/1965. *An Apology for Poetry or The Defence of Poesy*, edited by Geoffrey Shepherd. Manchester: Manchester University Press.

Speed, John. 1631. *A Prospect of the Most Famous Parts of the World*. London: Printed by John Dawson for George Humble.

Swift, Jonathan. 1726/2001. *Gulliver's Travels*, edited by Robert DeMaria. London: Penguin.

Treaty of Lisbon amending the Treaty on European Union and the Treaty establishing the European Community, signed at Lisbon, 13 December 2007. The Member States [of the European Union]. Official Journal of the European Union 1. December 13. http://eur-lex.europa.eu/legal-content/EN/NOT/?uri=CELEX:12007L/TXT.

Part I
Others

1   Europeans before Europe
Modernity and the Myth of the Other

David Blanks

Although the shelves in my office are filled with books that have titles such as *Europe in the Middle Ages, The European Mind from Antiquity to the Present*, and *Everything You Ever Wanted to Know about Early Modern Europe*, and while I teach courses called "Early Modern Europe (c. 1450–1700)" and "Europe in the Age of Revolution and Reform," the introductory chapters of these books, and my introductory remarks in such classes, are always given over to explaining *why* using the term 'Europe' in the medieval or early modern period is something of a misnomer. I say 'something of a misnomer' and not, flat out, an error, because although 'Europeans' did not know they were Europeans at the time, there was, nonetheless, a certain nascent Europeanness bubbling up in the fifteenth, sixteenth, and seventeenth centuries. It was in the early modern period that the cultural values and practices emerged that would later be identified as European not only by the citizens of Europe but also, and just as importantly, perhaps more importantly, by the scholars who studied them. We can put it that way.

It is difficult to know how most 'Europeans' identified themselves at the time. Most were poor and illiterate, and, as we shall see, this is one of the core problems when it comes to examining early modern constructions of the idea: for the most part, we simply do not have the data we require to answer the question. What we do possess are the observations of elites, and even those are few and far between—not sufficient, really, for building an informed case, but we do the best we can because there is little else to go on in this period. Trouble ensues when scholars get caught up in rushing to the finish line, 1989 and all that, and end up glossing over cultural constructions they know are more complex than they have allowed for (cf. Delanty 1995, 2013; Said 1978).

Historians and literary critics have carefully sifted through the writings of their predecessors from Herodotus to Hobbes; they have catalogued, collated, compared, and compiled; and some impressive analyses have resulted therefrom (cf. den Boer 1993). And yet, this 'nominalist' approach is not entirely satisfying, as the editors and some of the authors of this volume suggest, not only because meanings change over time, and from person to person, and even for one person in the course of a career, but especially because at the end of the day we are still entirely at the mercy of sources written by and for the educated classes. Most 'Europeans' did not see themselves that way. They were far more likely to identify themselves as part of a particular family or clan, or perhaps, in broader terms, as coming from a specific place, or maybe simply as Christians. Peter Burke notes, for example, that in the sixteenth and seventeenth centuries even members of the upper classes considered themselves Bretons or Catalans or what have you; that Erasmus self-identified as being from Rotterdam; Montaigne, as a Gascon; and the French poet Pierre de Ronsard, despite using the term 'Europe' so frequently in his writings, nonetheless thought of himself as a "gentilhomme Vandomois" (Burke 1980, 27).

And although we begin to see the word used by intellectuals rather more frequently after 1450, it was not until the late nineteenth century that it had any sort of currency among the majority of people living on the continent, and it probably did not entirely crystallize across broad spectrums of the population until after World War II. Yet we persist in using this anachronism in our writings and our lectures, not only because it is convenient, and because without it, it is hard to make sensible generalizations and comparative analyses about this period, but also because there *was* something there. There was something to it. The answer to Peter Burke's question is, no, Europe did not exist before 1700—but 'Europeans' most certainly did (cf. Bohrer 2012).

When Burke first asked this question, it was the early 1970s,[1] and the principal work that had been done by then, the work that he was using as his stepping-off point, was the product of scholars who had witnessed not one but in some cases two world wars, who were living through the Cold War, and who joined in the general hand-wringing and soul-searching about what had happened, what it meant, and, most relevant to the concerns we are addressing here, what it meant to be European: who was in, who was out, and how 'Europeans' could be brought together in such a way so as to prevent this from happening again.

It was just after the war in 1946 that Winston Churchill first called for a United States of Europe; the Hague Conference, seen by many as the wellspring of the European Union, was held in 1948; both the Council of Europe and the College of Europe were established in 1949; and, on the academic side, the School of European Studies opened its offices at the University of Sussex in 1963. With but a single exception *all* of the work upon which Burke bases his essay was produced in these years by scholars who shared this overall sense of cultural crisis (Burke 1980, 27–28).

It was around this same time or shortly thereafter—indeed, at the very time that Burke was looking into these issues, in the late 1960s and early 1970s—that identity studies became a notable discipline. Although this was primarily a move aimed at creating cultural and intellectual space for those who had been disenfranchised by the establishment, or who had never found a voice to begin with, members of the 'establishment' continued to ask questions about identity themselves: hence the appearance of a raft of studies aimed at understanding the origins of Europeanness.

Given these circumstances, it is hardly surprising that those inclined to examine the roots of European identity in the medieval and early modern periods should have found some essential 'European characteristics' that were rooted in the ancient world and that came to the fore in reaction to that seemingly ubiquitous medieval enemy, the Muslim other. When one reads the *Chanson de Roland* or other *chansons de geste*, the enormously popular crusading poems of the High Middle Ages, it is difficult to escape the conclusion that this is where the European—or in this case more appropriately Latin Christian—sense of 'us' versus 'them' was born. But one wonders whether the villagers and warriors who enjoyed (not reading but) listening to the troubadours perform these epic tales came to the same conclusions that we do in thinking back about them. Certainly there was great variation depending upon where they lived. Those closer to the Mediterranean—sailors, merchants, pilgrims, and the like—and those with first-hand knowledge of real life Muslims, undoubtedly felt differently than, say, a Yorkshire farmer watching a mystery play that pitted the pharaoh, devotee of Mahomet, against Moses, follower of the true God (Tolan 2002, 130). My sense is that the farther away you were from the centre of action, the less nuanced your interpretation (Jones 1942, 213)—an observation that, as we shall see below, is perhaps equally valid for academics today.

It was also in the 1960s that Norman Daniel, a devout Catholic with long experience in the Muslim world, provided the framework for much subsequent work that was more specifically focused on the emergence of the idea of Europe. Daniel believed that Western attitudes towards Islam were 'canonized' in the Middle Ages. This was a view shared by Edward Said, who himself was enormously influential in shaping the scholarship of succeeding generations, especially among those of the identity studies camp who were writing a counternarrative to the received wisdom of the 1970s and 1980s. Said bought into the accepted narrative vis-à-vis the Muslim other that had initially been posited by Daniel, Richard Southern (1962), and others (Said 1980; Daniel 1960, 1975; Manselli 1965; see also Blanks 1999, 25–29). Daniel devoted his scholarship specifically to trying to understand the sources of modern attitudes towards Islam, which is precisely what we are doing here in trying to understand the early modern (and in this case late medieval) sources of attitudes toward the European self. In Daniel's view, the way in which medieval Christians thought "has always been and still is part of the make-up of every Western mind brought to bear upon the subject" (1975, 301). "If we have to choose a date to end the western European Middle Age," he wrote, "we might do worse than take 1939" (1975, 2).

A generation later, in another influential book, Robert Bartlett also went looking for the origins of Europeanness (1993). Bartlett was somewhat more ecumenical in his outlook as befitted the post–Cold War, post–1960s academic and political climate. As is typical of such works, he provides the appropriate caveats in his introduction, then plunges ahead and talks about Europe as if it was the way in which the people of the region normally referred to it. As suggested above, this was necessary in order to compose a study that holds together and makes sense to us today—rather in the same way, I suppose, as we discuss feudalism, the Crusades, and the Renaissance even though these terms were not in use at the time. But the important thing for our purposes here is this: Bartlett is searching for those intangible qualities that really do seem to be taking shape in this period even if they have as yet no name. This I suppose could fall under the heading of a 'realist' approach, and in truth it seems the only viable way of trying to grasp the essence of this emerging culture before 1700—before, that is, the Enlightenment and, more significantly still, before the late nineteenth and early twentieth centuries, by which time people really did have a sense of what Europe was and what it meant to be European even if it remained (and still remains) a vigorously contested discourse.

The notion that there was both an intensification and an extensification of Christian identity between 950 and 1350 is central to Bartlett's thesis, and Muslims play a leading role in his narrative. He has quite a bit to say about the cultural aftermath of the Crusades, devoting two chapters to what he calls "race relations on the frontiers of Latin Europe." The argument is more subtle than it sounds, however, focusing on the widely used medieval notion of *gens* and applying it not only to Christendom's Muslim neighbours to the south and east but also equally to the pagan peoples of the north and northeast. Here is a new turn. It is not just a matter of constructing European identity in regards to (1) people who conquered you (the Muslims) and (2) people you conquered (the Indians): in addition, Bartlett is able to demonstrate that the same approach to the other that was in operation in the Mediterranean world was equally at play in German and Slavic lands as well, as it also was in peripheral regions such as Scotland, Ireland, and Wales.

In his essay Burke had cautioned that "despite the excellent books on the idea of Europe, the social history of the consciousness of Europe remains to be written" (1980, 22). Here, too, Bartlett moves in new directions as he is able to get away from purely elite records and show, through a variety of different types of sources, that the intangible quality that we will all later recognize as quintessentially European is spreading its roots in the fourteenth and fifteenth centuries:

> By 1300 Europe existed as an identifiable cultural entity. It could be described in more than one way, but some common features of its cultural face are the saints, names, coins, charters and educational practices. ... By the late medieval period Europe's names and cults were more uniform than they had ever been; Europe's rulers everywhere minted coins and depended upon chanceries; Europe's bureaucrats shared a common experience of higher education. *This is the Europeanization of Europe.*
>
> (Bartlett 1993, 291; emphasis mine)

It is still something of a stretch to use the term 'Europe' when referring to the late Middle Ages, but Bartlett has advanced the argument considerably, especially by tapping into nonelite sources, and he points to something at the end of his book that should be highlighted when thinking about the emergence of new discourses in the early modern period, that is, the role of the universities in homogenizing a European sense of self. This factor will have great resonance not only within Latin Christendom as it is gradually transformed into a more secular society, but also in the colonies, first and most significantly in the sixteenth, seventeenth, and eighteenth centuries in Latin America, where the Spanish introduce their model of higher education, and then later in Africa and other areas of Western colonization (Carnoy 1974; Roberts, Rodríguez Cruz, and Hurbst 1996; Shils and Roberts 2004).

Another significant shift towards a more nuanced interpretation came two years later with the publication of Gerard Delanty's foundational text, *Inventing Europe: Idea, Identity, Reality* (1995). It was a solid contribution to the literature, a widely read work that was translated into seven languages. Identity studies were at their peak; the Berlin wall had just come down; the European Union had just been formed; and Delanty was interested in critiquing what he calls the Grand Narrative of Europe, arguing (in line with the academic tenor of the times) that it was not so much a reality as it was a contested cultural construction.[2] He ran through the history of the idea of Europe in an attempt to discover how this discourse could be put to use as "the basis of a collective identity unencumbered by the narrow normative horizons of national identity and the chauvinism of the 'Fortress Europe' project" (Delanty 1995, 1). He warned (again in line with the political tenor of the times) that since World War II Europe as a concept had in an ironic way actually reinforced a narrow nationalism built upon deep prejudices and an opposition to immigration, that it was exclusive rather than inclusive. What he wished to advocate, instead, was an idea of Europe linked to multiculturalism and postnational citizenship (Delanty 1995, 156–163; see also Nelson, Roberts, and Veit 1992).

In regards to *early modern* constructions of Europe, however, this led Delanty into some difficulty. His overarching cultural and political aims tended to reinforce the notion that western European identity was formed in opposition to the Muslim and, with Bartlett, the eastern European other. Such theories of alterity were *au courant*, and on the whole Delanty did a better job than anyone else had done until then of providing an overview of the subject, especially in that he took it all the way to the present day. However, because he relied heavily on the existing secondary literature— making, in addition to Bartlett, significant use of such tried and true classics as Gollwitzer (1951), Hay (1957), and Daniel (1960)—his analysis of this period and its relation to what he was primarily interested in, namely, the nineteenth and twentieth centuries, ended up being rather reminiscent of, and indeed in part took its cue from, Edward Said's thesis in *Orientalism*. Avoiding the Grand Narrative of progress and western superiority, this type of anti-Eurocentric narrative had its heart in the right place, but in some ways unwittingly reinforced the stereotypes it was trying to challenge. Despite wanting to establish a collective, political identity, this narrative tends to reinforce an exclusive version of the idea of Europe. Said used many of the same secondary sources for his introductory chapter on western attitudes prior to the nineteenth century (1978, 49–73). Both works were insightful for the post–1800 world, but both accepted certain rather time-worn generalizations about the premodern period that historians by then had come to question. It was clear that there was far more variety in the premodern encounters, especially with Islam, than either Delanty or Said acknowledged (Blanks and Frassetto 1999; Blanks 1997; Tolan 1996).

Nearly two decades later, when Delanty thought about issuing a new edition of *Inventing Europe*, he came to the same conclusion: that alterity did not provide an entirely satisfactory explanation as a source for the idea of Europe and European identity. Times had changed—intellectually, socially, and politically. Delanty came to feel that he needed to rethink his previous thesis as a result of new trends in history and sociology, as well as new developments in Europe and the world that had taken place since the early 1990s. *Formations of European Modernity: A Historical and Political Sociology of Europe* (2013) marks a real sea change in his assessment of the idea of Europe and, especially for our purposes here, in his assessment of the *origins* of the idea of Europe. It seeks to question not only older Eurocentric conceptions of the European heritage, but also what Delanty now argues are the equally skewed critiques of Eurocentrism. That one of the major contributors in this field should find the need to revise his theoretical frame-work is, I believe, commendable, to be sure, but also ample justification in and of itself for revisiting Burke's question at this time. And what are his new conclusions? Twenty years ago Delanty answered Burke's question in the affirmative; today he no longer believes that Europe existed before 1700.

In *Formations of European Modernity*, Delanty incorporates newer and more fashionable theories of modernity and cosmopolitanism to try to uncover what he calls the "fundamental structure of Europe" (2013, ix). Again, he is trying to develop a more nuanced analysis. He wants to pose questions about the limits and possibilities of Europe in the *present* day and to reevaluate the European heritage in the light of *present* concerns, most nota-bly, the failure of the EU to turn its dreams into reality, and, faced with the pressures of ever increasing immigration from non-European countries, espe-cially Muslim ones, the mounting crisis of European identity. Consequently, whereas in his earlier book the idea of Europe had become an "institutional-ized discourse" *in the early modern period*, by 2013 he characterized the idea of Europe as a "product of the modern age" (Delanty 1995, 10; 2013, 160).

Let us take a moment to pull this apart. Delanty has now come around to the view that alterity cannot be the sole source of a European self or identity; it played a role, but so did other factors. This is absolutely correct. Where we part ways is that Delanty then goes on to argue that the European self did not even exist before 1800. There simply was no European heritage before then. This assertion reflects, in part, recent trends in social science that are open to the category of 'construction,' where the tendency is to focus on modernity and the past 200 years, where references to the Middle Ages and the early modern period become introductory in nature, where the more distant past is largely cut off from the present (cf. Molho 2007). This view also reflects some deeper unspoken ideological positions. It is an attempt to rescue the EU project. It wants to back away from notions of othering that reinforce difference in order to embrace similarity. It wants to see Muslims not as victims of crusaders but as victims of colonial discourses, which presumably are easier to overcome. It is a shying away from discussions of race, ethnicity, and difference because these run counter to the political utopia of unity-in-diversity. It is an unconscious realization that any attention paid to alterity cuts across these goals. To the extent that there was alterity in the past, it is not really what Europe is all about, this discourse says; no, Europe is modern, it was created by modernity, it did not exist in the bad old days. Europe is a modern discourse that we need to urge along in the right direction. Let us not emphasize differences in the past, *especially* religious differences with other cultures. This tendency is to be avoided. In fact, to the extent that there were differences, they were internal. If there is anywhere one can see traces of modern Europe in the past, it would be here, in a sort of premodern diversity. Again, Delanty: "Plurality might be the best starting point for an adequate appreciation of the shaping of Europe since the Middle Ages" (2013, 138).

Moreover, this line of reasoning says, Europe did not create modernity; rather, it is a product of modernity, just like every other culture, and therefore it can neither be blamed for getting us into this mess nor take credit for modernity's successes—thus avoiding triumphalism, essentialism, any claims to European superiority, and so on. What we end up with then is a Europe that was created by modernity and therefore not responsible for its own (or anyone else's) circumstances; an other that is not really an other; and a present that is the site of competing discourses that, we hope, will turn out in a certain way—hence the psychologically and emotionally satisfying appeal of these recent theoretical moves.

> One is tempted to ask these scholars: why rely on such traditional schemes of historical periodization? Why conceive of the past as if it comprised distinct historical periods? Can there not be cultural characteristics—forms of social organization, types of political allegiance, psychological perceptions, etc.—that traversed the course of European history from one historical period to another? Does 'modernity' ... necessarily imply a sundering of 'modern' from 'premodern' Europe? What bearing do experiences from before (even long before) the middle of the eighteenth century have on an understanding of our own, contemporary Europe?
>
> (Molho 2007, 8)

There is a level at which this particular sociological approach simply does not trust history, but there is an inherent contradiction in that view. On the one hand, Delanty wants to argue *après* Habermas, Derrida, Foucault et al. (see Delanty 2013, 290–291) that there really was no European heritage before the nineteenth century; on the other hand, this same theoretical approach necessarily sees history as a "learning process" and culture as a "domain of critique and reflection." This creates an awkward situation because it means that even if we think of modernity as being multicivilizational we are still in the position of having to admit that certain attitudes or worldviews or practices might be thought of as properly belonging to a "European model of modernity." And even if we think of Europe as being the product of modernity, we are still in the position of having to ask where the culture of critique and reflection came from. Whence the critical reason associated with modern thought?

By now it will be obvious where this discussion is heading. The European model of modernity might well indeed mean a constitutional and democratic state, human rights, the integrity of the human person, social solidarities, and civil society as Delanty suggests, but cultural constructions are not built out of thin air. There was a capacity to think in certain ways that really did emerge in a certain place and at a certain time. "It is well and good to talk about construction and shifting meanings, but on the basis of what elements, one wishes to ask, does this construction take place?" (Molho 2007, 8). The answer is, on the basis of the building blocks that were formed in Europe between 1450 and 1700. This learning process, the ability to critique history, to reflect upon it, to learn its lessons: this *is* what constitutes European culture. Europe might be the product of modernity, but Europeanness comes from the premodern world.

So, to recap for a moment, the move away from saying that the idea of Europe is a function solely of encounters with the other is welcome. This is correct. There was more to it than that. But to say that such encounters had no appreciable impact on the formation of European identity swings too far back in the other direction. I am still persuaded that ideas about what it meant to be a Western Christian were born, in part, in the Middle Ages, in opposition to the Muslim other, and that new constructions of the idea of Europe emerged in the sixteenth and seventeenth centuries due to encounters with peoples of the New World. It makes sense, too, that the expansion of Latin Christendom in the late Middle Ages into German and Slavic areas led to a certain 'westernization' of the idea of Europe and that a new political sense of the term 'Europe' was appearing among a tiny, educated elite in the sixteenth and seventeenth centuries in opposition to the Habsburg and later the Bourbon dynasties. So far, so good.

And presumably the sense of being a Latin Christian eventually sank fairly deeply into the population—in part because the crusading elites were not all that far removed from the population culturally, intellectually, or socially; in part because commerce and crusading went hand in hand

(Phillips 1998, 24–51). This was far less true, however, when we consider the evidènce we use to chart the appearance of the term 'Europe' in the nominalist sense. Burke is undoubtedly correct vis-à-vis the seventeenth century when he points to such sources as street ballads, pamphlets, and diaries to suggest that the notion of Europe must have had some currency among the general population (Burke 1980, 26–27). I can accept that. But this is where we have to be careful in terms of what questions we are asking because "Did Europe exist before 1700?" can be interpreted in different ways.

Burke wanted to shift the discussion in the direction of not just whether the term was employed, not just how it was used, but also if it is possible to "change the perspective slightly from the history of an idea to what the French call the history of *mentalités collectives*" (Burke 1980, 21). To push it a bit further, I want to know if we can detect—from a realist perspective—any of the ways in which ideas of Europe which later came to be more closely associated with the term were actually bound up with the concept of modernity itself. My conclusion is that we can detect them, but that they are not all functions of some form of alterity as was once thought.

And so, to bring this back around to where we left off, what can be seen as a uniquely new and modern way of seeing the world, the very tools that we use to construct our analyses today, the fact of interrogating the past and asking the questions at all, of asking what it all means, Delanty's "learning process": this is the Europeanness that evolved in a sort of cultural or civilizational process of self-organization in the late medieval and early modern period.

This concept is perhaps best expressed through what the Canadian philosopher Charles Taylor (2007) calls the "immanent frame." Modernity, which I maintain here *is* Europeanness, was a function primarily of internal processes of cultural development/evolution. It came straight out of the Christian reform movement of the Middle Ages and then bubbled up through the Reformation, the Scientific Revolution, and the Age of Enlightenment.[3] In other words, it was the internal process of developing the ability to see things in new and *unique* ways that led to the cultural model of Europeanness and, after 1700, in conjunction with the various other factors here outlined, to the idea of Europe.

The constructionist approach is valid at an elevated level, but this was not what Burke was thinking about. It is not the question he was asking. And it is not really the question we should be asking here now either, especially to the extent that this renewed interest in the origins of western attitudes and worldviews is largely the result of shifting *mentalités collectives* today. If for no other reason than this, in order to understand how people actually thought and acted in the past, then we are going to have to shift away from analyses of the contested meaning of words to something more akin to what anthropologists used to call a "thick description."

The "immanent frame" was an emergent way of seeing and thinking about the world in the early modern period. Before 1450, nearly everyone in Europe believed that God created us, that we had souls, that there was life after death, and that whatever happened in this world was designed or controlled or at least heavily influenced by powers that were not of this world; after 1700, 'Europeans' had a choice as to whether or not they wanted to believe this. This was the immanent as opposed to the transcendent frame. There is a long-standing debate about what secularity means, and it can be defined in a variety of ways: most commonly, it is seen either as the expulsion of religion from public life or as the decline of religious beliefs and practices. Taylor emphasizes a third way of thinking about secularity in terms of the *conditions* of belief. We are now living in a "secular age," he argues, because the conditions of belief have changed. Sometime between 1450 and 1700 a threshold was crossed, and this immanent frame, Taylor writes, is "a distinction *tailor-made for our culture*" (Taylor 2007, 16; emphasis mine).

The roots of this change were in the reform movements of the medieval church. It was the result of what Taylor calls a "rage for order" (2007, 61–89). What he means by this phrase is that churchmen desired to do a better job of making sure that the members of their communities acted like good Christians. They wanted to reduce the levels of violence and superstition that they saw all around them. To accomplish this goal, they worked on reforming the practices of the Church from within, which required gaining a better knowledge of how nature worked. All manner of beliefs and practices needed to be thought through and tested. Scholasticism, when directed towards more pressing problems than trying to figure out how many angels could dance on the head of a pin, resulted in some serious reevaluation of what it meant to be Christian, the nature of God, and the ways in which God operated in the world. In the long run, this led through Calvinism and the neo-Stoic programmes of the seventeenth century to the Deism of the eighteenth—the goal being always to "inculcate some of the norms of civility and a properly ordered life in *everyone*" (Taylor 2007, 120).

But it was not a straight path. There were many dead ends, many variations, many differences of opinion, successes, failures, and plenty of ruptures. And through it all there were still (and still are) people who maintained their medieval belief systems more or less intact even as the culture around them changed. For these reasons this cannot be termed a Grand Narrative. It is not teleological. It could have gone, and could still go, in a different direction altogether. It is the source of where we are now, those building blocks that led to the creation of the modern world. It did not necessarily have to turn out this way. It could have happened somewhere other than Europe. But like similar emergent cultural practices, such as the printing press, or gun technology, once it was 'invented' in one area, it quickly spread to others and there was no need to reinvent it all over again. Indeed, its appearance in a new region precluded independent development of these technologies and, in our present case, of these new ways of seeing the world. The immanent frame came from Europe and spread outwards. There was nothing colonial or triumphant about it (even if that was how it was explained later on). It was just what happened.

Throughout the early modern period, then, there was a gradual diffusion among the people who lived in a region that later came to be popularly known as Europe of a new way of thinking about themselves and about their relation to God and nature: one that eventually came to characterize an entire society, or, if you prefer, although not everyone likes the term, an entire civilization. There arose, in the period in question, a certain disenchantment, an inclination to believe that more things could be explained naturally, through a combination of science and common sense, than through recourse to the supernatural. Over time people felt less at the mercy of demons, spirits, and magic forces. They developed what Taylor calls "buffered selves," meaning that their minds and bodies no longer seemed at risk of supernatural invasion. In the long run this led to disengaged reason and an exclusive humanism. It was unique in the history of the world.

Likewise, it is not a Grand Narrative because it is understood, and implicit in this analysis, that these practices and ways of thinking/being are what Taylor (2004) explains as social imaginaries—but this does not mean that they were any less real or any less forceful for all that. Contested, fine; anemic, no. This is about ideas. This is about discursive practices. But it is also about that '*je-ne-sais-quoi*' that constitutes European culture. Central to western modernity is a new conception of the moral order of society, the very one that frames our inquiries here and now—a self-structuring order that emerged unplanned from within. In Taylor's words:

> The great invention of the West was that of an immanent order in Nature, whose working could be systematically understood and explained on its own terms, leaving open the question whether this whole order had a deeper significance, and whether, if it did, we should infer a transcendent Creator beyond it. … Western modernity, including its secularity, is the fruit of new inventions, newly constructed self-understandings and related practices, and can't be explained in terms of perennial features of human life. (2007, 15–22)

What it means to be African or Arab, Asian, Native American, Latin American, North American, Indian or Aborigine; the very concept of identity; the notion of varying discourses about identity; historical periodization—everything that constitutes aspects of what we regard as proper academic analysis of peoples, their self-perceptions, and their place in the world—all of it is at base some form of Enlightenment project. A scientific, taxonomizing worldview. A European one. There is really no way around this and certainly no reason to be apologetic about it. Indeed, it has been put forth time and again that one of the fundamental drives/urges that makes Europe what it is, that makes European culture European—along with artefacts such as man as a political animal, the rule of law and custom, mixed government and self-governance—is this need to know, this drive toward self-realization, self-reflection (Horcher 2014). To deny this is to "fall into the trap of writing to the theory, rather than to the history or the text" (Festa and Carey 2009, 24).

It might be argued that this is a gross overstatement, that the outlook of the vast majority of people who live or ever lived in Europe is actually not that different from that of people in other parts of the globe. Perhaps there is some truth to that, and yet, something did change in the early modern period, and this has worked its way into the culture. It can certainly be seen as part of its intellectual heritage. On the popular level an argument can be made that westerners in general, and now, by extension, people everywhere, are obsessed with identity whether or not they recognize this in themselves. This is precisely why this question is coming to the fore yet again.

From the perspective of an outside observer, an American who has been living and working in the Middle East for more than 20 years, and one who has been reading and writing about Europe, and travelling and occasionally living there, for even longer, it seems to me that there is more anxiety and more public discussion about identity than there has ever been. And when it comes to Europe's relationship with Islam, there might be more anxiety today than there has been at any time since the Ottomans laid siege to Vienna in the summer of 1683. It is little wonder that academics and nonacademics alike are doing a great deal of thinking about what it means to be European. There is a general consensus among historians that European identity was formed at least in part in the sixteenth and seventeenth centuries in the process of trying to beat back the Turks. Is this happening again now?

It is not the full story, of course. As we have seen, there are also internal dynamics at play that have led to the emergence of a European identity, processes that were self-sustaining and independent from the mirror of the other. But it is part of the story—and maybe one way we can think about this is to compare attitudes toward the Muslim other today with those in the past. In Europe we have gone from being anti-Muslim in one way, which is to say, having negative attitudes toward Muslims because they believe wrong things about God, to being anti-Muslim in another way, that is, having negative attitudes toward Muslims because they still believe in God. The story of the rise of the idea of what it means to be European is how we got from the first thing to the second thing. And that most certainly happened before 1700.

Notes

1. The article was a revised version of a lecture Professor Burke had first given in a series on "The Idea of Europe" for the School of European Studies, University of Sussex, in 1975.
2. For an example of this sort of Grand Narrative, see Duroselle (1990).
3. Delanty would surely see that as part and parcel of that bogeyman the Grand Narrative, but it is not, for reasons I am about to explain; that is, it was diverse, contested, and so on.

Works Cited

Bartlett, Robert. 1993. *The Making of Europe: Conquest, Colonization and Cultural Change (950–1350)*. Princeton, NJ: Princeton University Press.

Blanks, David. 1999. "Western Views of Islam in the Premodern Period: A Brief History of Past Approaches." In *Western Views of Islam in Medieval and Early Modern Europe: Perception of Other*, edited by David R. Blanks and Michael Frassetto, 11–53. New York: St. Martin's.

Blanks, David, ed. 1997. *Images of the Other before 1700: Cairo Papers in Social Science* 19:2. Cairo: American University in Cairo Press.

Bohrer, Karl Heinz. 2012. "'Europe' as Utopia: Causes of Its Decline." Translated by Ciaran Cronin. *New Literary History* 4 (43): 587–605.

Burke, Peter. 1980. "Did Europe Exist before 1700?" *History of European Ideas* 1 (1): 21–29.

Carnoy, Martin. 1974. *Education as Cultural Imperialism*. New York: MacKay.

Daniel, Norman. 1975. *The Arabs and Medieval Europe*. London: Longmans.

Daniel, Norman. 1960. *Islam and the West: The Making of an Image*. Edinburgh: Edinburgh University Press.

Delanty, Gerard. 1995. *Inventing Europe: Idea, Identity, Reality*. New York: Palgrave Macmillan.

Delanty, Gerard. 2013. *Formations of European Modernity: A Historical and Political Sociology of Europe*. New York: Palgrave Macmillan.

Den Boer, Pim. 1993. "Europe to 1914: The Making of an Idea." In *The History of the Idea of Europe*, edited by Kevin Wilson and Jan van der Dussen, 13–82. Milton Keynes: The Open University.

Duroselle, Jean-Baptiste. 1990. *Europe: A History of Its Peoples*. London: Viking.

Festa, Lynn, and Daniel Carey. 2009. "Some Answers to the Question: 'What Is Postcolonial Enlightenment?'" In *The Postcolonial Enlightenment: Eighteenth-Century Colonialism and Postcolonial Theory*, edited by Daniel Carey and Lynn Festa, 1–33. Oxford: Oxford University Press.

Gollwitzer, H. 1951. *Europabild und Europagedanke: Beiträge zur deutschen Geistegeschichte des 18. und 19. Jahrhunderts*. Munich: Beck.

Hay, Denys. 1957. *Europe: The Emergence of an Idea*. Edinburgh: Edinburgh University Press.

Hörcher, Ferenc. 2014. "Europe Reloaded: Tradition, Reality, Project—An Introduction." In *Transfigurations of the European Identity*, edited by Bulcsu Bognár and Zsolt Almási, 1–20. Newcastle upon Tyne: Cambridge Scholars.

Jones, Meredith C. 1942. "The Conventional Saracen of the Songs of the Geste." *Speculum* 17: 201–225.

Manselli, Raoul. 1965. "La res publica christiana e l'Islam." In *L'Occidente e l'Islam nell'alto medioevo*, 115–147. Spoleto: Centro Italiano di Studi sull'Alto Medioevo.

Molho, Anthony. 2007. "A Harlequin's Dress: Reflections on Europe's Public Discourse." In *Finding Europe: Discourses on Margins, Communities, Images*, edited by Anthony Molho and Diogo Ramada Curto, 1–17. New York: Berghahn.

Nelson, Brian, David Roberts, and Walter Veit, eds. 1992. *The Idea of Europe: Problems of National and Transnational Identity*. London: Bloomsbury.

Philips, J. R. S. 1998. *The Medieval Expansion of Europe*. 2nd ed. Oxford: Clarendon Press.

Roberts, John, Águeda María Rodríguez Cruz, and Jurgen Hurbst. 1996. "Exporting Models." In *A History of the University in Europe*, Vol. 2, edited by Hilde de Ridder-Symoens, 256–282. Cambridge: Cambridge University Press.

Said, Edward. 1978. *Orientalism*. New York: Vintage Books.

Shils, Edward, and John Roberts. 2004. "The Diffusion of European Models Outside Europe." In *A History of the University in Europe*, Vol. 3, edited by Walter Rüegg, 163–229. Cambridge: Cambridge University Press.

Southern, Richard. 1962. *Western Views of Islam in the Middle Ages*. Cambridge, MA: Harvard University Press.

Taylor, Charles. 2004. *Modern Social Imaginaries*. Durham, NC: Duke University Press.

Taylor, Charles. 2007. *A Secular Age*. Cambridge, MA: Belknap—Harvard University Press.

Tolan, John. 2002. *Saracens: Islam in the Medieval European Imagination*. New York: Columbia University Press.

Tolan, John, ed. 1996. *Medieval Christian Perceptions of Islam: A Book of Essays*. New York: Garland.

2 *Ūrubba* in Early Modern Arabic Sources

Nabil Matar

This chapter focuses on the 'idea of Europe' in the early modern period and how that idea was understood by those who lived just across the sea from Europeans: the Arabic-speaking peoples from Tangier to Alexandretta. Given the twentieth- and twenty-first-century political and economic consolidation of western and central Europe, scholars have examined the historical record to see whether there was or has been a cultural 'idea of Europe,' too. Denys Hay (1957, 25) noted that the first use of the term 'Europeans' appeared in the wake of the battle of Tours in 732, thereby suggesting that a religious-Christian idea of Europe had emerged as a result of the encounter with Islam. If such a territorial-cum-religious appellation came about as a result of the confrontation with Islam, it will be necessary to inquire whether it was an appellation that the 'Europeans' projected to the Muslim Arabs (and Berbers) across the sea, and whether they defined themselves to themselves as having a common "economic and cultural and legal base … in the western half of the old Roman Empire" (Hulme 1994, 193).

By the sixteenth century, there were extensive exchanges between the northern and southern shores of the Mediterranean, ranging from trade to piracy and from captivity to travel. A century later, those exchanges had increased to include diplomatic visits and treaties, alliances, and invasions, and by 1700, European fleets and traders were assuming a major role in the commercial and naval control of the western Mediterranean. But as the peoples of Spain and Italy, France and Britain, Holland and Malta—the only regions about which North African Arabic writings have survived from the early modern period—encountered Arabic speakers, they presented themselves to them as *Naṣārā* [Christians]. Their self-definition as recorded in Arabic sources was religious, not geographical, which is why the self-definition that the North Africans assumed in those encounters was also religious: *Muslimūn* [Muslims]. Alternatively, when the Muslims encountered the Ottoman Turks/*Türk*/*Atrāk* after 1516–1517 and the expansion into all of North Africa (except Morocco), they defined themselves against these fellow Muslims as '*Arab*,' emphasizing their cultural and ethnic distinction even when they praised the Ottomans for defending them against the attacks of the *Naṣārā*.

By examining in a chronological order Arabic sources from both North Africa and the Levant, this chapter documents how the Arabic-speaking societies used the name 'Europe.' The emphasis on Arabic is necessary because of the frequent possibilities of mistranslation in the European sources.[1] This chapter shows why *Ūrubba* was not preeminent in Arabic writing and thinking.[2]

* * *

From the seventeenth century onwards, the regencies of Algeria, Tunisia, and Libya began to draw away from the central authority of Istanbul and to pursue their own political and military agendas. Along with Morocco, they sent frequent ambassadorial delegations and emissaries to the European capitals and negotiated commercial, peace, and captive-exchange treaties. During and after their visits, some emissaries reported with relative admiration and envy about what they saw in technological and administrative innovation and cultural and social differences. But their descriptions were always focused on the specific regions they had visited and did not encompass a larger geographical or continental unity. All but one of the surviving travelogues were written for the Moroccan court about Spain, France, Holland, Malta, Sicily, and Italy. Curiously, while the second account of c. 1640s mentioned the name of 'Europe,' the other accounts, written in 1690, 1766, and 1779–1788, did not.

The Arabs had their own rich legacy of geographical writings in the medieval period, and in Shams al-Dīn Abi 'Abdallah al-Dimashqī's fourteenth-century geographical treatise, 'Europe' is a name that is associated with the division of the world by Alexander the Great. "He divided the inhabited world into four parts, the first of which he called Urūfā in which is found al-Andalus, the Slavs, the Franks, Tanja and the Byzantines" (1923, 24). But Europe did not have any specific importance or character for Alexander. Similarly, in an anonymous sixteenth-century rendition of a ninth-century geographical text, Europe does not appear since the author divided the world into *aqālīm* [zones] in which he situated "Bilād al-Rūm" [lands of the Byzantines] and "Roma al-kubrā" [Great Rome] in the fifth and sixth zones.[3] All the major travellers in the period under study who left accounts of journeys and geographies described lands extending from Morocco to Iraq to India, not Europe, because it was in those countries that they found education, bought books, fulfilled religious duties, joined Sufi circles, studied at the feet of learned scholars, or conducted trade. 'Europe' was not a destination they sought, and therefore their information remained so limited that even the name of the continent was variously spelled and pronounced—notwithstanding the fact that Europeans traded extensively with the Ottomans, who possessed a wide array of maps of the Mediterranean, Europe, and the New World. Ottoman cartographers had prepared numerous maps for their fleets and military commanders, including the first Islamic maps of the New World by Piri Reīs (d. 1554).[4] But these maps and atlases remained confined to the Ottoman elite and were not shared among the public, most certainly not among those in the subjugated Arabic (and Berber) provinces.

The first 'Mappamundi' or world map by Tunuslu Hajj Ahmed was not really done by a Tunisian, and its companion text was written in Ottoman, not Arabic. In translating some of the cartouches on this map, Giancarlo Casale (2013, 81) included the following sentence: "Europe: This is the part of the world that they also call 'Frengistan'"—perhaps a throwback to al-Idrīsī's twelfth-century *"bilād al-ifranjiyyīn"* [land of the Franks] (1984, 730, 742). Because the map was drawn by a Venetian dragoman, the name 'Europe' appears on it. But as with other maps, it did not make its way into the Arabic provenance—as can be seen in the most important bibliographer of Arabic writings since Ibn al-Nadīm's *al-Fihrist* [The index] (d. 990). Mustafā ibn 'Abdallah/Ḥajjī Khalīfa/Kātip Celebī (1609–1657) travelled widely among the mosques and libraries of the Ottoman empire and beyond, after which he alphabetically (unlike Ibn al-Nadīm's thematic arrangement) organized the titles of about 15,000 books into a massive compendium that he called *Kashf al-zunūn fī asāmī al-kutub wa-l-funūn* [Survey of the names of books and arts]. The books covered all areas of Arabic and Islamic knowledge, but no title in the Arabic list includes anything associated with the geography or cartography of early modernity. There are references to the usual classics by al-Mas'ūdī, Ibn Baṭṭūṭa, Ibn Jubayr, and a few others, but when Celebī, interestingly, transliterated and wrote down in Arabic the word 'atlas' in the preface to the geographical units, he did not have any Islamic, Turkish, or Arabic work in mind: rather, he had consulted Mercator's atlas in a Turkish version. In light of the wording that appeared in the European atlas, Celebī used the term *'Ūruffa,'*[5] seemingly rejecting the earlier designation of *Frengistan;* and he did that too in his monumental *Jahanama:* *'Ūrubba.'*[6] His contemporary, Abu Bakr al-Dimashqī (d. 1691), translated W. J. Blaeu's *Atlas Major* into Ottoman in 1675 (Krachkovski 1987, 712), but his work remained in the confines of the High Porte of Sultan Mehmed IV, his patron, never reaching the wider Arabic public. When an Arab writer from Ottoman Lebanon, Aḥmad ibn Aḥmad al-Khālidī al-Ṣafadī (1969), wrote the first Arabic account about Italy and Malta in the 1610s, he had no access to the term 'Europe' and used *bilād al gharb* [lands of the west] (208), and *bilād al-Naṣārā* [lands of the Christians] (220). He also mentioned cities such as Livorno, Pisa, and Rome, along with the kings of Spain, France, and the Grand Master of Malta, but he did not seem to have a view of these regions and their rulers as constituting a continental entity: rather, they were lands of the Christians and not of the 'Europeans' because they were united, in his view, by the religion of Christ—whatever that might have meant to him, given his largely Qur'ānic understanding of it.

Arab sailors and sea captains possessed portolan maps for Mediterranean navigation, but these maps identified the ports that ships used, rather than described the hinterlands or the continental layout.[7] As a result, Arabs did not get to 'see' maps of continents and so did not conceive of geographical divisions: they had no opportunity to locate 'Europe' on a map, which is why when they thought of regions to their Mediterranean north, they used nomenclature that reflected

1 cities,
2 countries that bore the names of languages, or
3 an overarching religion—*Nuṣrāniyya.*

As religious wars flared in western Europe from the mid-sixteenth to the mid-seventeenth centuries, the *Naṣārā* in Arabic writings started to break down into national groups associated with specific languages: *Inglīz* [English], *Ifransīs* [French], *Flamink* [Flemish], *'Ajam* or *Isbanyol* [Spanish], and *burtuqāl* [Portuguese]. Although they followed different denominations of Christianity, to the Muslims, they appeared to belong to different religions altogether: the enmity and violence which the Protestants (English and Dutch) showed to Catholics (Spanish) could not but have meant to North African writers that the former were totally separate from the *'abadat al-ṣalīb* ["worshippers of the Cross"].

Such a perspective on the Protestant–Catholic divide was confirmed by the expelled Andalusians (Moriscos) from the end of the sixteenth century onwards. The Andalusians were familiar with the geographical nomenclature used among their former compatriots: that is why they were the only writers to use terms for Protestants in a geographical context: *Latārīn* and *Kluūniyyīn*, Lutherans and Calvinists. As they settled in North Africa, from Salé to Tunis, the Andalusians described their experiences among the Christians and prepared texts that they hoped would be useful to their new coreligionists. The most significant of these texts was a lengthy account about the casting of canons and the use of artillery, written by Aḥmad ibn Ghānim. It was taken from Spanish sources (and he himself wrote it in Spanish) and was translated into Arabic in the 1640s by Aḥmad ibn Qāsim. As the author described his life among the Spaniards, he wrote that he had lived in the "best countries of Europe," and "the meaning of that name is one quarter of the world and for us it is *hayyat al-joof,* and contains many dominions of the Christians, one of which was the land of al-Andalus, which is the best land in that quarter, known among the non-Arabs as *Ūrubbā.*" He continued by mentioning "the countries of the English and the Franks and the Flemish and the Italians, which meant those who belonged to the country of Italy." There were also *bilād maghribiyya* (19), *maghribiyya* sultanates (233), and *bilād al–Islam* (*passim*).[8] Europe was taking shape, but not against Africa (the term itself had a different meaning in Arabic): perhaps for Ibn Ghānim, *Ūrubba* was simply a synecdoche for Christians/Christendom/*bilād al-Naṣārā.*

The translator Aḥmad ibn Qāsim (1997) wrote one of the most detailed autobiographies in early modern Arabic. After fleeing Spain to Morocco, and because he was fluent in both Arabic and Spanish, he became the court translator to three rulers, from the late 1590s to his death in the 1640s. On one occasion, he recorded how the Moroccan ruler, Mulay Zaydān (reg. 1603–1627), ordered him to translate a "large *'ajamī* book" which was in the "language of the *ifranj*": it showed in *muṣawwara* [illustration] all the "regions of the world, including lengths and widths of countries, rivers, courses of rivers, cities on their banks and all the seas, islands, and *aqālīm*" (93). This "book" was the first atlas that Ibn Qāsim had seen—although he did not use that word. Later, after he recounted the numerous disputations that he had had with Christians in France, he returned to geography to inform the reader that the world was divided into four parts, each of which had its own name, and that *Ūrubba* was the name given to the inner quarter that is near the North Pole: "It starts in the Black Sea and reaches the boundaries of al-Andalus" (120).

While he and the exiled Andalusians had access to a geographical terminology that included the name of Europe, other Muslims in North Africa did not, nor did they think in continental terms. If "the inhabitants of the European continent *thought* and *acted* as European long before they spoke of themselves as European" (Bohrer 2012, 587), it was a Europeanness that was not at all evident to the *only* outside people who observed and wrote about them. For the Arabic-speaking peoples who were dealing and wheeling with Europeans, there was not even an "imagined" European community (*sensu* Benedict Anderson)—again because when North Africans signed peace and commercial treaties, they named specific countries, since neither the English nor the French nor others ever presented themselves to their Muslim counterparts as 'Europeans' united in a common identity. Nor, most importantly for Arabic speakers, were the *Naṣārā* united in language; and while there was a lingua franca in the Mediterranean basin, as Jocelyne Dakhlia has shown, all official treaties were written in English or French, Dutch or Italian (and of course translated into Turkish or Arabic). Such differences in languages and 'religions' were in stark contrast to Dar al-Islam where it was possible for Moroccans and Egyptians and Syrians to see themselves as culturally, intellectually, and (most importantly) linguistically *Muslimūn,* from Fez to Musil and from Aleppo to Mecca.

Another reason for not seeing 'Europeans' was that Arabic geographical knowledge remained Ptolemaic, where the world was divided into *aqālīm* [zones] that listed cities, mountains, rivers, and seas, but not continents.[9] As late as the nineteenth century, a well-travelled Moroccan such as Abu al-Qāsim al-Zayyānī still referred to Ptolemy and his *aqālīm* (1967, 309), although other writers/travellers by that time had begun to use continental designations. In this context, it is important to note that no Arab writer, traveller, or pilgrim ever added a continental epithet to his name. Arabic nomenclature did not include allusions to African or Asian origination (Leo Africanus was of course the papal name given to Ḥasan al-Wazzān at his baptism) because names were associated with cities and/or regions: one came from Taza or Dimyat or Meknes or Bukhara or Khurasan or Jerusalem or Musil—(and such associations, by the way applied to both native Muslims and Christians and Jews)—and so the epithet in the name became Tazi, Dimyati, Miknasi, Bukhari, Khurasani, Maqdisi/Jerusalemite, Musili, and the like. In turn, Arabs could not conceive of others as understanding themselves differently, and so when an Englishman converted and settled among them, he was given the surname *Inglīzī* [English]; or *Fransīs* if he was French or *Jenawī* if he was Genoese. As Arnon Groiss has observed: "Generally speaking, territorial identities in the Middle East were far less important traditionally than in the West. Their role in the local society was minor compared to that of the religious, ethnic or linguistic identities, and they barely had any political significance" (2011, 30).

That North Africans and other Muslim Arabs had very limited information about the geography of other countries does not mean that they did not have, by far, more direct information about the daily customs and behaviors of the Euro-Christians than the other way round (see Matar 2011). In the major port cities of the Arab Mediterranean, from Tetuan to Algiers to Tunis to Alexandria to Beirut to Iskenderun, there were always clusters of French or English, Venetian, or Dutch factors and traders, consuls and clerics, sometimes living with their families, who facilitated commercial exchange between their countrymen and the local population. An average Aleppan or Miknasi stood a much greater chance of bumping into an English merchant or a Spanish priest than a Londoner or a Parisian had of seeing Muslim shaykhs or merchants or emissaries. While such daily knowledge about the *Naṣārā* was attainable by numerous other means, too—directives from the rulers, Friday sermons (denouncing the enemy), *taqāyīd* [news reports], jurisprudential decisions, and oral narratives of captives—it never took shape in books about the countries and peoples of western Europe. The numerous ambassadorial accounts that have survived from Moroccan emissaries were confined in their readership to the court, although they could not but have trickled down to families and friends, as the letters of 'Abdallah ibn 'Aisha show (see Matar 2015a). Still, it is significant that not a single sea traveller crossing from Tangier to Izmir, from al-Tamjarouti in the 1590 to al-Miknāsī in the 1780s, ever mentioned continental names: rather, the three divisions of the landmass around the Mediterranean Sea (a name that was very rarely used in the Arabic writings of the period under study) were designated not in accordance with geography but religion and ethnicity: *barr al-'Arab* [coastline of the Arabs], *barr al-Naṣārā* [coastline of the Christians], and *barr al-Türk* [coastline of the Turks]. In a seventeenth-century tract on tobacco, the anonymous author wrote:

It [tobacco] first appeared in *bilād al-Ifranj* at the end of the tenth century [the sixteenth century AD]. They [the infidels] became attached to it and pointed out its benefits. And so it spread to the islands of the Maghrib and the regions of *bilād al-Hind* [India], beyond the Sea of Salt [the Mediterranean]. Then it reached *bilād al'Arab* where it had been forgotten and ignored ... and finally it reached *arḍ al-Türk* and *al-'Ajam* [the Persians] where it became famous.[10]

North African Muslims did not see 'Europe': they saw *Naṣārā* and *ifranj*, exactly like most other Muslims, even as far away as the Maldive Islands.[11] The landmass that Muslims could cross from Fez to Tunis to Jerusalem and Istanbul, or from Aleppo to Baghdad to Mecca appeared to be one; and while religion and ethnicity (Turk and Arab and Berber, Muslim and Christian and Jew) marked important differences, geography or language did not, and therefore a traveller did not have any sense of crossing from one continent to another. Only in the case of America was there a sense of a new and different entity: and although no North African is known to have travelled there and written about his journey, the term was first picked up in Spain and appeared in the 1690 ambassadorial report of Muhammad Wahāb al-Ghassānī: "Marka." Later, other ambassadors described America in the context of narrating Spanish history and Anglo-Spanish conflict in the eighteenth century. But it is not clear if any of the writers understood "Marka" to mean a continent.

Meanwhile, in the eastern part of the Mediterranean basin, Christian Arabs, both Maronite-Catholic and Orthodox, had some conceptualization of Europe, even if they might not have had the maps. The Maronites of Lebanon (and Syria) had extensive relations with Italy and France as missionary priests arrived in the Levant to proselytize at the same time that local Maronites went to Rome to acquire an education in theology, philosophy, and languages. These latter priests became familiar with Catholic culture and on returning to their homeland not only instructed their own communities about the countries they had inhabited, but also debated with the Orthodox 'schismatics' in the hope of converting them to Roman Catholicism. The Arabic exchanges among the Orthodox and the Catholics are extensive and range over all topics, from discussions of the *per filium/filioque* divide to the new calendar introduced by Pope Gregory VIII (of which the Catholics tried to convince the Orthodox—who refused to accept it) to the pride of the Catholics about the diffusion of Catholicism around the world, unlike the limited range of Orthodoxy. In such discussions and disputations, there were references to the world and its various regions and continents. Thus, in a "Report on the kingdoms that are under the jurisdiction of the Roman Church and of the countries in each kingdom," there is a list of kingdoms, principalities, and the number of Catholic clergy in them: for instance, the king of France has 166 metropolitans, 117 princes, 100 presbyters, 11,629 monasteries, 5,515 *qasabāt*; then Austria, Florence, Genoa, Venice; and then regions in Africa and the "New World" (*al-dunyā al-jadīda*), Mexico, Granada, Brazil, Goa. But strangely in this anonymous manuscript of the seventeenth century, there is no mention of Europe. Rather, it makes the following declaration:

> Learn that the world is divided into four parts: the first is known as *bilād al-ifranj*; the second is Asia which begins in Constantinople and ends in China; the third is known as Africa and extends from Egypt to *bilād al-Ifranj*, and the fourth is known as *yenki dunya*, I mean the New World.[12]

In 1668, a Catholic priest from Musil in Iraq went on the pilgrimage to Jerusalem and then boarded an English ship from Iskenderun headed for *bilād Ŭrubba*. He used that phrase, the lands of Europe, at the outset of his account, but as he continued, he used *bilād al-Naṣārā* for the countries he visited—France, Italy, and Malta. He recorded his journey in a manuscript of which numerous copies have survived, but the information remained confined to Catholic scriptoria (al-Mawsūlī 1906, 4, 5).[13]

The most extensive geography book that appeared in this period was published in France in 1717. It was written in Greek by the patriarch of Jerusalem, Chrysanthus Notaras, and subsequently translated into Arabic (by translators who admitted that they were not good in either Greek or Arabic).[14] Notaras had studied mathematics in Paris, and while his book was rich in classical allusions, it presented a Ptolemaic-based geography of zones and a Catholic-based cosmography that rejected the heliocentric system as a false claim of 'moderns' such as the *Kūpernīkkiyyīn* [Copernicans]. Be that as it may, the book included detailed information about Europe, although the translator/s never seemed to get the name right and used *Ŭrubba, Ŭr Ŭbī, Afrobā, Afrobī*, and others even on the same page. In the units about "the borders of Europe which are very beautiful," the author wrote:

> All of Europe is fertile and fruitful, of moderate climate, and densely inhabited. It has many special characteristics, distinctive flora and flowers and animals, spices, precious stones and pearls. But there are no lions, elephants, dragons or wild and savage beasts. … Most of the people of Europe are courageous and many are very intelligent. How many a wise man has been born there, and scientist, and physician, and rhetorician, and exegete of scriptures and law; and how many military leaders who have conquered the peoples of the world and others with the power of their actions, tongue, and arm! In Europe are the two kingdoms of the Greeks and the Romans that are widely famous; and in it appeared all the sciences and crafts, courage and good manners and wit: one can justly call it the ornament of the world.[15]

Russian Orthodox emissaries frequently visited the Ottoman regions that had high numbers of Orthodox Arabs in order to give them financial support. In turn, Arab priests travelled to Moscow where they acquired texts about the new geographies that they subsequently translated into Arabic. Furthermore, and as they interacted with the European merchants in their cities, they picked up names and news that gave them an informed picture of the world. In the 1660s, the patriarch of Antioch, Makarios, went on a journey from Aleppo to Moscow about which his deacon Būluṣ wrote the longest travel account in Arabic regarding a European country in the early modern period. Būluṣ knew the history of Syria, from the days of the Mamelukes to his own days, and asserted that he placed much greater trust in histories written by his own community than in those written by the *ifranj* (3r).

But to a large extent, his geography remained unchanged in its nomenclature: there were *bilād al-Masīḥiyīn* (4v, 7, and *passim*); *bilād al-'Ajam* [non-Arab/ Persian]; Damascus and Aleppo in *bilād al-'Arab* (8v); *bilād al-Rūm* and *bilād al-Kozak wa-l-Maṣkof* [Cossacks and Moscow] (14r). Būluṣ recognized different peoples in different countries without a continental unity that endowed them with some kind of communal identity.[16]

A century later, in 1758, a treatise about Russia which praised *Ürubbā* was translated into Arabic.[17] The title of the manuscript is "A Popular Account of Modern Russia," and it was based, as the anonymous author/ translator indicated, on the writings of modern travellers as well as on the works of cartographers and wanderers who had gathered information about all races, tribes, and kingdoms of the world.[18] "That is why we have called it *al-Tārīkh al-maskūnī* [*The Universal History*]." The author promised to start with Russia since it was the northernmost kingdom, and then, after "we describe Europe, we will move to Asia, then Africa, and finally America." The author did not complete his history since the manuscript consists of a detailed account of every region in Russia, along with long sections on culture, customs, religious history and institutions; but nothing else. Still, the description of Europe with which the author opened is the longest that had appeared in Arabic until then:

> The world is divided into four parts: *Ürobbā*, Asia, Africa and America. ... The first part is Europe which, if compared and con-trasted with the other parts, appears to be small in size and space, but in the light of its success, it is the greatest and most attractive. It has been very productive because its inhabitants have been attentive to science and technology. The dear reader should know that those who have mapped the earth, the historians, the law-givers, and those who have developed urban cultures, those who are advanced in wars and the heroes famous among soldiers and kings and sultans have all been born and raised in Europe. Honesty and truthfulness prevail in Europe more than in any other part of the world. What is more, it has a higher number of inhabitants than the other parts of the world which has enabled it by means of its large number of soldiers to build mighty naval and land forces that have dominated many kingdoms and countries in other parts of the inhabited world. They have pre-vailed and imposed their laws on the peoples of those regions: they have subjugated them by their technology and science, their learning and military strength. Thus the kingdom of Great Russia is obeyed by the peoples of Great Tartaria and Siberia in Asia who have bent their necks before it. Also, its priests have taught at the courts of rulers and have spread the Holy Gospel drawing many people away from idol worship and into the fold of the true faith. We intend to show this very clearly in our book. Similarly, the French and the Spanish, the English and the Flemish have come to rule over many regions in America and

in Africa, even various regions in the East Indies. From there they have carried vast possessions and enriched their kingdoms. This is proof of what we are saying: Europe is blessed with bounties more than others.

The location of Europe in the inhabited world is excellent and is better than others. For that reason, it is more abundant in fruit and people because it is not below the Equator, nor is it too near to it like the hot countries, nor too far, like the cold countries with snow and ice. It is between 35 and 73 degrees in width, from the south to the north. As for its length, it is between 9 and 93 degrees below the Equator, from west to east. For that reason, the length of Europe from the River Tukalia and ending in Ofion [Onega], a river in Muscovy, is 3600 *ifranjī* miles and its width starting in Sweden and reaching to Lada [River] is about 2200 *ifranjī* miles. Europe is surrounded by the sea from all sides except in the east where it is connected to Asia. To the north, there is the frozen sea, I mean, the North Sea which cannot be crossed, and to the east, it is surrounded by the Western or Atlantic Sea which separates it from America. To the south, it is surrounded by the Strait of Jabal Tar [Gibraltar], and the sea that runs between the two land masses separates it from Africa. To the east, it extends to the archipelago, the strait of Gallipoli, the Marmara Sea, the Strait of Constantinople, the Black Sea and the Lake of Mioti [Azov Sea]; and from the Hatanayīn River, it extends in a straight line to the Ofion River which reaches the North Sea. These are the boundaries of Europe.

Europe includes the following kingdoms and dominions: Muscovy which is in Europe, and Safiḥa [Sweden], Denmark, Lehiyyī [Poland?] and Germania which is Austria (which encompasses monarchies and subjects, rulers and potentates); and Turkey in Europe; also the kingdoms of France and Spain and Portugal and Italy (which encompass various governors and rulers). It also includes the islands of Britain, I mean the kingdom of England, with islands that are governed by its kings. About all these we intend to write in this book which we have called *Khabariyāt al-ʿālam* [*News about the World*]. (fos. 4–5)

… Europe contains rivers, lakes, mountains, and islands, as well as dry land and other natural features. It also has man-made institutions such as denominations, customs, languages and beliefs, either as a result of nurture or of habit or of inheritance. … As for the religions of *ahl Ūrubbā* [Europeans], the foremost and the most accurate is that of the Christians, which is divided into three churches: Eastern, Western, and Lutheran and Calvinist. There are also the religions of the Turks and the Jews, and some idol worshipers in the northern part of Muscovy, Sweden and Denmark; I will describe their religions in due course. As for the languages that are common in Europe: they are four, Greek, Latin, Līrkī [Slavonic] and Tiftonīkī [Teutonic/Germanic]. As for Greek, it is the vernacular now, I mean the *Rūmī*, which is used in all parts of European Turkey. Latin has evolved into Italian, French and Spanish; by Old Līrkiyā, I mean Slavonic, from which evolved the Muscovite, Līhī [Polish], Ankarī, Ghominkī [Ukrainian?], Serbian, Slavonic, Fusianiki, and Bulgarian languages. And from Tiftonīki developed the Austrian, Dutch, English, and Danish languages. From Latin and Līrkiya developed by default the Fulakhiyya; the Arna'ūtī [Albanian] evolved by default from Latin, Līrkiyā and Turkish. These are the languages that are used in Europe. So too is the Turkish language which prevails among the Ottomans in all the regions adjacent to the borders with Europe.

According to all historians, Europeans are gentler and better-mannered than all the uncouth peoples living in the other three parts of the world. They are kind and compassionate to strangers, gracious in their greetings, courteous and orderly, lovers of mercy and justice, generous and affable, obedient to the law of nature, with placid behavior and possess a philosophy of manners, either as a result of habit or of nurture. (fos. 6–7)

Strangely, the manuscript makes no reference to the American continent. While the geographical information about the boundaries and parameters of Europe is relatively accurate, the description and transcription of languages suggest limited understanding of the original texts and/or limited translation ability. It is possible that the author used some kind of map, although it is unclear why there is no reference to America: the new continent does not have a place in the world which is being presented to the Arabic readers. Nor, for that matter, does the author elaborate on the Ottoman empire in which the Arabic-speaking population—for whom the manuscript was presumably intended—lived. Given the paucity of Arabic sources about Europe and the rest of the world, the description could be useful to its readers, and it is possible that the author intended to describe the geography and ethnography of the Arabic-speaking world later in the work. But the emphasis on the superiority of the Europeans would have been both perplexing and dangerous to readers: perplexing because readers would not know why they were expected to celebrate that superiority or to accept the statements about the Europeans; and dangerous because it turned their perspective away from their own regions and history to foreign parts. It is likely that the manuscript circulated among members of the Orthodox community, at whom it was obviously aimed, but it never reached a larger audience, probably because at times of military conflict between the Ottomans and the Russians, such praise of Russia would have been viewed with suspicion. The manuscript was definitely not available to another Orthodox priest writing in the same period in Aleppo. Mikhā'īl Brayk explained that world news reached him via the letters sent to the merchants and to the *Ifranj* [Franks] in Damascus (32). As he described the earthquake of 1755, he used *"bilād Arobā* [the country of Europe] in the West" (1930, 31). But then, and perhaps relying on oral information, Brayk wrote/pronounced the name 'Europe' quite differently from his predecessors: recording a prophecy that had been found in Hebrew near the city of Paris in 1754, he wrote that in the year 1757, there was going to be war in the lands of *Afrobī*/Europe (Brayk 1930, 57).

While Christian Arabs possessed some writings about Europe, without always having first-hand experience of any country there, the absence of 'Europe' is most noticeable in the three travelogues written by the Moroccan ambassador 'Uthmān ibn Muḥammad al-Miknāsī (d. 1799), who spent two to three years in European countries. No other writer in the premodern Arab World travelled as much as he did into different regions of the Christian West—Spain, Malta, Naples, and Sicily—and then into the Ottoman empire, Tunisia, Algeria, and Morocco. Al-Miknāsī was the most diversely travelled of Arab writers before the *Nahḍa* (renaissance) of the nineteenth century, and yet much as he interacted with the Spaniards and the Maltese, the Neapolitans and the Sicilians; and much as he listened to their accounts of history, which he carefully summarized; and much as he recalled Arabic accounts about medieval encounters, he never used the term 'Europe.' In Spain, the country that was most difficult for North Africans to visit because of its anti-Muslim legacy, he saw *Naṣārā* wherever he turned; and he saw cities that gave him no reason to mention a large continental concept such as Europe. The second journey took him into the Mediterranean Sea (a name he does not use) and into Valletta and Naples and Palermo; the third journey took him to Istanbul after which he travelled through Anatolia to Damascus and further south to Mecca and Medina. On the return segment of his journey, he passed through Jerusalem and Acre, sailed to Tunis (on board a Christian ship), and continued on land to Morocco. On this journey, he travelled through three continents, and yet, at no point did he ever mention continental names (see Matar 2015b).

Al-Miknāsī was quite good at geography. His itineraries are accurate, and his descriptions of cities and ports, monuments and mosques, castles and monarchs are mostly based on first-hand observations. Arab itinerants always used descriptions from previous travellers (sometimes crediting them, sometimes not), and al-Miknāsī was no exception. He relied in his description of Spain on the earlier accounts of two Moroccan ambassadors, al-Ghassānī (1690) and al-Ghazzāl (1766). But in regard to Malta, the kingdom of Naples, and Sicily, he does not mention prior sources and so must be presumed to have recorded what he saw and, importantly, what he heard. He was extremely inquisitive and in his texts mentioned how he had asked about what he did not understand or know. The description of his encounters with the vast variety of peoples, both Christian and Muslim, always highlighted specific cultural aspects and either expressed condemnation or admiration. But his focus was always on cities and ports and individuals rather than on larger units or groups. The countries in which he travelled and the sea that he crossed did not appear to be geographical composites: they were religious or ethnic composites—the Arab coastline, the Turkish coastline, the Christian coastline, not continents.

Sometime about 1796, just under a decade after al-Miknāsī returned from his last journey, another Moroccan scholar, Abu al-Qāsim al-Zayyānī, went on the pilgrimage to Mecca. In his *al-Tarjumāna al-kubrā fī akhbār al-ma'mūr barran wa baḥran* [*The Great History of the World by Land and Sea*], he included a geography of the world as he knew it. He was a widely read diplomat and a man of many travels, but when he came to describe the Mediterranean and the peoples around it, he wrote the following:

> *Baḥr al-Maghrib wa-l Shām wa-l Rūm* [the Sea of the Maghrib and Syria and the Sea of the Byzantines]: begins in the fourth *iqlīm* [zone] and is called *Baḥr al-Zuqāq* [Sea of the Strait] because it is eighteen miles wide. It then proceeds east in the direction of *arḍ al-Barbar* [land of the Berbers] and the north of *al-Maghrib al-Aqsa* [the Farthest Maghrib] until it reaches *al-Maghrib al-Awsat* [Middle Maghrib] and connects with *arḍ Ifrīqiya* [Tunisia] unto *Wadī al-Raml* to *arḍ Barqā* and *arḍ Lūqā wa Marāqiya*—to *al-Iskandarīya* [Alexandria] and the northern part of *arḍ al-Tīh* to *Filasṭīn* [Palestine] to the rest of the coasts of *Shām* [Syria] until it reaches *Suwaydiya*. There it turns back toward *al-Maghrib*. It links up with the Constantinian Gulf, to the island of *Bilonch* and *Kashmīl* to *Ardant*. There it reaches the Gulf of Venice and links up with the Sicilian *majāz* [strait] unto *Bilād Rūmiya* then to *Bilād Seqobyā* [land of the Slavs] and *Aryonā*. It passes by the mountains of *Yunān* [Greece] and East Andalusia where in the south it reaches the two islands, where it had started. (1967, 294)

That a well-travelled and deeply learned jurist did not see a 'Europe' on the northern coast of this multifarious sea is significant. Al-Zayyānī was not an average traveller: he was able to read maps (*al-karīta*) and to determine the location of his ship (1967, 129); he knew French and/or Spanish (1967, 130), and he had studied every major travelogue by Arabic writers (but mentioned nothing by European authors). He knew the ports from Tetuan to Izmir and throughout his travels tried to verify information and so corrected whatever errors he encountered. But he never mentioned 'Europe.' Nor did Shihāb al-Dīn al-Qalyūbī in his "Epistle about City Names," copied in 1804: he organized place-names not by continents but alphabetically, with very few names from the 'European' regions: Rome, Cordoba, Malaga, the Island of Majorca, Venice, al-Andalus, and Seville. His geography was of North Africa and the Middle East, all the way to "Sind" and "Hind."[19]

* * *

As far as the Muslim Arabs of the Mediterranean basin were concerned, *Ūrubba* was not a name they encountered in their exchanges with the *Naṣārā*. Rather, they encountered Christendom/*bilād al-Naṣārā*. Part of the reason was that emissaries, merchants, sailors, and others who arrived in the North African Mediterranean ports from the lands of the Christians always presented themselves (and were identified by their dress) as Christians. These Christians strongly saw themselves as belonging to the new national entities that, after the Reformation, had split Christendom into denominational states. It is very unlikely that North Africans ever heard the term 'European' from any of the English or the Dutch or French—showing that in their encounter with the North African Muslim polities, the national designations were as important to the English or the Dutch or the French as the denominational identities, and did not include geographical-continental composites. Only the eastern Christians and the Andalusian exiles seemed to have come into contact with the name of *Ūrubbā* and used it in their writings. But they did not and could not influence Arabic geographical discourse since their writings remained either private or in manuscript. Nor did their knowledge about Europe arise from developments in native learning or exploration, but rather from translations and adaptations from European languages.

For early modern Europeans, 'Christian' had not yet been replaced by 'European' nor "the common corps of Christendom" by 'Europe' (Baumer 1945, 136). As a result, *Ūrubbā* remained a foreign and infrequent conceptualization among Arabic-speaking Muslims and Christians—the non-Europeans with whom the Europeans most widely interacted.

Notes

I am grateful to Professor Galina Yermolenko, De Sales University, for her comments on this essay.

1. In 1682, for instance, a translator of an Arabic letter sent to King Charles II from Morocco opened with the following address: "To the Governour of Europe and their Prince Charles the second." But the Arabic had made no mention of 'Europe' (TNA CO 279/30/76 [15 September 1682], a translation of the Arabic letter in TNA SP 102/4/112).
2. Bernard Lewis (1982, 299) argued that it was because of the absence of "curiosity" that Muslims did not bother about Europe. In reaction, Khālid Ziyādah (1983) tried to show the wide Islamic interest in Europe. See also Shams al-Dīn al-Kīlānī (2001). All authors, however, assume that there was a well-established Arab-Islamic conceptualization of 'Europe.'
3. Anonymous, title page.
4. Studies of Ottoman cartography are numerous; see Emiralioğlu (2014).
5. Fleugel (1842) 3:101. It is the name that had been used by al-Baṭṭānī (d. 929): see Krachkovski (1987, 120).
6. For the influences on his work, see Krachkovski (1987, 689–693): they included Abraham Ortelius, Gérard Mercator, Philipp Cluver, and Giovanni Lorenzo, among others.
7. See the discussion of the Sfaxi 'workshop' of maps in Krachkovski (1987, 496–500). For the map see Bodleian Library, Oxford, MS Marsh 294.
8. Al-Hajarī, *Kitāb*, fos. 17–18.
9. See, for example, al-Khawārizmī (1926).

10. "Tract on Tobacco," Princeton, MS Landberg 365, p. 2 in microfilm reel 12, University of Jordan, Center for the Study of Bilād al-Shām.
11. See, for instance, the references to *al-Naṣārā al-ifranj* [Frankish Christians] repeated in Sirāj al-Dīn (1984), 18 and *passim*.
12. University of St. Joseph, Beirut, Lebanon, Bibliothèque orientale, MS 691, p. 554 in microfilm reel 749, University of Jordan, Center for the Study of Bilād al-Shām.
13. See my translation of the text in Matar (2003).
14. The BnF catalogue states that it was translated in the eighteenth century, but at the end of the manuscript, the translators mention that they finished the work in 1802.
15. BnF, MS Arabe 2249, 92r.
16. BnF, MS Arabe 2761. For the translation of the account, see Matar (2003).
17. British Library, IO ISL 2449.
18. One of those works is the above-mentioned by Notaras.
19. Al-Qaylūbī c. 1803.

Works Cited

Anonymous. *Kitāb hay'at ashkāl al-arḍ* [Book of the images of the world], BnF MS Arabe 2214.

Baumer, Franklin Le Van. 1945. "The Conception of Christendom in Renaissance England." *Journal of the History of Ideas* 6 (2): 131–156.

Bohrer, Karl Heinz. 2012. "'Europe' as Utopia: Causes of Its Decline." *New Literary History* 43: 587–605.

Brayk al-Dimashqī, Mīkhāīl. 1930. *Wathāiq tārīkhiyya li-l-kursī al-malakī al-anṭākī* [Historical documents of the Antiochean Melkite Patriarchy]. Edited by Qustantīn al-Basha. Lebanon: Ḥarīṣā.

Casale, Giancarlo. 2013. "Seeing the Past: Maps and Ottoman Historical Consciousness." In *Writing History at the Ottoman Court: Editing the Past, Fashioning the Future*, edited by H. Erdem Çipa and Emine Fetvacı, 80–99. Bloomington: Indiana University Press.

al-Dimashqī, Shams al-Dīn Abi 'Abdallah. 1923. *Nukhbat al-dahr wa 'ajā'ib al-barr wa-l-baḥr* [Selections about the wonders of land and sea]. Edited by A. Meran. Leipzig: Otto Harrassowitz.

Emiralioğlu, M. Pinar. 2014. *Geographical Knowledge and Imperial Culture in the Early Ottoman Empire*. Burlington, VT: Ashgate.

Fleugel, Gustavus, ed. 1842. *Lexicon bibliographicum et encyclopaedicum Mustafa ben Abdallah*. London: R. Bentley.

Groiss, Arnon. 2011. "Communalism as a Factor in the Rise of the Syria Idea in the 1800s and the Early 1900s." In *The Origins of Syrian Nationhood: Histories, Pioneers and Identity*, edited by Adel Beshara, 30–54. London: Routledge.

al-Hajarī, Aḥmad ibn Qāsim. 1997. *Kitāb Nāsir al-Dīn 'ala 'l-Qawm al-Kafirīn* [Book of the supporter of religion against the unbelievers]. Translated and introduced by P. S. Van Koningsveld, Q. al-Samarrai, and G. A. Weigers. Madrid: Agencia Espanola de Cooperacion Internacional.

al-Hajarī, Aḥmad ibn Qāsim. C. 1642. *Kitāb al-'izz wa-l-manāfi' li-l-mujāhidīn fī sabīl Allah bi-ālāt al-ḥurūb wa-l-madāfi'* [The book of glory and benefits for the fighters struggling in the cause of God with instruments of war and artillery]. Rabat, National Library of Morocco, MS Jeem 87.

Hay, Denys. 1957. *Europe: The Emergence of an Idea.* Edinburgh: Edinburgh University Press.

Hulme, Peter. 1994. "Tales of Distinction: European Ethnography and the Caribbean." In *Implicit Understandings*, edited by Stuart B. Schwartz, 157–197. Cambridge: Cambridge University Press.

al-Idrīsī, Muḥammad ibn Muḥammad al-Šarīf Abū 'Abd Allāh. 1984. *Opus Geographicum.* Edited by E. Cerulli et al. Amsterdam: Brill.

Khālidī, Aḥmad ibn Muḥammad. 1969. *Lubnān Fi 'ahd Al-Amīr Fakhr Al-Dīn Al-Ma'nī Al-Thānī* [Lebanon during the period of Prince Fakhr al-Din II]. Edited by Asad Rustum and Fu'ād Afrām al-Bustānī. Beirut: Lebanese University.

al-Khawārizmī, Muḥammad ibn Mūsā. 1926. *Kitāb ṣurat al-arḍ* [Book of the images of the world]. Edited by Hans v. Mzik. Leipzig: Harrassowitz.

al-Kīlānī, Shams al-Dīn. 2001. *Ṣūrat Ūrubbā 'ind al-'Arab fī-'aṣr al-wasīṭ* [The image of Europe among the Arabs in the medieval period]. Damascus: Wizārat al-thaqāfa.

Krachkovski, Ignati Iulianovich. 1987. *Istoria Arabskoi Geografischeskoi Literatury.* Trans. Salāḥ al-Dīn 'Uthmān Hāshim, [Tārīkh al-adab al-jughrāfī al-'arabī. 2nd edition]. Beirut: Dār al-gharb al-islāmī.

Lewis, Bernard. 1982. *The Muslim Discovery of Europe.* New York: W. W. Norton.

Matar, Nabil. 2003. *In the Lands of the Christians: Arabic Travel Writing in the Seventeenth Century.* New York: Routledge.

Matar, Nabil. 2011. *Europe through Arab Eyes, 1578–1727.* New York: Columbia University Press.

Matar, Nabil. 2015a. "Abdallah ibn Aisha and the French Court, 1699–1701: An Ambassador without Diplomacy." *French History* 29: 62–75.

Matar, Nabil. 2015b. *An Arab Ambassador in the Mediterranean World: The Travels of Muḥammad ibn 'Uthmān al-Miknāsī* London: Routledge.

al-Mawsūlī, Ilyās ibn Ḥannā. 1906. *Riḥlat awwal sharqiyy ilā Amrīka* [The voyage of the first easterner to America]. Edited by Antoine Rabbat. Beirut: Imprimerie catholique.

al-Qaylūbī, Shihāb al-Dīn, c. 1804. *Risāla fī asmā' al-bilād* [Epistle on city names]. In microfilm reel 395, University of Jordan, Center for the Study of Bilād al-Shām.

Sirāj al-Dīn, Hasan Taj al-Dīn Muḥammad Muḥibb al-Dīn Ibrāhīm. 1984. *The Islamic History of the Maldive Islands.* Edited by Hikoichi Yajima. Tokyo: Institute for the Study of Languages and Cultures of Asia and Africa.

al-Zayyānī, Abu al-Qāsim. 1967. *al-Tarjumāna al-kubrā fī akhbār al-ma'mūr barran wa baḥran* [The great history of the world, by land and sea]. Edited by 'Abd al-Karīm al-Filālī. Rabat: Wizārat al-Anbā'.

Ziyādah, Khālid. 1983. *Taṭawwur al-nadhra al-islāmiyya ilā Ūrubbā* [The development of the Islamic view of Europe]. Beirut: Ma'had al-inmā' al-'Arabī.

3 Europeanizing the Turks in Robert Greene's *Alphonsus, King of Aragon*

Ladan Niayesh

The Comicall Historie of Alphonsus, King of Aragon (c. 1587), Elizabethan author Robert Greene's first dramatic attempt, is one of several heroic romances written in the wake of Christopher Marlowe's *1 Tamburlaine*, which was staged earlier during the same year. Like *Tamburlaine*'s other "weak sons,"[1] such as George Peele's *The Battle of Alcazar*, *Soliman and Perseda* attributed to Thomas Kyd, or *John of Bordeaux* and *Selimus* attributed to Greene himself—all of them written within five years of *Tamburlaine*'s *premiere*—*Alphonsus* capitalizes on the success of that landmark conqueror's play, as well as on an overall literary interest in chivalric material in the bellicose context of the Armada years.[2] Following the Marlovian precedent and the conventions of dramatic romance,[3] the play stages the exploits of its fictitious eponymous hero over vast territories, from his native Aragon to Asia Minor by way of Naples and Milan, as he fulfils fantasies of chivalric and erotic conquests over enemies east and west.[4] Unsurprisingly, the over-reaching hero's triumphs culminate, as in Tamburlaine's case, in his defeating the Great Turk and his forces, the great eastern Mediterranean Muslim power threatening Christian Europe in the sixteenth century. But what is more surprising is the build-up to that final triumph, starting with the fact that contrary to Tamburlaine, Alphonsus does not fully dominate the action of the play that bears his name. The character is even totally absent from the stage for a long central section of the play, from 3.2 to 4.3,[5] and even when he comes back late into the final scene of Act 4, he speaks a total of only 25 lines before the end of the act. In his absence, the stage is most spectacularly filled by the Great Turk Amurack and his people. The Turk is shown, as could be expected, with his court, tributary kings, and janissaries, but he is also more unusually accompanied by an Amazon for a wife, an equally Amazonian though marriageable daughter, and the sorceress Medea conjuring for them. These characters appear alongside Mahomet's temple and his priests, with that false god's misleading prophecy (predicting victory to Amurack if the Turks attack Alphonsus, while telling his priests in private that the opposite will in fact happen) ultimately determining the course of action for all. With the exception of the desolate no-man's-land of 4.2 in which Alphonsus's father Carinus, the rightful heir to the throne of Aragon, finds and kills his old enemy, the treacherous Duke of Milan, all these scenes take place in Turkish territory, so that despite the Aragonese promise of the play's title, Ottoman land becomes the main locale and the centre of attention. Ottoman land is also where the play concludes, not with the Turk getting caged, tortured, and falling to an inhumane death in the manner of Marlowe's Bajazeth, but with his granting his daughter's hand to his victor and celebrating with him the union of the two houses, completing a fantasy of a European community that includes Turkey, a dream that has not yet come true in our own time.

This intriguing plot distribution and the play's unconventional final incorporation of the Turks call for an attempt at interpretation. This is what this chapter purports to do, by both looking at the play's own construction of the Turks and searching for possible precedents and analogues. My argument here is that Greene's treatment of his Turks is not an isolated case, but an example of an alternative, Europeanized view of the Turks still existing in the early modern period, and more specifically in heroic romances—contrary to our received idea that the Turks were solely or at least primarily seen at the time as "the present terrour of the world," according to the often quoted passage from Richard Knolles's *The Generall Historie of the Turkes* (1603, sig. B1^r).

One of the features that strike us most when looking at the Turkish scenes in *Alphonsus* is their abundance of classical and mythological references. It is true that the recourse to Greek and Latin mythological frames was characteristic of plays composed by the University Wits, regardless of their subject matter. So Greene, who particularly boasted of his background as a graduate from both Oxford and Cambridge and whose name was frequently accompanied by the mention "master of arts" on the title pages of his published works,[6] could not be expected to be sparing in his use of classical allusions. But it is worth noticing that in *Alphonsus*, a large amount of classical references used by or about the Turks links them to the Homeric background of the Trojan War, as if the plot was to a certain extent a variation on (or a reenactment of) that archetypal confrontation between Europe and the European-constructed Asia of the *Iliad*.

Analogies with Troy appear as early as the first of the scenes involving the Great Turk. Belinus, the king of Naples earlier defeated by Alphonsus and seeking refuge at Amurack's court, first describes their respective situations by using a Trojan analogy:

> But as poore *Saturne*, forst by mightie *Iove*
> To flie his Countrey, banisht and forlorne,
> Did craue the aide of *Troos*, King of *Troy*,
> So comes *Belinus* to high *Amurack*. (3.2.871–874)

Tros, to whom Amurack is compared here, was an early ruler of Troy and the city's eponym.[7] The rest of the analogy appears incorrect, since according to Roman mythology, after his defeat by Jupiter, Saturn fled not to Troy but to Latium and Rome, where he was received by Janus. But perhaps the forced reference to Tros prepares us for the rest of the plot, in which we see Amurack lose his daughter Iphigina to his victor Alphonsus, just as the mythological Tros lost his son Ganymede to Zeus, who abducted the handsome youth. The reference may also be seen as an ironic reversal of the expected Troy-to-Rome translation in the *Aeneid*, with an Italian prince here seeking succour from Troy's equivalent, rather than a Trojan prince looking west for a fresh start. But whether or not it is intentional, this opening reference in the first of the Turkish scenes to a classical past and to the supposed common ancestors of so many Europeans, from Romans to Britons, posits right away the Turks as part of the same cultural sphere as the rest of the nations involved in the play's capacious plot.

A further Trojan foreshadowing appears, however forcedly, later into the same scene. There, Medea, the sorceress from Colchis, who is yet another Europeanized Asiatic mythical figure, conjures for Amurack by specifically calling up the spirit of Calchas. The latter was the soothsayer whose prophecy at the start of Homer's *Iliad* entailed the sacrifice of Agamemnon's daughter Iphigenia to the goddess Artemis—whom Agamemnon had offended—so as to gain favourable winds for the Greek fleet to sail towards Troy. The circumstances of Calchas's prophecy are explicitly recalled here, as if to make sure that the allusion and parallel are not lost on the spectators:

> Thou which wert wont in Agamemnons dayes
> To vtter forth *Apolloes* Oracles
> At sacred *Delphos*, *Calchas* I do meane,
> I charge thee come. (3.2.941–944)

This reference to Agamemnon immediately follows the first entry of Amurack's daughter, whose name, Iphigina (a name almost the same as Agamemnon's Iphigenia), was introduced and repeated twice over the preceding four lines. Again Greene gets part of his mythological referencing wrong, since the Homeric prophecy did not take place at Delphi but in Aulis. It is possible that a larger portion of the audience was likely to have heard of Delphi rather than of Aulis, but whether the will to reach out to the audience or a limited mythological literacy is the cause of Greene's misreferencing is hard to establish. The Trojan parallel is nonetheless put forward, however confusedly, since the sacrificed Iphigenia of the *Iliad* was of course a Greek rather than a Trojan princess. True to its programmatic title, *The Comicall Historie of Alphonsus* eventually presents a much toned down version of the sacrifice, since despite several threats on Iphigina's life in the course of the play, only her virginity gets 'sacrificed' to the victor, whom she marries in the end because the prophecy wills it so.

Meanwhile, in 3.2, the prophecy first meets the hostility of both Iphigina and her mother Fausta, revealed to be an Amazonian queen and vowing to bring in her armies to counter the western forces of Alphonsus and his tributary kings. Again the parallel with the Trojan War is there, with Iphigina the Amazon getting defeated in 5.2 in the manner of Homer's Penthesilea overcome by Achilles, and as in the *Iliad* the moment of defeat for the Amazon corresponds to that of her victor's falling in love with her.

The Trojan parallel is pursued right to the end of the play, which offers a happy ending variation on the Homeric model, celebrating a wedding and the reconciliation of former enemies rather than the utter destruction of the defeated or their being taken into slavery, even though both prospects are averted *in extremis* in the play. The set of Trojan parallels reaches completion in the final lines of the play, with Amurack's last speech in which he gives his daughter away to Alphonsus and wishes him to "liue King *Nestors* yeeres" (5.2.2078). Nestor, the wise king of Pylos, was of course the oldest of the Greek leaders fighting against Troy and one of the victorious survivors of the war.

As the above examples show, the Trojan allusions are too persistent in Greene's *Alphonsus* to be accidental. Yet none of the play's past editors has attempted an explanation for them. John Churton Collins (1905, 73) dismisses their overall effect as "a phantasmagorical medley," the work of a *debutant* playwright overdoing it with his approximate classical culture, while Nicholas Storojenko (1964, 174) finds fault with the play's "strange conglomerate of epochs." But I believe these allusions contribute not just to classicizing the Turks but more importantly to familiarizing and culturally claiming them by recalling the closer-to-Europe theory of their Trojan origin. This was a minority view held by a few Renaissance authors against the dominant belief in the Turks' more threatening "obscure and base" origin in Scythia or Central Asia, which is better remembered by the readers of Knolles's *Generall Historie of the Turkes* (1603, sig. A4[r]). Yet even Knolles himself starts his account of the Turks' origin with that minority view, if only to say he does not adhere to it:

> Some ... deriue them from the Trojans, led thereunto by the affinity of the words *Turci* & *Teucri*; supposing (but with what probabilitie I know not) the word *Turci* or Turks, to haue beene made of the corruption of the word *Teucri*, the common name of the Trojans: as also for that the Turks haue of long most inhabited the lesser ASIA, wherein the antient and most famous citie of TROY sometime stood. (1603, sig. B1[r])

The term *Teucri* noted by Knolles, which derived from the name of Teucer, founder of Troy, was indeed recurrently used as an alternative for 'Trojan' in classical times, for example, by Virgil in the *Aeneid*.[8] As for the conflation of Turks and Trojans, it occasionally occurred throughout the Middle Ages. But it is worth noting that for a short time it became the dominant view at the end of this period, in the specific context of the writings connected to the fall of Constantinople in 1453.[9] Terence Spencer (1952, 330–333) cites as an illustration of this phenomenon an extract from Isidore of Kiev's eyewitness account of the siege, which contains a description of Mehmed II referred to as "Teucrorum princeps et dominus" ("prince and chief of the Trojans").[10]

James G. Harper (2005, 152) interprets this "reoccupation of the symbolic territory of the Trojan legend" as a way of ideologically compensating for the Ottomans' unstoppable territorial expansion. The idea could be either to find a rationale for the Turks' advances—Trojans only reclaiming their own, and hopefully stopping once they got it—or at least imaginatively to come to terms with this fact by incorporating the Turks as ultimately "part of us" through a shared mythical ancestry. In this manner, the Turks would be accounted for as one of the many European claimants to a Trojan line, such as the Franks supposedly descending from Trojan Franco or the Britons claiming descent from Trojan Brutus, not to forget of course the most famous of all Trojans, Aeneas, the legendary founder of Rome. Taking their place in the *translatio imperii* scheme, howbeit in a tangent way rather than in the habitual east–west course, the Turks would fit an established memory pattern, and their conquests could be explained through a supposed symbolic connection to Trojan virtue, nobility, or manifest destiny.[11]

Accordingly, Harper (2005, 158) notes the frequent appearances by turbaned figures alternating with those wearing a Phrygian cap in iconographic representations of Trojans in fifteenth-century paintings and tapestries. The amalgamation was vehemently opposed in the following years by Pope Pius II, who in 1456 commissioned Nicolo Sagundino's *De Turcarum origine* to buttress the theory of the Turks' Scythian—read Caucasian or Central Asian—origin so as to better prepare the ideological grounds for the Crusade he hoped to launch against them.[12] Yet, belated artistic and literary iterations of the Trojan hypothesis still survive well into the later decades of the sixteenth century, as we saw in the case of *Alphonsus*, in which even Amurack's first words, as his character is introduced in the play, are to welcome Belinus king of Naples as a cousin: "Welcome *Belinus* to thy cosens Court" (3.2.851). Taking his place among the princes of Europe who used to address each other as "cousins" in their correspondence, Amurack is straightaway introduced as "one of us" (European princes) rather than "one of them" (Muslim enemies). Another contemporary example of the same conflation of Turk and European is Pistol's exclamation "Base Phrygian Turks!" in Shakespeare's *Merry Wives of Windsor* (1.3.83) composed around 1597, although most modern editors either dismiss it as a "Phrygian mystery" (Shakespeare 1904, 44) or otherwise uninformatively gloss it as "a term of abuse" (Shakespeare 1974, 295).

The classicized and romanticized Turks of Greene's "comicall historie" convey little of the terrifying image one would expect in a century during which Europe experienced such traumatic episodes as the siege of Vienna (1529) or the falls of Rhodes (1522) and Cyprus (1570). At the most, Calchas's surplice and cardinal's mitre as his ghost is conjured at the court of the Great Turk (3.2.951–952) briefly evoke Luther's assimilation of the Pope and the Turk as two incarnations of Antichrist.[13] But even there the analogy could be said to help bring the Turks closer to home and interpret them and their ways in European terms, even if the reference recalls a background of

European religious strife and division rather than one of European cultural unity.

It is true that the costumes for Amurack and his janissaries, the elite corps admired and feared in the accounts of the Sultan's armies, may have introduced additional Turkish stereotypes onstage, possibly in the vein of the "Turkish cap, / A black mustachio and a fauchion" mentioned by Hieronimo as the costume notes needed for the part of Soliman in the play-within-the-play of *The Spanish Tragedy* (Kyd 1959, 4.1.144–145), or "thy croune thy robe / & semester" which Bacon snatches away from the Great Turk Amurack / Ameworth in the anomymous *John of Bordeaux* (1936, ll. 171–172), another Turk play composed around the same years as a sequel to Greene's own *Friar Bacon and Friar Bungay* (c. 1589). But as it is, neither the stage directions nor the dialogues in *Alphonsus* provide any such explicit details about the Turks and their costumes, while the famed janissaries themselves merely provide a fleeting measure of local colour alongside a group of tributary kings appearing in Tamburlainian fashion in a single stage direction at the start of the battle against Alphonsus's forces: "*Enter* Amuracke, Crocon *King of* Arabia, Faustus, *King of* Babilon, Fabius, *with the Turkes* Ganesaries" (4.3.1471–1472).

The one and only specifically Turkish characteristic that is foregrounded in the portrayal of Amurack and his followers in *Alphonsus* is their religious faith. This is introduced as early as the Great Turk's first speech, in which he invokes Mahomet in his words of welcome and comfort addressed to Belinus: "now mightie *Mahomet* / Hath giuen me cause to recompense at full, / The sundry pleasures I receiu'd of thee" (3.2.856–858). But interestingly, here too, despite the topical name given to Greene's Sultan—probably after the incumbent Sultan Murad III (reg. 1574–1595)—the portrayal of Islam in the play is far from reflecting the contemporary state of western knowledge about that religion, at least among the more scholarly spheres.[14] The idol-worshipping Muslims of *Alphonsus* rather recall traditions inherited from medieval propagandist writings dating back to the Crusades, such as Raoul de Caen's *Gesta Tancredi* (c. 1112–1131), which described, for example, how Tancred's armies found and destroyed a silver idol of Mahomet in the temple of Solomon in Jerusalem.[15] In such accounts, as well as in the Carolingian *chansons de geste* translated into English in the thirteenth and fourteenth centuries, Islam is by no means presented as the aniconic—and even anti-iconic—priestless religion of the prophet Muhammad. Instead, it is either an extension of classical paganism or a heretical offshoot of Christianity, or even possibly both, based on the unholy worship of a trinity of hotchpotch idols from different systems, Apollyon, Tervagant, and Mahomet, who together make up a conflated distortion of both classical and Christian references.[16]

Accordingly, the medievalized Mahomet of *Alphonsus*, discovered in 4.1, is a fire-spitting, oracle-pronouncing idol served by two terrified priests. His apparent function is to help the Turks by giving them superior knowledge

about the future, but as in many Saracen romances, such as the anonymous fifteenth-century *Sowdone of Babylone*, the one and only effect of this
false god's intervention is to lead his own people to their defeat. At once
fantastic and spectacular with his infernal fire-breathing brazen head, and
comic and down-to-earth through his propensity to take offence and his
consulting with his priests over the prophecy that will make him even with
Amurack, Mahomet fully discredits the Turks' side with his rough magic
and immediately provides the instruments of their future defeat. What he
ultimately contributes to the plot is the conditions for what Norman Daniel
(1984, 141) calls the "Tervagant convention" of Saracen romances—that
is to say the obligatory scene of renunciation in which the Muslim leader,
disappointed by his gods, publicly rejects them and offers to destroy their
statues as a preliminary to (or an acknowledgement of) the Christians' utter
triumph. As an illustration of such scenes, Samuel Chew (1937, 392) quotes
from the above-mentioned *Sowdone of Babylone*, in which the defeated
Sultan Laban orders his idols to be brought before him and beaten: "Fye
upon thee, Appolyn. Thou shalt have an evil end. And much sorrow shall
come to thee also, Termagant. And as for thee, Mahound, Lord of all the
reste, thou art not worth a mouse's turd."

A similar fate awaits Mahomet in Amurack's prescient dream in *Alphonsus*,
making the Great Turk and the people he stands for *toujours déjà* Christian
converts:

> And doest thou think thou proud iniurious God,
> *Mahound* I meane, since thy vaine prophesies
> Led *Amurack* into this dolefull case,
> To haue his Princely feete in irons clapt,
> Which erst the proudest kings were forst to kisse,
> That thou shalt scape vnpunisht for the same?
> No, no, assoone as by the helpe of *Ioue*,
> I scape this bondage, downe go all thy groues.
> Thy alters tumble round about the streets.
> And whereas erst we sacrifisde to thee:
> Now all the Turks thy mortall foes shall bee. (3.2.996–1006)

This preordained renunciation completes the incorporation of the already
classicized, familiarized, and Trojanized Turks, making them fully assimi-
lable on European and Christian terms. This paves the way for the happy
union of Iphigina and Alphonsus, a union through which the Christian and
European champion legitimately inherits Amurack's empire, completing a
fantasy of hegemony over the entire Mediterranean, from the Iberian Peninsula
to Constantinople.

Ultimately, through the romantic conventions of conversion and cross-
cultural marriage, what *Alphonsus* achieves is thus a classically inherited
dream of assimilation, rather than one of annihilation of the Turkish other.
The play thereby explores alternative scenarios for overcoming otherness, in

preference to sheer military victory, even though military victory remains an obligatory passage for an epigone of Marlowe's Tamburlaine. In so doing, Greene's play remains true to the rationale of Saracen romances, a genre that according to Benedict S. Robinson (2007, 16) was from its very beginnings in late twelfth-century crusading Europe "a transnational form," belonging to no nation in particular, but engaged in a logic of incorporation of otherness, not just in its plots, but also through its circulations and adaptations in many languages and traditions. With such stereotypical go-between characters as the converted Saracen champion, the Muslim princess falling in love with a Christian knight, and the humbled Sultan turning his back on his ineffectual gods,[17] popular romances like *Sir Bevis of Hampton* (c. 1300), circulating in Anglo-Norman, French, Dutch, and Italian versions (Martin 2014), or the many versions (including the above-mentioned *Sowdone of Babylone*) of the story of Fierabras, the Saracen knight who became one of Charlemagne's 12 peers, encoded inclusive conceptions of race, gender, religion, and nation, so as to follow the evolution of medieval Europe's contacts with Muslim lands around the Mediterranean. Such romances also envisaged in their peripeties corollary, self-questioning fears of intermarriage, shared inheritance, and divided allegiance. These fantasies and fears in turn found a renewed relevance for late sixteenth-century Europe, a period marked by religious divisions and cross-cultural encounters achieved through the various means of war, diplomacy, piracy, and commerce in the Mediterranean.

Expansive, transcultural scenarios held a particular appeal for early modern England, at a time when Elizabeth I herself entertained a correspondence with Murad III—Greene's Amurack's possible namesake—and his Albanian wife Safiye. The same period was also shortly to see the foundation of the Levant Company (1592) and such examples of occasional transmediterranean alliances as the five Moroccan ships that joined Essex's forces for the 1596 raid against Cadiz.[18] Read against this background of what Jonathan Burton (2005) calls "traffic and turning," Greene's play no longer appears as a belated example of a medieval genre rooted in the historical frame of the Crusades alone, nor can it be dismissed as an outdated iteration of a long refuted theory on the supposed Trojan origin of the Turks. Rather, like other early modern romances of cross-cultural contact with a Muslim east, such as Richard Johnson's *Seven Champions of Christendom* (1596) and *Tom a Lincoln* (1599 and 1607, adapted for the stage at an unknown date) or Greene's own *The History of Orlando Furioso* (1592), it engages with that "space of negation, negotiation and confusion of identity" which Daniel Vitkus sees as a highly non-Saidian characteristic of early modern Turk plays (2003, 13).

Many of the images of Islam in early modern works of fiction are "imaginary resolutions of real anxieties about Islamic wealth and might," writes Vitkus (2000, 7). As a genre that lends itself particularly well to happy-ending cross-cultural encounters through its heroes' quests and exploits in far-away lands, romances of conquest are an ideal vehicle for offering such imaginary resolutions, well beyond their medieval crusading context of apparition. In his own modest way as a tyro playwright, Greene in his first play attempts one such-like resolution in the late sixteenth century, echoing such short-lived contemporary dreams of European and Christian unity capable of stopping the Turks as the battle of Lepanto (1571). Reversing the logic of sustained Ottoman advances on Europe throughout this century, both before and after Lepanto, into a territorial as well as a cultural conquest of his classicized Turks and medievalized Muslims, Greene's play attempts what Benedict Robinson (2007, 2) calls a typically romantic "polytemporality," one that under the surface of a few topical allusions, such as the name Amurack or the fleeting reference to Janissaries, brings the novelty of the encounter back to well-established models, thereby facilitating the coming to terms with it. Limited though the artistic merits of this beginner's play may be, Greene can be said to position himself as a continuator of a whole line of late medieval romances revived and adapted in the early modern period, which all try to cope, in fantasy if not otherwise, with an ever-widening world of mixed identities and conflicting allegiances.

Notes

1. I borrow this expression from the title of an article by Peter Berek (1982), "*Tamburlaine*'s Weak Sons: Imitation as Interpretation Before 1593."
2. On the chivalric revival in Elizabethan literature, see Davis (2003).
3. For more on the conventions of romance, see Cooper (2004).
4. Greene's protagonist may be loosely modelled on Alfonso V of Aragon (1396–1458), who invaded Naples as a claimant to the crown, but who of course defeated no Turkish sultan and married no Turkish princess at any point. Greene may have conflated this figure with that of Alfonso I of Aragon, nicknamed "the Battler" (fl. 1104–1134), who lived long before the Ottoman empire was founded by Osman I at the end of the thirteenth century and had no connection with Italy, but was famous for his many victories over Muslim armies in Andalusia.
5. The act and scene divisions in this chapter follow those inserted by W. W. Greg in his facsimile edition for the Malone Society Reprints (1926). All subsequent quotes are also from this edition.
6. The mention appears in particular on the title–pages of his plays *Friar Bacon and Friar Bungay* (1630 edition), and *The Scottish History of James the Fourth* (1598 edition).
7. For more on the mythological references in this chapter, see Grimal (1991).
8. One example is Aeneas's being called "captain of the Teucrians"; see Virgil (1983), book 6, line 743.
9. For a brief summary on the background of this phenomenon, see Schwoebel (1967, 148–149).
10. Spencer (1952, 331) quotes Isidore's account from the version of his letter in Bernard Breydenbach's *Peregrinatio ad terram sanctam* of 1486.
11. This argument is developed by Harper (2005, 156).
12. On Pius II's position and the debate on the origin of the Turks in his time, see Hankins (2003, 330–332).

13. See Chew (1937, 101–102).
14. For more on this, see Dimmock (2013).
15. Quoted in Tolan (2002, 119–120).
16. See for details Metlitzki (1977, 117–120).
17. For more on the Saracen stereotypes in crusading romances, see part one ("The People") in Daniel (1984) and chapter 6 ("History and Romance") in Metlitzki (1977, 117–219).
18. For more on this, see Pettegree (2011, 130).

Works Cited

Anon. 1936. *John of Bordeaux, or the Second Part of Friar Bacon.* Ed. William Lindsay Renwick. Oxford: Malone Society Reprints.

Anon. 1990. "The Romance of the Sowdone of Babylone and of Ferumbas His Sone who Conquered Rome." In *Three Middle English Charlemagne Romances*, edited by Alan Lupack, 1–103. Kalamazoo, MI: Medieval Institute Publications.

Berek, Peter. 1982. "*Tamburlaine*'s Weak Sons: Imitation as Interpretation Before 1593." *Renaissance Drama* 13: 55–82.

Burton, Jonathan. 2005. *Traffic and Turning: Islam and English Drama, 1579–1624.* Newark: University of Delaware Press.

Chew, Samuel. 1937. *The Crescent and the Rose: Islam and England during the Renaissance.* New York: Oxford University Press.

Collins, John Churton, ed. 1905. *The Plays and Poems of Robert Greene*, Vol. 3. Oxford: Clarendon Press.

Cooper, Helen. 2004. *The English Romance in Time: Transforming Motifs from Geoffrey of Monmouth to the Death of Shakespeare.* Oxford: Oxford University Press.

Daniel, Norman. 1984. *Heroes and Saracens: An Interpretation of the* Chansons de Geste. Edinburgh: Edinburgh University Press.

Davis, Alex. 2003. *Chivalry and Romance in the English Renaissance.* Cambridge: Brewer.

Dimmock, Matthew. 2013. *Mythologies of the Prophet Muhammad in Early Modern English Culture.* Cambridge: Cambridge University Press.

Greene, Robert. c. 1587/1926, *The Comicall Historie of Alphonsus, King of Aragon.* Ed. W. W. Greg. Oxford: Malone Society Reprints.

Greene, Robert. c. 1590/2000, *Selimus, Emperor of the Turks.* Ed. Daniel Vitkus, *Three Turk Plays from Early Modern England.* New York: Columbia University Press.

Grimal, Pierre. 1991. *The Penguin Dictionary of Classical Mythology.* Trans. A. R. Maxwell-Hyslop. London: Penguin.

Hankins, James. 2003. *Humanism and Platonism in the Italian Renaissance*, Vol. 1. Rome: Edizioni di storia a letterature.

Harper, James G. 2005. "Turks as Trojans; Trojans as Turks: Visual Imagery of the Trojan War and the Politics of Cultural Identity in Fifteenth-Century Europe." In *Postcolonial Approaches to the European Middle Ages: Translating Cultures*, edited by Ananya Jahanara Kabir and Deanne Williams, 151–179. Cambridge: Cambridge University Press.

Knolles, Richard. 1603. *The Generall Historie of the Turkes.* London: Adam Islip.

Kyd, Thomas. c. 1589/2014, *Soliman and Perseda*. Edited by Lukas Erne. Manchester: Malone Society Reprints.

Marlowe, Christopher. 1587–1588/1999, *Tamburlaine the Great*. Ed. Mark Thornton Burnett, *The Complete Plays*. London: Everyman.

Martin, Jean-Pierre. 2014. *Beuve de Hamptone, chanson de geste anglo-normande de la fin du XIIème siècle*. Paris: Champion.

Metlitzki, Dorothee. 1977. *The Matter of Araby in Medieval England*. New Haven, CT: Yale University Press.

Peele, George. c. 1589/2005, *The Battle of Alcazar* Ed. Charles Edelman, *The Stukeley Plays*. Manchester: Manchester University Press.

Pettegree, Jane. 2011. *Foreign and Native on the English Stage, 1588–1611: Metaphor and National Identity*. Basingstoke: Palgrave Macmillan.

Robinson, Benedict. 2007. *Islam and Early Modern English Literature: The Politics of Romance from Spenser to Milton*. New York: Palgrave Macmillan.

Schwoebel, Robert. 1967. *The Shadow of the Crescent: The Renaissance Image of the Turks*. Nieuwkoop: de Graaf.

Shakespeare, William. 1904. *The Merry Wives of Windsor*. Ed. H. C. Hart. London: Methuen.

Shakespeare, William. 1974. *The Riverside Shakespeare*. Ed. Harry Levin et al. Boston, MA: Houghton Mifflin.

Spencer, Terence. 1952. "Turks and Trojans in the Renaissance." *The Modern Language Review* 47: 330–333.

Storojenko, Nicholas. 1964. *Robert Greene: His Life and Works—A Critical Investigation*. Trans. E. A. Brayley Hodgetts, in *The Life and Complete Works in Prose and Verse of Robert Greene and George Peele*, edited by Alexander Grosart, Vol. 1. New York: Russell & Russell.

Tolan, John. 2002. *Saracens: Islam in the Medieval European Imagination*. New York: Columbia University Press.

Virgil. 1983. *Aeneid*. Trans. Robert Fitzgerald. Harmondsworth: Penguin.

Vitkus, Daniel. 2000. *Three Turk Plays from Early Modern England*. New York: Columbia University Press.

Vitkus, Daniel. 2003. *Turning Turk: English Theater and the Multicultural Mediterranean, 1570–1630*. New York: Palgrave Macmillan.

Part II
Genres

4   The Survival of Medieval Antiquity

Fifteenth-Century Transformations of the *Roman Antique* Tradition in Castile and Beyond[*]

Clara Pascual-Argente

Europe, or rather a specific idea of Europe at a given moment, can productively be conceptualized as a "space–time package" akin to Mikhail Bakhtin's notion of the chronotope, as Peter Burke (2006, 236) has recently suggested.[1] The different iterations of this complex "cultural construct" (Burke 2006, 237) feature a diversity of spatial and temporal characteristics. My point of departure here, 'medieval antiquity,' describes one such chronotope, manifesting itself in the genre known as romance of antiquity, *roman d'antiquité*, or *roman antique*.[2] While the *romans antiques* may not create a chronotope of Europe in any strict sense, they do fashion a chronotope of antiquity as the place of European origin—a fundamental piece, as I shall explain, for the construction of a shared cultural memory of the classical past for courtly elites across western Europe.

The virtual identification between chronotope and literary genre posited by Bakhtin (1981, 84–85) is borne out in the medieval *romans antiques*, situated in a playfully anachronistic pagan past and thematizing stories of Greek territorial expansion around the Mediterranean (see also Baumgartner 1995). The *romans antiques* made available, for the first time in the vernacular, narratives about the wars between Oedipus's sons, and between Greeks and Trojans, as well as about wandering heroes and monarchs such as Aeneas, Alexander the Great, or Apollonius of Tyre. This generic label was initially used to refer to a group of Francophone romances created around the middle of the twelfth century: the so-called classical trilogy including the *Roman de Thèbes*, *Roman d'Énéas,* and *Roman de Troie*, sometimes complemented with the *Roman d'Alexandre* and only on rare occasions with the fragmentary *Roman d'Apollin de Tyr*.[3]

In traditional narratives of French cultural and literary history, the *romans antiques* remain a transitional genre that served to pave the way for, and was soon superseded by, its younger cousin, the Arthurian romance. Re-creations of the classical past in the form of romances had, nonetheless, a long and fruitful life throughout medieval Europe. The early Francophone *romans antiques* continued to be copied, illustrated, translated, and variously transformed, and new ones appeared in French as well as in other European vernaculars. Indeed, some thirteenth- and fourteenth-century works that have become canonical in the study of medieval literature in Spanish (*Libro de Alexandre, Libro de Apolonio, Historia troyana polimétrica*), Italian (Boccaccio's *Teseida* and *Filocolo*), and English (Chaucer's *Troilus and Cressida* and the *Knight's Tale*) are situated squarely within what Barbara Nolan (1992) has called the tradition of the *roman antique*.

The *romans antiques* remain a uniquely European genre not only because of their continued success and wide circulation but also, and more importantly, because their spread is directly linked to what historian Robert Bartlett has labelled "the Europeanization of Europe." This term refers to the process of cultural homogenization brought about by the progressive adoption of common practices, such as the Roman Latin liturgy or the worshipping of specific saints, and institutions, such as chanceries or universities (Bartlett 1994, 243–291). The Europeanizing process intertwined with the expansion of the Frankish and Norman nobility across Europe through military conquest and colonization that pushed the boundaries of Latin Christendom, as well as through additional means such as dynastic alliances (24–59).

The *romans antiques* are closely related to the Europeanization of Europe: as it turns out, they were initially shaped by clerics connected with universities and chanceries. Further, the creation and diffusion of these works were frequently tied to dynastic or territorial expansion: many *romans antiques* arose out of courtly milieus near the borders of Latin Christendom, while their diffusion across political frontiers was often associated to dynastic alliances. Perhaps for this reason, they often deal with processes of territorial, dynastic, and cultural expansion and homogenization akin to those I have described above. But even more than this, the *romans antiques* were part and parcel of the Europeanization of Europe in quite a literal way, by constructing a common classical past shared by courtly elites across Latin Christendom.

Pervasive narratives such as Troy's, Alexander's, or Apollonius of Tyre's provided the lay nobility's higher echelons with a shared history to which they often felt genealogically connected and in which, thanks to the deliberate use of anachronism, they saw themselves, their aspirations, and their vulnerabilities reflected. Thus the *romans antiques* fashioned a common ancient origin and identity for their courtly publics, becoming a key tool in the creation of a European vernacular cultural memory of the classical past. It is for this reason that art historian Hugo Buchthal (1971, 65) could say that the medieval versions of the Trojan myth "represented in [their] odd way an assertion of the unity of Western Europe, which shared not only a common religion but also a common origin"—an evaluation that may conceivably be extended to the whole narrative world of the *romans antiques*.

While the enduring hold that the *romans antiques* came to have on the medieval imagination has finally started to be recognized, this tradition's continued existence and cultural relevance during the fifteenth century remains a blind spot in literary history. The scholarly erasure of medieval antiquity's active presence during early modernity is part of the old, but persistent, critical paradigm that would still define the Renaissance as the true beginning of European engagement with the classical past (or with the past *tout court*).[4] My aim in this chapter is to refute the pervasive assumption that, by the fifteenth century, the tradition of the *roman antique* had become no more than an irrelevant holdover of medieval culture, quickly vanishing as humanist culture became more prominent. Instead, I shall show how some narratives closely connected to the *romans antiques* remained politically and culturally relevant in the fifteenth century, engaging with and eventually integrating within vernacular forms of humanism.

To this end, I shall explore the fifteenth-century trajectory of three such narratives in Castile, a literary space often marginalized, like the *romans antiques* themselves, in the discourse of European literary history. Castilian *romans antiques* concentrated around three main stories: those of Alexander the Great, Apollonius of Tyre, and the Trojan War. The three strands of this tradition appeared in the thirteenth century with two pioneer poems, the *Libro de Alexandre* and the *Libro de Apolonio*. The first of these works recounts the life of Alexander the Great, but it also includes a long retelling of the Trojan War, which Alexander narrates to his troops. One of the earliest works to be influenced by the *Libro de Alexandre* was the *Libro de Apolonio*, which focuses on the misadventures of King Apollonius of Tyre. In the fourteenth century, the standalone Trojan story became prominent within Castilian literary imagination in works such as the *Historia troyana polimétrica*, the *Crónica troyana*, or the *Sumas de historia troyana*, all of which ultimately derived from Benoît de Sainte-Maure's *Roman de Troie*.

The late fourteenth century and, especially, the fifteenth century bring about the beginnings and rapid expansion of Castilian vernacular humanism, "the translation and adaptation of classical works for the entertainment and instruction of noble and unprofessional readers" (Lawrance 1990, 222)—a development that, like the *roman antique* tradition, is hardly exclusive of Castile.[5] Within the Iberian kingdom, two important elements differentiate, generally speaking, the textual products of vernacular humanism from the earlier *romans antiques*. First, there is a generic shift: vernacular humanism is defined by the proliferation of literal translations of historiography and moral philosophy from classical antiquity, in contrast with the actualized refashioning of heroic narratives as romances that characterize the *roman antique* tradition. Second, they tend to be interested in the Roman world as their main model, in stark contrast with the Greek imaginary that pervaded the *romans antiques*.

The following pages consider different forms of interaction between the *roman antique* tradition and the world of vernacular humanism through three case studies, which also take up the three main narratives I have mentioned: the history of Alexander's achievements in Gutierre Díaz de Games's *El Victorial*, where *romans antiques* are used as a corrective to the perceived dangers of vernacular humanism; the story of Troy in the compilation known as *Sumas de historia troyana*, where a *roman antique* narrative travels through courtly networks across political and linguistic frontiers; and, finally, the biographical tales related to Apollonius of Tyre in the incunabulum entitled *Vida e historia del rey Apolonio*, where the worlds of the *roman antique* and of vernacular humanism come together as they circulate, once again, across Europe, this time in printed form. In addition to showing the continued presence and relevance of the *roman antique* tradition, the last two examples are representative of the preservation and expansion of the European (and Europeanizing) networks that gave birth to these travelling texts.

Looking Back: A Fifteenth-Century Alexander

The early fifteenth century witnesses a true explosion in the number of classical texts in vernacular translation available to Castilian readers, providing them with a novel route of access to the pagan past. The abundant translations, mostly of historical or philosophical works, respond to the demand of a rapidly growing class of lay readers (Lawrance 1985), and prominent members of the nobility are often their direct commissioners or dedicatees. The leading figures among these would-be literate aristocrats were powerful lords actively involved in military endeavours, but also keenly aware of the need to secure a place in the royal court during peacetime, if they were to maintain and augment their power. Thus the pursuit of knowledge became for these noblemen "an essential training not only for military prowess, but for more general lessons, and especially for fitting noblemen for their role in the governance of the polity" (Lawrance 1986, 70). Such political and intellectual ambitions would not go unchallenged, since bookish learning and the political role it facilitated were at that point the province of the *letrados*, a bureaucratic class of university-educated clerks who held important courtly positions. As a consequence, the so-called debate on arms and letters as it takes shape in Castile attempts to determine whether it is legitimate for the lay nobility to access the kind of learning (much of it of classical origin) that they believed would allow them to fulfil a greater political role—"to conquer a political function in peacetime," in Carlos Heusch's words (2010, 324).[6]

The Roman 'knights' held up as examples in many ancient texts became a crucial model for those Castilian noblemen aspiring to undertake martial and intellectual pursuits, since they had combined their military function in wartime with governmental tasks during peacetime (Rodríguez Velasco 1996). From the predominantly Greek and Trojan world of the medieval *roman antique*, then, vernacular humanism moves antiquity's main geographical and chronological centre of gravity to Rome: authors such as Livy, Valerius Maximus, Sallust, or Lucan become favourites, and Castilian writers pepper their own narratives with examples from Roman antiquity. The continued relevance of the *roman antique* tradition is, nonetheless, evident in works such as the chivalric biography that will be the focus of this section, Gutierre Díaz de Games's *El Victorial*. Díaz de Games makes abundant use of the thirteenth-century *Libro de Alexandre* in his work, in what I would argue is a calculated nostalgic gesture: the writer presents narratives associated with the *romans antiques* as the only legitimate form of access to classical antiquity for lay noblemen. It is therefore on ideological grounds, as shall become clear, that *El Victorial* sets up a relationship of competition between vernacular humanism and *roman antique*.[7]

El Victorial, written during the 1430s, recounts the life and deeds of the author's patron, nobleman Pero Niño. The *Libro de Alexandre* is a key subtext for this work, as Rafael Beltrán (2011) has convincingly demonstrated, on four different levels. First, Díaz de Games (2014, 20–23) includes in his own book 18 stanzas from the old Castilian romance, part of Aristotle's advice to young Alexander. Second, this fragment appears in *El Victorial* within a brief recounting of Alexander's life (one of the four biographies of model knights that head the book), whose main events and organization closely follow the *Libro de Alexandre*'s take on the Macedonian king (19–27). Third, Díaz de Games purposefully echoes the *Libro de Alexandre* in specific episodes retelling Pero Niño's exploits (Beltrán 2011, 168–170). Finally, the bond between the two works goes much deeper than the inserted biographical sketch or occasional echoes: in *El Victorial*, the Alexander legend in general, and the *Libro de Alexandre* in particular, functions as the underlying model structuring the narration of Pero Niño's life and deeds.

Díaz de Games's choice of the *Libro de Alexandre* as the main exemplar for his own literary endeavour carries, I believe, ideological connotations directly related to the shadowy presence of vernacular humanism within his work. As Jesús Rodríguez Velasco (2001) and Heusch (2010) have demonstrated, *El Victorial* takes a hostile stance against those aristocrats with intellectual and political aspirations who were avidly commissioning and consuming translations of classical works. Díaz de Games presents his subject, nobleman and ideal knight Pero Niño, as their polar opposite. For example, Niño does not have any particular interest in bookish knowledge, having been told by his tutor that "he who has to learn and practice the art of knighthood does not benefit from spending a long time learning his letters" (Díaz de Games 2014, 91).[8] We are also informed that Niño, beloved by the king, refuses to take on governmental responsibilities, despite having ample opportunity to do so, because he fears that in becoming the monarch's favourite, there would be "things that do not partake of the craft of knighthood" (116).[9]

Niño's image is thus moulded in accordance with his biographer's beliefs about society in general, and nobility's military role in particular. Díaz de Games views social orders as immutable and divinely ordained, since God

grants to some the grace of being clerks, and to others that of being good merchants, and to others that of being good workmen, or being labourers, and to others that of being knights and good defenders. … And if the labourer or the merchant wants to make use of letters, he does not know how, because it is not in his nature; and so mounting a horse and taking arms is a hard thing for him. (115)[10]

As a consequence, knights have no business performing tasks that are the province of clerks; a knight's worth, *El Victorial* makes clear, is directly proportional to his suffering during wartime and is greatly diminished if he enjoys courtly comforts. Through both his portrait of Pero Niño and his own reflections on chivalry, then, Díaz de Games mounts an attack on the legitimacy of the 'Roman' model of chivalry beloved of some Castilian noblemen and associated with vernacular humanism. It is perhaps for this same reason, as Heusch (2010, 321) suggests, that *El Victorial*'s author is eager to stress the limitations of pagan knights and their inherent inferiority to Christian ones.

Díaz de Games's position in the 'arms and letters' question is, therefore, quite clear: lay noblemen must perform an exclusively military function and do not require intellectual preparation. It is in this context that his use of the *roman antique*'s narrative universe makes political sense. Despite the criticism mentioned above, *El Victorial*'s author hardly rejects classical antiquity as a valid model for lay aristocrats: as he recognizes, and enables through his use of Alexander as an overarching model, Christian knights must take the example "of those who worked so hard to have honour and fame, whether they are believers or infidels" (Díaz de Games 2014, 49).[11] Pero Niño's biographer offers a tried-and-true alternative to the problematic world of Roman 'knights' and vernacular humanism: the old *romans antiques*, such as the *Libro de Alexandre*, which not only provide alternative heroes but also fashion a noble culture wholly dependent on clerkly tutelage.[12] Alexander may well have been a master in all seven liberal arts, as Díaz de Games cannot but acknowledge in his short retelling of the Macedonian's life; however, the part of the *Libro de Alexandre* that he deems worthy of reproduction within his own work is that in which Aristotle instructs Alexander on general behaviour and, above all, on military strategy—a knight's true function.

The presence of the *roman antique* tradition in *El Victorial* goes beyond the Alexander legend. Díaz de Games's book includes numerous short stories that interrupt, punctuate, and ornate the overall narrative arc defined by Pero Niño's life, of which several draw from the classical world as re-created in the *romans antiques*. The stories of the two Amazons Calestia (from the Alexander legend) and Pantasilea (from the Trojan legend), together with that of Dido, serve to illustrate a reflection about love. Later, the beginning of Pero Niño's English campaigns gives Díaz de Games the chance to provide his particular version of the Brutus story in the "Tale of Brutus and Dorothea," a short romance in which the Trojan hero marries, abandons, and finally reunites with Greek princess Dorothea, Menelaus and Helen's daughter. All of these stories go back to the Greek- or Trojan-based past of the *romans antiques*, as opposed to the Roman leanings of vernacular humanism. More importantly, Díaz de Games uses these narratives to high-light the areas that he deems appropriate for noble culture: love and warfare, rather than the pursuit of knowledge for the better government of the realm.

The ideological leanings of Díaz de Games provide an important key to understanding the inclusion of some inserted stories in *El Victorial*, whose apparent gratuity has often puzzled critics. It is not just that, as Heusch (2010) has proposed, the writer took the chance to 'publish' literary pieces on which he had been working for a long time: the stories set in the pagan world draw from the world of the *roman antique*, and remain an ideologi-cally charged alternative to the similarly charged Roman narratives that had become favourites of those members of the nobility who held intellectual aspirations. Díaz de Games looks back on the *romans antiques* as represen-tatives of an ideal, reactionary social order that he feels may crumble under the pressure of would-be literate knights.

Díaz de Games's nostalgic view of the *romans antiques* appears to reinforce the critical narrative I mentioned above, which characterizes them as a medi-eval holdover in the age of humanism. However, the fact that a clerk like Díaz de Games used the tradition of the *roman antique* as an implicit attack against lay noblemen invested in vernacular humanism does not mean that those noblemen were at all hostile to such a tradition. On the contrary, the emergence of vernacular humanism in the Castilian literary scene was undoubtedly enabled by the courtly familiarity with the matter of antiquity that the *romans antiques* had facilitated, and it served to give a new lease on life to the oldest Iberian *roman antique*, the *Libro de Alexandre*: it is significant that one of its two extant manuscripts dates from the fifteenth century, while the second one (copied in the late thirteenth or early fourteenth century) was owned by one of the most prominent figures within vernacular humanism, Íñigo López de Mendoza. A similar case can be made for the compilation of ancient Greek narratives that is the focus of the following section, the *Sumas de historia troyana*.

Looking Ahead: A Travelling Troy

El Victorial makes evident the centrality of Troy within the tradition of the *roman antique*. Even if the Alexander story serves to structure the whole book, Díaz de Games is careful to include narratives from the Trojan cycle among the alternatives to Roman matter that he is keen to offer. Conserva-tive clerks like Díaz de Games are, however, hardly the only fifteenth-century Castilians—or, for that matter, Europeans—interested in medieval retellings of the Trojan legend, which also figures prominently within the readings of those knights with a penchant for humanistic learning. This section considers the trajectory of a fourteenth-century Castilian version of the medieval Trojan narrative, the *Sumas de historia troyana* (hereafter *Sumas*), first in the hands of one such knight, Diego de Valera, and later in those of a clerk, Raoul Lefèvre, in the ducal court of Burgundy. Both Valera and Lefèvre reclaim, through the *Sumas*, the chronotope of medieval antiquity in courtly contexts infused with vernacular humanism. And unlike Díaz de Games, both Valera and Lefèvre look ahead, seeking to further new cultural or political projects.

The *Sumas* was created and first started circulating during the second half of the fourteenth century (Rey 1932, 14). By this time, the Castilian *romans antiques* had shifted from verse to prose and become focused on Troy. At the heart of the *Sumas* remains the traditional arc of medieval romance narratives about the Asian city: Jason's quest for the Golden Fleece; Troy's first destruction by some of Jason's companions, most notably Hercules; the city's reconstruction and the Trojan War, which results in its second and final destruction; and the Greeks' return, including Ulysses's death. Benoît de Sainte-Maure first articulated this sequence in the *Roman de Troie*, and Guido de Columnis followed its main lines in his Latin *Historia destructionis Troiae*, based on Benoît's poem and one of the main sources of the Castilian compilation. The *Sumas* sets out to amplify this basic narrative: the most significant additions are the early history of Troy; the insertion of a detailed recounting of Hercules's life; the inclusion, after the Greeks' return, of the stories of Aeneas and Brutus; and the closing of the book, breaking the rough chronological order followed so far, with two additional stories about Greeks, those of Philomena and Oedipus.

It is not until the 1400s that the wide-ranging influence of the *Sumas* is really felt in Castile and beyond. And it is then that, among the many readers of the Trojan compilation, we find Diego de Valera, who has been called the "paradigmatic figure of [the] Castilian cultural renovation" (Di Camillo 1996, 230)[13] that crystallized in the form of vernacular humanism. While not a member of the high nobility, Valera was brought up in the court of King Juan II of Castile and became one of the most important public voices in a kingdom fraught with civil strife, from Juan's troubled reign up to that of the Catholic Monarchs. From his youth Valera became well known, not only in Castile but also in other European courts, for his combination of enthusiastic chivalric action and extensive book learning, thus embodying the ideal of the literate knight.

Evidence that Valera knew and appreciated the *Sumas* can be found in his short treatise *Origen de Troya y Roma* (c. 1455–1460), in which the Castilian writer uses the fourteenth-century compilation as the main source for a rapid overview of Trojan and Roman history (Sanmartín Bastida 1998). At the beginning of his work, Valera explains that he writes to satisfy the curiosity of his dedicatee, Juan Hurtado de Mendoza, lord of Cañete. Hurtado de Mendoza, who is obviously one of those noblemen newly fascinated with the Roman world, has expressed to Valera on several occasions his desire to know "who was the first founder of the Roman city."[14] The writer feels the need to go beyond the stated question and declares that,

> even though you only asked about Rome, [I shall] write not only about it, but also about Troy, a much more ancient city ... because—when

considering Rome—, since it had this name we can well say that it was founded, or rather, enlarged and fortified, by the Trojan lineage. It seemed therefore convenient to keep the natural order by speaking first about Troy and then about Rome.

(Penna 1959, 155)[15]

It is, therefore, the genealogical connection between Troy and Rome that makes the story of the Asian city necessary knowledge for those noblemen interested in the Roman world.

Unlike the competitive relationship set up in *El Victorial*, Valera's use of the *Sumas* suggests a collaboration between old and new narratives: in this respect, the *Origen de Troya y Roma* is representative of the genealogical, chronological, and narrative contiguity between the tradition of the *roman antique* and the world of vernacular humanism. By including the story of Troy as recounted in a popular compilation like the *Sumas*, Valera creates a bridge between the kind of narratives that had long been the province of noble culture and those that had only recently been incorporated into it, thus countering positions like Díaz de Games's. It is true, nonetheless, that Valera mines the *Sumas* exclusively for their general structure and historical data (Sanmartín Bastida 1998, 175–176), subordinating the Trojan story to the all-important Roman connection and showing nothing similar to the fascination with the narrative mechanisms of romance that Díaz de Games demonstrates in his rewriting of Brutus's story.

To find a reader of the *Sumas* that makes fruitful use of not only the compilation's narrative content but also its generic features, it is necessary to follow the Castilian work as it travels from Castile to the Burgundian ducal court. There, Raoul Lefèvre, secretary and chaplain to Duke Philip the Good, used it as a source for his *Recueil des histoires de Troye* (hereafter *Recueil*), a romance that he completed around 1464. In its four projected books, Lefèvre sets out to recount four destructions of Troy, carried out, respectively, by Hercules (on two separate occasions); the Greeks at the end of the Trojan War; and a Roman consul (Lefèvre 1987, 125). However, the Burgundian writer finished only two books, and as a consequence the *Recueil* became, rather than a story about Troy, one about Hercules. The acknowledged main source, much reworked, for Lefèvre's *Recueil* is Boccaccio's *Genealogia deorum gentilium*, yet for much of the romance's treatment of Hercules, and in particular (but not exclusively) for the parts that deal with his deeds in the Iberian Peninsula, Lefèvre made use of the *Sumas*, which he sometimes identifies as the "Croniques d'Espaigne" (Lefèvre 1987, 341, 372, 375).

The reasons for Lefèvre's interest in the *Sumas* as a source for his own work are directly related to the particular configuration that ancient matter had taken at the Burgundian court of Philip the Good. Vernacular forms of humanism that paid particular attention to Roman historiography were hardly an exclusive feature of Castilian cultural and political life: the same constellation of works that had become central for Castilian literate aristocrats was widely available in French, as a result of the translation project started under Charles V of France in the second half of the fourteenth century.[16] All of those works were often copied, read, and discussed in the Burgundian court; however, the dukes became particularly invested in the Greek, rather than the Roman, past as a model for self-fashioning. Thus, Greek antiquity became prominent in Burgundian political imagery, both in the romance forms tied to the tradition of the *roman antique* and the translated historiographical works dear to vernacular humanism.

The clearest way in which the Greek classical past comes to the forefront of Burgundian courtly life is the foundation of the chivalric Order of the Golden Fleece by Philip the Good on the occasion of his marriage to Isabel of Portugal in 1429. This brings Jason and his quest into the spotlight; other Greek heroes like Hercules and Alexander the Great would also become prominent figures within the literary production promoted by Philip and his son, Charles the Bold. The older duke appears to have been partial to retellings of these heroes' lives in the tradition of the *roman antique*: Jean Wauquelin's *Les faicts et les conquestes d'Alexandre le Grand* (1448) rewrites the old Alexander romances, while Lefévre's own *Recueil* (primarily concerned with Hercules) and his earlier *Histoire de Jason* (c. 1460) are also situated within this genre's parameters (Pinkernell 1972).[17] Charles preferred instead to promote translations from classical historiography on similar topics, such as Vasco de Lucena's versions of Quintus Curtius and Xenophon, dealing, respectively, with Alexander and Cyrus.

Estelle Doudet (2005) has cogently connected this Greek fascination with the diplomatic, political, and military ties that Burgundy sought to establish with Byzantium, and, after Constantinople's conquest, with Philip's preparations for a crusade that would retake the city from the Ottomans. The dukes' efforts to construct a Burgundian cultural and political space independent from that of France are, in my view, no less important. They would explain the dukes of Burgundy's apparent disinterest in exploiting politically the *exempla* found in Roman historiography that had become so popular in some Castilian and French quarters. Many of those *exempla*, and particularly those crafted by Valerius Maximus, had been central to the construction of an argument in support of the French crown by authors writing in the vernacular, such as Christine de Pizan or Alain Chartier.[18]

It is in this context that the particular features of the *Sumas* take on their full value. First, the compilation remains one of the few works dealing with Trojan matter that include a story about the origins of the Golden Fleece, which would have been particularly relevant in the Burgundian court. Second, the Castilian work deviates from the standard Trojan narrative, closely associated with the French monarchy.[19] Indeed, the *Sumas* would be better described as a general compilation of Greek matter than as a retelling of the Trojan narrative; as such it was particularly useful for Lefévre, who sought, in his *Recueil*, to displace the story's weight from Troy to Hercules.[20] If the value of the *Sumas* to Valera was, as I have argued, the satisfactory genealogical continuity between Troy and Rome that the compilation provides, one that follows the habitual east–west direction of the *translatio imperii* topos, Lefèvre seems to have appreciated exactly the opposite quality: the way in which the Castilian work disrupts this smooth line, bypassing chronology or going off on tangents like the story of Hercules, who, as Jason's companion, goes east to get the Golden Fleece and destroy Troy, but also west to conquer Spain.

In some ways, Lefèvre's use of the *Sumas* is not unlike that of Díaz de Games, in that both authors live in a context where they are undoubtedly aware of the cultural force of the Roman narratives associated with vernacular humanism and purposefully choose to sidestep them in favour of the ideological and narrative possibilities offered by the *romans antiques*. Nonetheless, unlike Díaz de Games—nostalgic for a status quo that feels under siege—Valera and Lefèvre are looking forward rather than back, seeking to put old stories to use in the service of new interests: in the case of the *Origen de Troya y Roma*, those of would-be literate aristocrats; in that of the *Recueil*, those of an emerging principality that attempts to carve a new political and cultural space out of ancient narratives.

This use of the *roman antique* as a tool in the Burgundian state-building process would seem to clash with the tradition's long-established function as a Europeanize cultural force, one that created a cultural memory of antiquity shared by European courtly elites. But it is precisely the role that these and other classical narratives were still performing as foundations of a European courtly identity that made them effective as a launching pad for protonational identity formation, which needed to be carried out in a symbolic language recognisable and legitimate across political borders.[21] Indeed, the status of the Trojan story as a key ingredient in a successful performance of courtly identity, intelligible across frontiers, goes a long way towards explaining why an Iberian visitor would have travelled with a manuscript of the *Sumas* to the northern court.[22]

That Iberian visitor may have been Diego de Valera himself, who visited Burgundy in 1442 in order to participate in the *pas d'armes* set up by Pierre de Bauffremont near Dijon. Alternatively, in view of the closeness of Castilian and Portuguese courtly literatures during this period, the *Sumas* could have arrived at the duchy through one of the many Portuguese courtiers who visited or established themselves in the duchy as a consequence of the marriage of Duke Philip the Good to Isabel of Portugal. Being able to provide a novel version of the Trojan story would have been a sure way of establishing a common cultural identity with Burgundian courtiers, those "men brought up with certain extraordinary stories about Troy"[23] that Lefèvre (1987, 125) mentions in his prologue to the *Recueil*. The Trojan narrative's role as a foundation for both individual and collective self-fashioning, then, explains why "everybody talks about the Trojan stories" (Lefèvre 1987, 125),[24] "everybody" meaning here 'everybody who is anybody' in the Burgundian and western European courtly spheres.

New Horizons: A Printed Apollonius

The third narrative that I consider, that of Apollonius of Tyre, takes us back to the Iberian Peninsula, although once again with an important northern European connection. After the thirteenth-century *Libro de Apolonio*, the story of the Greek king does not seem to have surfaced independently in Castilian until the *Vida e historia del rey Apolonio* (hereafter *Vida e historia*),[25] printed not in Castile but in Zaragoza—one of the main cities of the crown of Aragon—by Juan Hurus (c. 1488).[26] The *Vida e historia* retells the misadventures of King Apollonius of Tyre, who is intent on marrying King Antiochus's daughter, only to discover through a riddle that Antiochus has forced her into an incestuous relationship. Antiochus's subsequent attempt to have Apollonius murdered puts in motion a plot where the king of Tyre will suffer through shipwreck, marry, and temporarily lose his wife and daughter before finding them again in twin anagnorises. The *Vida e historia* is a beautiful quarto book of 46 pages (23 folia), most of them illustrated with woodcuts. The story is divided in 35 chapters, with a single column of text; each chapter is prefaced by a short sentence that functions as a chapter summary and is illustrated with a woodcut image.[27] This is, therefore, an abundantly illustrated book, with one and sometimes two images on most pages.

In the previous two sections, I have traced the ongoing friction and collaboration, in the middle decades of the fifteenth century, between the textual worlds of the *roman antique* and vernacular humanism. Díaz de Games sees the *roman antique* as the only legitimate mode of access to antiquity for lay noblemen; Lefèvre appropriates and actualizes the old genre in the service of a state-building project; and within the intellectual and political stances fuelled by vernacular humanism, Valera mines the Trojan narrative in order to provide a complete genealogy of Rome. Further, the *Sumas*'s arrival at Burgundy from Castile also shows that the medieval association between ancient narratives and European courtly memory and identity remained fully operative in the 1400s, allowing narratives focused on the pagan past to travel through courtly networks. The *Vida e historia* is significant not only in terms of the relationship between the two vernacular strands of classical narratives considered so far, but also as regards the widening European and, in many senses, Europeanizing networks through which ancient narratives travel in the early age of print.

Concerning the interaction between the *roman antique* and vernacular humanist traditions, the *Vida e historia* is almost the opposite of Valera's *Origen de Troya y Roma*: an unapologetic *roman antique* incorporating some key characteristics of vernacular humanism's textual production. The Zaragoza incunabulum makes exclusive use of what I have earlier called the chronotope of medieval antiquity: the story is set in the Greek Mediterranean at some point in the pre-Christian past, while its narrative structure takes the form of a romance (Gómez Redondo 1999, 1681–1682). On the other hand, the particular shape taken by the *Vida e historia* reveals clear humanistic influences. Its version of the Apollonius tale is a translation that follows quite closely a Latin (though not classical) model (Deyermond 1973, xiii); in fact, the language of the translation itself, with its abundant lexical and syntactic Latinisms and use, or maybe abuse, of the present participle, is in line with the efforts to renovate and illustrate the Castilian language led by those writers most closely associated with vernacular humanism around the midcentury. What is more, the text itself has been judiciously punctuated and corrected, in a display of the philological care characteristic of (Latinate) humanism, for which this particular printing press would receive warm praise.[28]

In addition to having some textual features typical of vernacular humanism, the context offered by the textual production of this press indicates that the printers probably conceived of the *Vida e historia* within this category. Pablo and Juan Hurus, two German brothers native of Constance, printed a significant number of translations of classical writings, producing versions of works by, or attributed to, Aesop (1482, 1489), Aristotle (c. 1488–1490), Sallust (1493), Seneca (1491, 1496), and Valerius Maximus (1495); in addition to others directly drawing from classical sources, like Boccaccio's *De claris mulieribus* (1494) or Leonardo Bruni's *Isagogicon* (1496) (Pallarés Jiménez 2008, 845–878). The inclusion of the *Vida e historia* among these texts, together with the linguistic and punctuation features noted above, suggests that, by the final years of the fifteenth century, the *roman antique* narratives had become integrated into the cultural world of vernacular humanism.

But the most remarkable aspect of the *Vida e historia* is, to my mind, the way in which the book itself reflects how the European courtly networks that we have seen at work in the case of the *Sumas* were expanding and reconfiguring in the early years of the printing press. Although seemingly homogeneous, the *Vida e historia* is actually a hybrid book: its three narrative levels (main text, images, and chapter headings) have two different origins, a fact that results in occasional misalignments between them. The main text of the *Vida e historia* contains a Castilian translation of the Latin version of Apollonius's story in the *Gesta Romanorum*, a late thirteenth- or early fourteenth-century tale collection. The xylographic programme, however, is one originally created to illustrate a slightly different version of the Apollonius narrative, the German version crafted by Heinrich Steinhöwel around 1460 and based not only on the *Gesta Romanorum* but also on Godfrey of Viterbo's *Pantheon*. Finally, the Castilian chapter headings translate, sometimes with amplifications, their German counterparts. The hybridity of the *Vida e historia* (not uncommon in early printed books) is the product of a web of relationships connecting German and Iberian printers, humanists, and courtiers.

A prominent figure in this web is that of Heinrich Steinhöwel (1412–1482), a popular German writer. While traditional scholarship refused to consider

Steinhöwel, who did not write in Latin, a "true" humanist, a more nuanced view has recently situated his work as part of a wider early humanist current (Flood 2007; Terrahe 2013, 17–19) focused on making available in German a variety of classical, humanist, and other Latin works.[29] Steinhöwel was a Swabian physician trained, among other places, at the University of Padua. Once back from Italy, he came into close contact with some aristocratic courts notable for their literary patronage, briefly including one mentioned in the previous section: in 1454, he travelled through soutwestern Germany with Philip the Good as the duke's personal physician (Classen 1997). Steinhöwel was also "one of the earliest German writers to recognize the benefits of printing" (Flood 2007, 780), and worked closely with printers Günther and Johann Zainer. The trajectory of this German humanist and courtier brings together courtly and printing milieus, to which he had access through his profession and his literary interests.

A different side of the network through which the *Vida e historia* took its particular shape is formed by the commercial relationships established within those printing milieus across western Europe. Steinhöwel's *Hystori des Küniges Appoloni* was printed in Augsburg, first as an unillustrated folio by Günther Zainer (1471), and later, as a quarto with a series of woodcuts, by Johann Bämler (1475) and Anton Sorg (1479). The book was reprinted many times after that, but not with the woodblocks used for the Bämler and Sorg editions, which would travel to Zaragoza sometime between 1479 and 1488 through the Huruses' trade connections.[30] These relationships bring about more than a visual programme and a chapter structure for the book: they are partly responsible for the book's existence itself, since awareness of the *Hystori des Küniges Appoloni*'s success must have played an important role in Juan Hurus's decision to print the Apollonius story.

The appearance of this kind of commercial relationship does not displace the courtly networks through which the stories of antiquity had traditionally been transmitted, such as the ties between the Iberian and Burgundian courts that led to the *Sumas*'s northern European travels. Rather, the trajectory I have just described makes clear that the two intertwine, as they had done in Burgundy, where printer William Caxton's courtly connections allowed him to come into contact with Lefèvre's *Recueil*, which he translated and printed as the *Recueyll of the Historyes de Troye*, the first book printed in the English language, in Bruges or Ghent around 1474. In the case of the *Vida e historia*, Steinhöwel was, as I have noted, in direct contact not only with printers but also with courts known for their literary activity, including that of the duke of Burgundy; similarly, the Hurus brothers created an intellectual circle around their press, collaborating with local writers and translators, many of whom had close connections to the court of the Catholic Monarchs or other aristocrats (Romero Tobar 1989, 564–565). With regards to the circulation of narratives set in classical antiquity, then, the *Vida e historia* is the product of the expansion of courtly networks through their links to "a new international class of educated entrepreneurs, artisans, and scholars whose interests and production increasingly responded to the economic incentives of the book market and the intellectual concerns of humanistic civic culture" (Pérez Fernández 2014, 54).

The trajectory I have traced through these three case studies is one of not only survival but also expansion of what I have called medieval antiquity, a group of stories that is defined by their setting in the world of the pre-Christian Greek Mediterranean and that became a common cultural ground for lay aristocrats across western Europe. It is possible, I would argue, to look at the impact of vernacular humanism and the printing press as reinforcing, renewing, and eventually expanding the reach (in terms of both content and circulation) of the cultural memory of antiquity shared by European courtly elites. These courtly elites were, admittedly, an extremely small group, but one with an outsized influence, especially for the upper bourgeois classes; the printing of stories of antiquity made them more easily available for those readers outside the court with a keen interest in courtly cultural forms. In this way, an important strand of the medieval European-ization of Europe, in the form of shaping and reshaping a common classical past, continued, pervading, ever more deeply, the European vernacular imagination.

Notes

* Research for this chapter has benefitted from the support of Rhodes College's Spence Wilson International Travel Fund and Faculty Development Endowment.
1. See this volume's Introduction for a brief exploration of this idea.
2. To avoid confusion, I use *roman antique* as the preferred label for the genre throughout this chapter.
3. It is worth noting that there is no generic continuity between the so-called ancient novel (or romance) and the *romans antiques*, which showed a strong preference for epics or historiography as their main sources. The lone exception is the story of Apollonius of Tyre, ultimately deriving from the *Historia Apollonii regis Tyri*, a late antique Latin text that probably translates a Greek romance.
4. For a recent, but still necessary and particularly effective, questioning of this paradigm, see Margreta de Grazia (2010).
5. The concept of vernacular humanism is most readily used in Iberian literary history, especially following the publication of Lawrance (1986). Nonetheless, similar developments can be found within other European vernaculars, for example, the programme of translations developed under Charles V of France.
6. "conquistar una función política en tiempo de paz" (all translations are mine).
7. I have very briefly sketched the opposition between *roman antique* and vernacular humanism in *El Victorial* in Pascual-Argente (2014, 162–163).
8. "[e]l que á de aprender e usar arte de cavallería, non conviene despender luengo tiempo en escuela de letras." This piece of advice contrasts starkly with coetaneous declarations about the full compatibility of arms and letters by noblemen invested in vernacular humanism, such as Íñigo López de Mendoza's famous dictum that "science does not blunt the spear's iron, nor does it loosen the sword from the knight's hand" ["la sçiençia non enbota el fierro de la lança ni faze

floxa la espada en la mano del cavallero"] (López de Mendoza 1988, 219). For a very similar statement by poet Gómez Manrique, see Heusch (2010, 325).

9. "cosas que non son de oficio de cavallería".

10. "[a] unos da gracia de ser letrados, e a otros de ser buenos mercaderes, e a otros de buenos mecánicos, e de ser labradores, e a otros de ser cavalleros e buenos defensores. ... E si el labrador o el mercader quiere usar de letras, non sabe, ca non es de su natura; pues subir en cavallería e usar armas esle dura cosa".

11. "de aquellos que tanto afanaron por aver onra e fama, agora sean fideles agora infideles".

12. The clerk who refashions old stories of antiquity is arguably the true hero in most *romans antiques* (Baswell 2000), and certainly in the *Libro de Alexandre*.

13. "figura paradigmática de la renovación cultural de Castilla".

14. "quién fuese el primero fundador de la romana cibdad".

15. "aunque sólo de Roma demandastes, no solamente de aquélla, mas de Troya, muy más antigua cibdad, escrevir ... porque—aviendo consideración a Roma—, desque ovo este nonbre, bien podemos dezir, de linaje de troyanos aver sido fundada, o, más verdaderamente fablando, engrandescida e fortificada. Así paresció cosa conviniente, guardando el orden natural, primero de Troya e después de Roma fazer minción".

16. In fact, many late fourteenth- and fifteenth-century Castilian translations used French (or Catalan) versions, rather than the Latin originals, as their main basis.

17. Philip also made preparations for a crusade that would retake Constantinople from the Ottomans, famously announced in a luxurious banquet imitating literary feasts—a self-conscious intertwining of literature and territorial expansion reminiscent of the early *romans antiques*.

18. This is particularly evident in Christine de Pizan's *Livre du corps de policie* (1407) and Alain Chartier's *Quadrilogue invectif* (1422), both of which were present in the ducal library, along with the French version of Valerius Maximus by Simon de Hesdin and Nicolas de Gonesse (Doutrepont 1909, 123–128, 277–278, 292–293, 300).

19. Doudet (2005, 188) lists some Burgundian attempts to appropriate the Trojan story and give the duchy a Trojan origin.

20. This is evident not only in the *Recueil*'s incomplete state, but also in the initial plan for a work in four parts, of which only the third one would touch on the Trojan War.

21. The tension between what we may call global and local impulses was already present in the early *romans antiques*; among the many treatments of dynastic and nationalistic uses of the Trojan story in medieval and early modern Europe, see, for example, Keller (2008) and Shepard and Powell (2004).

22. In this respect, it is not surprising to find that the *Sumas* arrived at the Burgundian court around the same time as two other Castilian works (translated into French around 1450) that take up courtly debates: Valera's own *Espejo de verdadera nobleza*, on what constitutes true nobility, and Juan Rodríguez del Padrón's *Triunfo de las donas*, on the *querelle des femmes* (Willard 1961; Vanderjagt 1981; Serrano 2008, 2010).

23. "hommes nourris en aucunes singulieres histoires de Troyes".

24. "des histoires [de Troyes] tout le monde parle".

25. The story of Apollonius takes up the last of the eight books in John Gower's *Confessio Amantis*, which was translated into Portuguese and then into Castilian, probably during the first half of the fifteenth century.

26. The only known surviving exemplar, kept today in the Hispanic Society of New York, does not provide these data. Homero Serís (1962) first brought the book to light and established its publication city and date, although he believed the printer to be Pablo Hurus, Juan's brother. Later studies have revealed that Juan was helming the printing press in Zaragoza around 1488 (Pallarés Jiménez 2008, 98–109).

27. I base my observations on the facsimile reproduction (*La vida e hystoria* 1966).

28. Gonzalo García de Santamaría noted of Pablo Hurus, "his work is advantaged in type and correction, of both of spelling and punctuation; something which, despite many fools not appreciating it in the vernacular, should not for that reason remain unappreciated, since correct spelling and punctuation do not harm the fool and benefit the wise" ["su obra lieva la ventaja en letra e correctión, assí de ortographía como de punctos, lo qual, ahunque en romance muchos necios no estimen, no deue ya por esso ser desestimado; ca la orthographía y punctuación no daña al necio y aprovecha al entendido"] (qtd in Marín Pina 1995, 86).

29. Research on translation in early German humanism has made enormous strides thanks to the research project, Marburger Repertorium zur Übersetzungsliteratur im deutschen Frühhumanismus, whose main achievements (including Terrahe's edition of Steinhöwel's Apollonius) are listed at <http://www.mrfh.de>.

30. Both brothers had ties to the Great Ravensburg Trading Company (Pallarés Jiménez 2008, 198–199), and Pablo travelled to Basel and Lyon, part of a route through which typographical materials were often traded (Romero Tobar 1989, 568n29).

Works Cited

Bakhtin, Mikhail. 1981. *The Dialogic Imagination: Four Essays*. Translated by Michael Holquist. Austin: University of Texas Press.

Bartlett, Robert. 1994. *The Making of Europe: Conquest, Colonization, and Cultural Change, 950–1350*. Princeton, NJ: Princeton University Press.

Baswell, Christopher. 2000. "Marvels of Translation and Crises of Transition in the Romances of Antiquity." In *The Cambridge Companion to Medieval Romance*, edited by Roberta L. Krueger, 29–44. Cambridge: Cambridge University Press.

Baumgartner, Emmanuèle. 1995. "Romans antiques, histoires anciennes et transmission du savoir aux XIIe et XIIIe siècles." In *Mediaeval Antiquity*, edited by Andries Welkenhuysen, Herman Braet, and Werner Verbeke, 219–235. Leuven: Leuven University Press.

Beltrán, Rafael. 2011. "Huellas de Alejandro Magno y del *Libro de Alexandre* en la Castilla del siglo XV: un modelo para la historia y la biografía." In *L'historiographie médiévale d'Alexandre le Grand*, edited by Catherine Gaullier-Bougassas, 155–172. Turnhout: Brepols.

Buchthal, Hugo. 1971. *Historia Troiana: Studies in the History of Mediaeval Secular Illustration*. London: Warburg Institute, University of London.

Burke, Peter. 2006. "How to Write a History of Europe: Europe, Europes, Eurasia." *European Review* 14 (2): 233–239.

Classen, Albrecht. 1997. "Heinrich Steinhöwel." *Dictionary of Literary Biography: German Writers of the Renaissance and Reformation, 1280–1580*, edited by James N. Hardin and Max Reinhart. Detroit, MI: Gale Research.

de Grazia, Margreta. 2010. "Anachronism." In *Cultural Reformations: Medieval and Renaissance in Literary History*, edited by Brian Cummings and James Simpson, 13–32. Oxford: Oxford University Press.

Deyermond, Alan D., ed. 1973. *Apollonius of Tyre: Two Fifteenth-Century Spanish Prose Romances*. Exeter: University of Exeter Press.

Díaz de Games, Gutierre. 2014. *El Victorial*. Edited by Rafael Beltrán. Barcelona: Galaxia Gutenberg / Círculo de Lectores.

Di Camillo, Ottavio. 1996. "Las teorías de la nobleza en el pensamiento ético de Mosén Diego de Valera." In *Nunca fue pena mayor: estudios de literatura española en homenaje a Brian Dutton*, edited by Ana Menéndez Collera and Victoriano Roncero López, 223–238. Cuenca: Ediciones de la Universidad de Castilla-La Mancha.

Doudet, Estelle. 2005. "Le miroir de Jason: la Grèce ambiguë des écrivains bourguignons au XVe siècle." *Cahiers de la Villa Kérylos* 16 (1): 175–193.

Doutrepont, Georges. 1909. *La Littérature française à la cour des Ducs de Bourgogne: Philippe le Hardi–Jean sans Peur–Philippe le Bon–Charles le Téméraire*. Paris: Champion.

Flood, John L. 2007. "Parallel Lives: Heinrich Steinhöwel, Albrecht von Eyb, and Niklas von Wyle." In *Early Modern German Literature, 1350–1700*, edited by Max Reinhart, 779–796. Rochester, NY: Camden House.

Gómez Redondo, Fernando. 1999. *Historia de la prosa medieval castellana, II: El desarrollo de los géneros. La ficción caballeresca y el orden religioso*. Madrid: Cátedra.

Heusch, Carlos. 2010. "De la biografía al debate: espejismos caballerescos en el *Victorial* de Gutierre Díaz de Games." *eHumanista: Journal of Iberian Studies* 16: 308–327.

Keller, Wolfram R. 2008. *Selves and Nations: The Troy Story from Sicily to England in the Middle Ages*. Heidelberg: Winter.

La vida e hystoria del Rey Apolonio. 1966. [Cieza]: La fonte que mana y corre.

Lawrance, Jeremy N. H. 1985. "The Spread of Lay Literacy in Late Medieval Castile." *Bulletin of Hispanic Studies* 62: 79–94.

Lawrance, Jeremy N. H. 1986. "On Fifteenth-Century Spanish Vernacular Humanism." In *Medieval and Renaissance Studies in Honour of Robert Brian Tate*, edited by Ian Michael and Richard Cardwell, 63–79. Oxford: Dolphin.

Lawrance, Jeremy N. H. 1990. "Humanism in the Iberian Peninsula." In *The Impact of Humanism on Western Europe*, edited by Anthony Goodman and Angus Mackay, 220–258. London: Longman.

Lefèvre, Raoul. 1987. *Le recoeil des histoires de Troyes*. Edited by Marc Aeschbach. New York: Peter Lang.

López de Mendoza, Íñigo. 1988. *Obras completas*. Edited by Angel Gómez Moreno and Maximiliaan Paul Adriaan Maria Kerkhof. Barcelona: Planeta.

Marín Pina, María Carmen. 1995. "La *Cárcel de amor* zaragozana (1493), una edición desconocida." *Archivo de Filología Aragonesa* 51: 75–88.

Nolan, Barbara. 1992. *Chaucer and the Tradition of the* Roman Antique. Cambridge: Cambridge University Press.

Pallarés Jiménez, Miguel Ángel. 2008. *La imprenta de los incunables de Zaragoza y el comercio internacional del libro a finales del siglo XV*. Zaragoza: Institución Fernando el Católico / Diputación de Zaragoza.

Pascual-Argente, Clara. 2014. "Remembering Antiquity in the Castilian *Confessio Amantis.*" In *John Gower in England and Iberia: Manuscripts, Influences, Reception,* edited by Ana Sáez-Hidalgo and R. F. Yeager, 153–164. Cambridge: Brewer.

Penna, Mario, ed. 1959. *Prosistas castellanos del siglo XV.* Madrid: Atlas.

Pérez Fernández, José María. 2014. "Translation, *Sermo Communis,* and the Book Trade." In *Translation and the Book Trade in Early Modern Europe,* edited by Edward Wilson-Lee and José María Pérez Fernández, 40–60. Cambridge: Cambridge University Press.

Pinkernell, Gert. 1972. "Lefèvre, Raoul." *Dizionario Critico della Letteratura Francese.* Edited by Franco Simone. Torino: Unione Tipografico-Editrice Torinese.

Rey, Agapito, ed. 1932. *Sumas de historia troyana.* Madrid: S. Aguirre.

Rodríguez Velasco, Jesús. 1996. *El debate sobre la caballería en el siglo XV: la tratadística caballeresca castellana en su marco europeo.* Valladolid, Spain: Junta de Castilla y León.

Rodríguez Velasco, Jesús. 2001. "El libro de Díaz de Games." In *La chevalerie en Castille à la fin du Moyen Âge: aspects sociaux, idéologiques et imaginaires,* edited by Georges Martin, 211–223. Paris: Ellipses.

Romero Tobar, Leonardo. 1989. "Los libros poéticos impresos en los talleres de Juan y Pablo Hurus." *Aragón en la Edad Media* 8: 561–574.

Sanmartín Bastida, Rebeca. 1998. "El tema troyano en *Origen de Troya y Roma* de Diego de Valera." *Cuadernos de Filología Clásica* 14: 167–185.

Serís, Homero. 1962. "La novela de Apolonio: Texto en prosa del siglo XV descubierto." *Bulletin Hispanique* 64 (1): 5–29.

Serrano, Florence. 2008. "La diffusion de la littérature espagnole à la cour de Philippe le Bon." *Romanistisches Jahrbuch* 59: 193–203.

Serrano, Florence. 2010. "Figures auctoriales et figures du pouvoir: Valera et Rodríguez del Padrón à la cour de Bourgogne." *Cahiers d'études hispaniques médiévales* 33 (1): 109–126.

Shepard, Alan, and Stephen D. Powell, eds. 2004. *Fantasies of Troy: Classical Tales and the Social Imaginary in Medieval and Early Modern Europe.* Toronto: Centre for Reformation and Renaissance Studies.

Terrahe, Tina. 2013. *Heinrich Steinhöwels 'Apollonius'. Edition und Studien.* Berlin: Walter de Gruyter.

Vanderjagt, Arie J. 1981. *Qui sa vertu anoblist: the concepts of noblesse and "chose publicque" in Burgundian political thought.* Groningen, Netherlands: J. Miélot.

Willard, Charity Cannon. 1967. "The Concept of True Nobility at the Burgundian Court." *Studies in the Renaissance* 14: 33–48.

5 Europe in Love

Contemporary History and Fiction in the German 'European Novel'

Nicolas Detering

In German literature, a faint awareness of some continental cohesion beyond mere geographical contiguity can be traced back at least to the sixteenth century. Laux Lercher's anti-Ottoman pamphlet *News of the Large man … Christian Great India, and How He Married the Maiden Christendom Europe* (1547) tells the allegorical story of the Gargantuan giant Christian, who is discovered by Portuguese sailors and whose body parts are analogous in size to the various European lands. At his request, the German emperor allows him to marry the maiden 'Christendom Europe,' and together they beget 30 children, representing 30 countries. United, the brothers stand strong against the Turks. Lercher's *News* is perhaps the earliest literary attempt to allegorize Europe in the German vernacular, but it seems to have gone entirely unnoticed at the time and is virtually unknown today. Even though foreign political works like Juan Luis Vives's satirical dialogue *De Europae dissidiis et bello turcico* ("Of the Strives of Europe and the Turkish War," 1526; German translation 1540) or allegorical plays like Jean Desmarets de Saint-Sorlin's *Europe* (1643) were promptly translated into German, they did not spark a genuine tradition of literary reflections on Europe.[1] To be sure, scattered works like Cyriacus Lentulus's didactic poem *Europa* (1650)—a versified textbook on topography—or the anonymous *Scena Europaea* ("The European stage," 1629)—an array of all the princes of Europe and various personifications unveiling their interests and bemoaning their fates—were published by German authors and printers during the Thirty Years' War, but they were mostly written in neo-Latin and seem to have had only limited impact. In light of these findings, one is tempted to adapt Peter Burke's provocative question (Burke 1980): Did German literature on Europe exist before 1700?

This chapter argues that it did but not for very long. Taking a "nominalist" approach—that is, limiting my research to literary works that use the term 'Europe' repeatedly or prominently (e.g., in the title)—I will examine the publication of a number of German 'European novels,' a fashion starting in the 1670s and continuing until the 1730s.[2] These were historical romances and novels that resembled the 'Asian' or 'African' novels of the time (see Simons 2001, 423–454) but were chiefly concerned with the current affairs of Europe. The European novel seems to have been a German phenomenon.

It started with the vastly successful novels by Eberhard Werner Happel, first with his *Europäische Toroan* ("The European Toroan," 1676), then continued with Happel's series of "annalistic" novels called *Europäische Geschicht-Romane* ("European History-Novels") in the late 1680s. The trend was carried on by works like Johann Beer's *Der verliebte Europeer* ("The Enamoured European," 1682), the anonymously published *Der europäische Firando* ("The European Firando," 1684), August Bohse's *Liebenswürdige Europäerin Constantine* ("The Lovable European Constantine," 1698), and Christian Friedrich Hunold's *Der Europäischen Höfe Liebes- und Helden-Geschichte* ("Romance of the European Courts," 1705).

Although critical studies on the history of 'European identity' abound, literary texts of the early modern period have seldom been analyzed. German literature of this era in particular has largely been neglected.[3] Suggesting that its roots lie in the merging of journalistic contemporary history with fiction, I will give a brief overview of one of their cornerstones, namely, the Baroque novel on Europe. The first section of this chapter shows that the term 'Europe' occurred particularly often in early periodicals, serial chronicles, and political pamphlets of the early and mid-seventeenth century. These media evolved earlier in Germany than elsewhere (Berns 1983, 95–96), and they played a pivotal role in the conceptualization of Europe as a chronotope: the continent becomes closely associated with its current state in time, that is, the space 'Europe' is conceptually blended with the present.[4] Just as periodicals in the seventeenth century have been said to produce a notion of the present as 'contemporaneity' (see Dooley 2010), I contend that they simultaneously construct the spatial notion of 'Europe.'

While earlier works like Lercher's or Lentulus's proved ineffective, the rapid rise of news media in Germany soon engendered literary reflections on the current state of the continent. One of the first 'journalist poets' of this time was Eberhard Werner Happel (who is discussed in the second part of this chapter). His successful novels were published serially and aimed at popularizing actual information on Europe by couching it in a fashionable love story.

A third and final part argues that starting in the 1680s, use of the term 'Europe' in a novel's title acquired new functions. It hinted not only at the narrated space but connoted generic features: As Johann Beer's *Der verliebte Europeer* and Christian Friedrich Hunold's *Der europäischen Höfe Liebes- und Helden-Geschichte* illustrate, 'Europe' could now imply a work's referential status (factual information integrated into fiction) as well as an intention of purpose (to instruct by telling an entertaining story).

Media of 'Contemporaneity' and the Emergence of 'Europe'

Beginning with the early semiannual publications by Michael Aitzing (c. 1530–1598) and Jacobus Francus (1550?–1620) in the 1590s, periodic news in Germany had a European focus. Francus, the publisher of *Historicae relationis continuatio* (Spring 1591, fol. A 2^v), proclaims that reading his periodical would enable the reader to learn "of many troubled things in France, Holland, England, and other countries, while being in a comfortable position, without danger, without strenuous travelling and difficulties."[5] The first weekly newspaper in history, the Strasbourg *Relation* by Johann Carolus (1575–1634), reported "all the best and memorable stories which will at times proceed and happen in Germany and the Netherlands, also in France, Italy, Scotland, England, Spain, Hungary, Poland, Transylvania, Valachia, Moldavia, Turkey etc. in the year 1609."[6] Of the *Relation*'s text, a total of 99 per cent concerned events from Germany (60 per cent) and other European countries (39 per cent) (Schröder 1995, 96–114). Of the 1,622 issues of the Hamburg newspaper *Wöchentliche Zeitung auß mehrerley örther* ("Weekly News from Various Places"), 57 per cent of all reports concerned Germany, 43 per cent the rest of Europe; by 1674, the ratio had been reversed, with 65 per cent of all messages now being on European countries other than Germany (see Wilke 1984, 151). Reports from outside the continent hardly existed in the first decades of German periodicals. Their focus on European events is reflected by the newspapers' tendency to name themselves 'European.' In the seventeenth century, 15 different enterprises were named *Europäische Zeitung* ("European News") or something similar, among them three different weeklies in Hamburg alone (Bogel and Blühm 1971, 87, 206, and 246).

The invention of periodicity implied a certain concept of time. While broadsheets and pamphlets could report recent events, they were nevertheless published *accidentally*, that is, after a specific event happened and only because this specific event happened. *Periodic* newspapers, however, were published at a certain moment in time (say, twice a year, every Tuesday, or every morning), no matter what incidents had occurred. Their publication was not dictated by specific events but by a rule of frequency. Publishers of periodicals simply assumed that newsworthy events were going to transpire before the next publication date. Thus, they reflected and consolidated a changed attitude towards the present time and its immediate future: by publishing continually, they expected and reinforced continuity. By fostering the notion of a continuous present, the periodicals also constructed a consciousness of "contemporaneity" (Landwehr 2014, 147–205; Dooley 2010). A German reader could now learn what happened at the same time in dozens of different places all over Europe. The various events were all connected by occurring simultaneously. Living in the same communicative present, newspaper readers became contemporaries through the shared reception of news in the way that Benedict Anderson has described for the genesis of the nation as an "imagined community" (cf. Anderson 2006, 22–36).

The early newspapers delighted in reporting as many events from as many places as possible. Theirs was a variegated panorama with little structure, but its variegation was a vital part of these media's intention to divert as well as to inform. The variety of spaces and countries made news more colourful and reflected the multitude of reported events spatially: a lot happened in a lot of places. The plurality of places was summarized by the umbrella term

'Europe' in their title. If the multitude of events were bracketed by happening in a continuous present time, then the multitude of places all shared a similar root—they were situated in Europe. Continuity and continent, contemporaneity and Europe, time and space thus became closely associated with each other. Both were collective terms for temporal and spatial plurality, and both were products of a communicative revolution around 1600.

And what a revolution it was. Between 1615 and 1640 alone, 80 newspapers were founded in Germany, most of which were short-lived. During the seventeenth century, roughly 200 publishing companies were set up in over 80 different places (Behringer 2003; Weber 1994b, 10). The average print run of weekly newspapers is estimated to have been around 350 to 400 (Weber 1997, 141–142), but the number of readers must have been much higher, due to contemporary reading habits like group subscriptions at courts, schools, and universities, public readings, as well as display of prints in public houses and inns (Böning 2002, 116). According to some calculations, weeklies could have reached up to 200,000 regular readers in the last third of the century: that is almost one quarter of all literate people in Germany (Weber 1994b, 20). The enormous success of a medium which at its core told of the variety of European events, and which frequently used the term 'Europe' on its title page and in its text, led to the formation of 'Europe' as a chronotope, a nexus of space and time. Whenever German pamphleteers, novelists, and dramatists used the term 'Europe' in the seventeenth century, they were likely to imply not only the plurality of countries and the unity of the continent, but also the plurality of current events and the unity of the contemporary present. Put simply, 'Europe' in German writing of the seventeenth century almost always meant 'the current state of Europe.'

There is no doubt that the Thirty Years' War (1618–1648) greatly facilitated this process. When Protestant Sweden began to support Catholic France in 1635 (at the latest), it became obvious that this was no longer a war about religion—if it ever had been—but about secular power and influence over the continent. The more continental the conflict became, the more the contemporary interest in European events increased (Weber 1997, 144). The term 'Europe,' closely associated with the current state of politics through its proliferation in news media, was now widely used in political writings of the time. Its increasingly pejorative use in pamphlets, broadsheets, and treatises reflected the anxieties of many contemporaries. The turmoil of war and the erratic instability of its coalitions are depicted as a critical element of the general state of threat and danger for the continent. A copper plate of 1644, translated from the Dutch, shows "Groß Europisch Kriegs-Balet" ("The Great European War-Ballet") in which the monarchs and their diplomats dance cheerfully with each other, apparently oblivious to the fate of their people (Figure 5.1).[7] The "European princes and peoples," confirms one pamphlet *Von dem gegenwertigen Zustande in Europe* ("On the Current State of Europe," 1640), "have kindled war against each other, and in doing so did not think of the common good, but only, and almost fervently of their individual interest."[8]

Figure 5.1 Groß Europisch Kriegs-Balet. Anonymous broadsheet after a Dutch prototype. Copper plate (around 1644). Herzog August Bibliothek Wolfenbüttel: Einbl. Xb FM 213.

European politics was characterized as a spectacle, a stage of superficiality, of transient coalitions and fickle fortune. This temporal perspective on the "present state of Europe" allowed for the rise of one of the most successful serial chronicles of the early modern period, the *Theatrum Europaeum*, first published in 1633 by the eminent printer and illustrator Matthäus Merian (1593–1660). The annalistic accounts, compiled and authored by changing contributors, were published serially every couple of years until 1738 and effected similar undertakings like the *Diarium Europaeum* by Martin Meyer (1659–1683). These chronicles aimed at informing the reader about current developments in European politics, selected important correspondences from the vast numbers of newspapers and historical relations, and combined them with original records and eyewitness reports (cf. Dethlefs 2004 and Schultheiß-Heinz 2011). Merian's and Meyer's annals were mostly neutral in tone, but the very design of their chronicles did provide a chronotopic interpretation of Europe's present as a particularly eventful and newsworthy period.

After the outbreak of the Dutch War in 1672, a new type of journal emerged that concentrated more on political commentary and reasoning (see Weber 1994a). These political journals were decidedly European in shape, too, and they often borrowed a fictional framework from the satirical tradition. For example, they presented a number of characters discussing the state of the continent in dialogue. "The disguised messenger of the Gods, Mercury, who, wandering through Europe, discovers some important discourses, speculations, and opinions," as the full title of *Der verkleidete Götter-Both Mercurius* (1674) reads, has been called the first of these new journals, even though it only appeared in four issues. The anonymous author relates how Mercury, the first-person narrator, is sent to different European countries by Jupiter in order to report everything that is new, but also all the rumours, opinions, and conjectures that are current. He first visits a public house in Amsterdam, where people discuss the war with France and possible options for the Low Countries. He then travels via Rotterdam to London, where a great number of people have gathered in front of the Royal Palace to argue about England's interest in the Franco-Dutch War. He goes to Paris to hear the French position, to Spain, to Turkey, and to various German cities. The *Götter-Both* follows a "European narrative"; that is, it constructs an additive plot that relies very heavily on a protagonist's continuing journey from country to country. Each fictional episode contains information on the current state and interests of the respective countries.

The 'European narrative' proved to be a fruitful form of political reasoning, and not just for early German journalism. Monthlies like *Der Europäische Mercurius* ("The European Mercury," 1689–1690, see Figure 5.2.)—which followed the same premise and was clearly a continuation of the earlier *Mercurius*—and journals like *Die Europäische Fama* ("The European Fama," 1683–1703), *Der Fliehende Passagier durch Europa* ("The flying passenger through Europe," 1698–1702), or *Der Europäische Niemand* ("The European Nobody," 1717–1721), all three probably written by Philipp Balthasar Sinold von Schütz (1657–1742), used a similar fictional narrative to relate alleged coffee house talk and widespread discussions about European politics. It may indeed appear difficult at times to distinguish the "European novel" from these political journals generically, since both existed within an

Figure 5.2 Mercury listening in on conversations at a public house. Frontispiece to the January issue of *Europäischer Mercurius oder Götter-Both* (1690). Bayerische Staatsbibliothek Munich: Res/4 Eur. 384,13. <urn:nbn:de:bvb:12-bsb11130004-5>.

"undifferentiated matrix of news and novels" (Davis 1983, 42–71). After all, some novels, like Eberhard Werner Happel's *Europäische Geschicht-Romane* ("European History-Novels"), were also published in serial form. Instead of artificially trying to separate the two, I would argue that "Europe" in the title of these novels hints precisely at the generic hybridization of political history within a fictional narrative frame.

Eberhard Werner Happel's Factual Fictions on Europe (1676–1690)

When Louis XIV's ambitions for power endangered European peace in the 1670s and 1680s, numerous new treatises, pamphlets, and histories focused on the present politics and histories of European countries (see Schmidt 2004; Wrede 2004, 324–474). The late seventeenth century also saw the rise of a new type of author in Germany: the commercial writer who aimed to sell more books by promising that they would not only be entertaining but also instructive.[9] The most prolific of these authors was Eberhard Werner Happel (1647–1690), a Hamburg-based journalist, polymath, and novelist, whose works established a form of Baroque "infotainment" on European matters that proved successful for decades.[10] Happel is today remembered for being the author of the *Relationes curiosae* ("Curious Relations," 1683–1691), one of the first learned journals in Germany (see Schock 2011). He began his career, however, in the 1670s as a writer of novels, and he continued to publish literary works until his death. His earlier oeuvre of fiction can be understood as an attempt to write a global pentalogy—four parts about the four continents, and a final part about all the islands of the world. Happel wrote *Der Africanische Tarnolast* ("The African Tarnolast") in the late 1660s (although it was not printed until 1689), then published *Der Asiatische Onogambo* ("The Asian Onogambo") in 1673, and *Europäische Toroan* ("The European Toroan") in 1676; and in 1682 he published his novel about the islands, *Der Insulanische Mandorell* ("The Insular Mandorell"). He announced the publication of an American novel twice but failed to complete it.

Unlike its predecessors, *African Tarnolast* and *Asian Onogambo*, which were not set in the present time, the third part of the pentalogy, *European Toroan,* was a story about all the states of Europe roughly from 1668 to 1673, the year in which Happel started to write the novel. Toroan, a Turkish prince and Christian convert who is forced to flee his cruel brother, seeks exile in 12 different European countries but is refused aid by all of their princes. Their justification for being unable to help a Christian refugee is always the same: given the troublesome political situation of the present, it would simply be too risky to prompt the wrath of the Ottoman sultan. The internal strife and wars of Europe—especially the Franco-Dutch War after 1672—are too many, the turmoil and rebellions within each state too threatening. Though smothered with digressions and encyclopaedic data, a clear argument hence pervades the *Toroan*: the European princes are incapable of standing up against the Ottoman empire because they are deadlocked by internal struggles, wars, and hegemonic ambitions. This was common-place in anti-Ottoman prints of the sixteenth and seventeenth centuries as well: Juan Luis Vives's *De Europae dissidiis,* for example, bemoaned the fact that the Christian princes were so distracted by fighting each other that they were unable to reconquer the Ottoman empire, which they could do in no time if only they stood united. A few years before Happel, the political writer Michael Praun wrote a treatise about the "amorous inclinations of the most beautiful Princess Europa" (*Relation von den Liebesneigungen Der Allerschönsten Princessin Europa*, around 1663), in which he, too, called for the European states and princes to end their internal strife, build a united federation of states, and fight the Turk. In his *Toroan*, Happel refers to these lamentations of external danger which aggravated the internal discord, but he transforms them from the public to the personal—a Christian knight is persecuted by his Ottoman brother, but the princes of Europe have other things to do than to help.

During Toroan's travels, which are motivated partly by his attempt to find shelter, partly by his quest for his love Borranda, the geography and history of all the states of Europe are described. Fact and fiction are intertwined in the process, or, as the title page puts it, the *Toroan* is "a brief description of all the kingdoms and countries in the whole of Europe, including their regents, depicted in a Turkish novel" (Happel 1676).[11] Happel's *Toroan* presented comprehensive information on Europe under the fictional garment of a Heliodorian romance, a complex story of lost love, search, and anagnorisis. Within this template, Happel described very recent events, thus illustrating and popularizing both political and other news. For example, an early chapter describes the earthquake of Ragusa (today's Dubrovnik) in 1668. Another chapter relates Toroan's participation in the czar's fight against the Stenka Razin rebellion (1670–1671) and informs the reader about the political situation in Russia at the time. Also, many chapters include opinions on the dangers of the Franco-Dutch War of 1672–1674. In other words, the fictional story progresses according to the chronology of real recent events, which Happel describes using newspapers and accounts from the chronicles of his time.

Toroan turned out to be one of Happel's more successful novels and was reprinted at least once (Happel 1689). Its concept, a semifictional novel about Europe in its current state, proved to be ahead of its time, too, as later novels like Hunold's *Der Europäischen Höfe Liebes- und Helden-Geschichte* would achieve commercial success as well. However, Happel's emphasis on topicality had one disadvantage. In his preface to *Toroan*, Happel reminds his reader that "Europe has, since I have finished the *Toroan*, changed considerably" (Happel 1676, fol. iv^v).[12] He entertains doubts "if this latest outline of Europe will last very long: The alliances are so marvellous that I think they'll last one year at best" (fol. v^r).[13] This notion that European coalitions were fickle was very common in broadsheets like the *Groß-Europisch Kriegs-Ballett* (see above), in chronicles like the *Theatrum Europaeum*, and in political pamphlets like "The Twisted Gamble of European Alliances" (*Das verkehrte Glücks-Spiel europäischer Alliantzen*, 1684) or "Unfortunate Change of Luck of the Campaigning Parties in Europe" (*Unglücklicher Glücks-Wechsel Der Kriegenden Partheyen in Europa*, 1691), which criticized the instability and contingency of European politics.

"One year at best"—perhaps it was his impression of inconstancy and eventfulness that gave Happel the idea to publish further novels on Europe once every year. Happel initiated the annalistic project of the *Sogenannte Europäische Geschicht-Roman* ("The So-called European History-Novel") in 1685 and every year released one novel with a focus on one European country, each divided into four parts that were published quarterly. The first *Geschicht-Roman* was *Italiänische Spinelli* ("Italian Spinelli"), written for 1685, followed by *Spanische Quintana* ("Spanish Quintana," 1686–1687), *Frantzösische Cormantin* ("French Cormantin," 1687, 1688), *Ottomanische Bajazet* ("Ottoman Bajazet," 1688–1689), *Teutsche Carl* ("German Carl," 1690), and *Engelländische Eduard* ("English Edward," 1691). Each novel bore the subtitle "that is: the so-called European History-Novel," followed by the year in which the novel was set. For example, the title of the *Italiänische Spinelli* was "The Italian Spinelli, or the so-called European History-Novel about the Year 1685." Hence, 'Europe' serves as an umbrella term for the totality of nations, just like it did in the weekly newspapers, the serial chronicles, and the monthly journals that Happel used for his novels. Each year corresponds to one country: continuity (year after year) and continent (country after country) are merged into a fictional account of contemporary Europe.

The typical *Geschicht-Roman* consisted of three elements: first, a fictional plot, namely, a high romance of a prince travelling through European countries in search of his lost love; second, a number of encyclopaedic digressions on topography, history, physics, or genealogy, compiled from travel books and compendia; and third, news from various nations and cities of the respective year, taken mostly from current newspapers or chronicles (Dammann 2011, 241–244). Both the "Discurse" (digressions) and the "Zeitungen" (news) are integrated into the fiction and are recounted, received, read, heard, discussed, or experienced by the protagonists.

The integration of news meant that Happel's fictions were by necessity set in the here and now of their year of origin. The four parts of the *Italiänische Spinelli*, for example, were set in the four seasons of 1685, the year it was published. With the exception of the *Europäische Toroan*, which was also set in the present time, this "actualization" of a fictional plot was highly innovative. Earlier novels had mostly been set in some distant past like antiquity or the Middle Ages, in a fictitious *locus amoenus* like Arcadia, or in some exotic and largely fictionalized country of Asia or Africa. Narratives that referred to the present and to European countries—let alone to German regions—were rare and almost entirely restricted to "lower" forms of literature like the Picaresque (see Dammann 2012, 469). Happel's European novels followed a different logic. Not only were they set in the immediate present, but they described their time emphatically as a period of unprecedented eventfulness: "In the past four or five months of this year," writes Happel in his *Italian Spinelli*, "we have experienced such strange things and changes that the importance of this material requires that it be put into writing for posterity's sake" (Happel 1685, Vol. 2, fol. 3ᵛ).[14] Happel's European novels depict the European continent in its temporal specificity: a space of such recurring novelty that any fictional account of it must indeed be serial, must be open to continuation from year to year. While spatially limited, the chronotope of Europe was temporally open; it changed constantly and thus required continuous literary reconstruction, very much like the periodicals and serial historiography that were published continually. While a finalized account of Europe like Happel's *Toroan* would simply be outdated within the year, a literary series of novels was more effective in creating European contemporaneity.

Disgusted by "Monotonous Matter": Johann Beer and Christian Friedrich Hunold

Although Happel was the most successful exponent commercially, there are other examples of factual fictions about then present-day Europe. One of the more prominent authors of a 'European' fiction was Johann Beer (1655–1700). Beer's odd *Der Verliebte Europeer* (1682) is less well known today than his other works and constitutes a "curiosity" in the eyes of many critics (Kremer 1984, 409). Beer's work, according to Richard Alewyn's pioneering study of 1932, marks a "breakthrough to reality" (Alewyn 2012, 201), a shift to formal realism in German literature,[15] but his European novel shows very few of the narrative qualities for which he is usually praised. Beer's *Europeer* is best understood by enquiring after its title's connection to other contemporary 'European' fiction, and by emphasizing the importance of the extensive factual digressions in the novel, which previous scholars have either ignored or trivialized.[16]

The antonomasia *The Enamoured European* refers to the protagonist Alexander, alternatively addressed by the narrator as "our European."[17] According to a preliminary address to the readers, Alexander is the (fictitious) author of his autobiography but recounted his life-story to a friend, one Amandus de Amanto, who has taken on the task of editing it and transforming the story into a third-person narrative. Alexander is a Sicilian prince who travels first to Madrid, then to Paris, Strasbourg, and finally Vienna. During the course of his travels, he is loved by four different women who belong to the various stations of his European journey. What seems like an erotic travelogue in the 'gallant' fashion is constantly interrupted by, as the afterword puts it, "rational discourses held by himself as well as others, so that the reader will not be disgusted by monotonous matter" (Beer 2002, 110).[18] These "discourses" include, for example, a longer monologue on France's need to fight the war against the Netherlands, spoken by a fictitious French minister (28–29), conversations on how to cure the bubonic plague, and descriptions of the sights and peculiarities of the places Alexander visits.

The typically Baroque title page alludes to this merging of fiction and factual "discurse" by indicating a number of binary pairs that seem to equal love and fiction on the one hand, and political history and nonfiction on the other:

> The Enamoured European, or truthful love-novel, in which are included Alexander's love story and brave heroic deeds, with which he not only endeared the women, but in which he also observed the most noble maxims of statecraft of various European kingdoms that he visits. For the respective profit of all curious women and prudent courtiers, collected by Alexander's good friend Amandus de Amanto.
>
> (Beer 2002, 5)[19]

The curious women, the title suggests, might be fascinated by the love stories of how Alexander endeared the "Frauenzimmer"; by the same token, the prudent courtier will delight in learning all the political maxims of the European states and in reading about Alexander's heroic deeds. If we extend the opposition and consider the tradition of Happel's encyclopaedic entertainment, the subtitle "a truthful love-novel" can also be read as a hint at its hybrid content: the amorous adventures of Alexander correspond to the term "love-novel," while the digressions on political theory and government are surely reported "truthfully." If we continue to follow the dualistic code even further, we might understand the main title, "The Enamoured European," to signal again the conveyance of factual information on European courts and heroes in the form of a love story.

The translation of "The Enamoured European" with "historical-political information conveyed within entertaining fiction" is underscored by the fictitious editor's note in the dedication, which announces that Alexander "could have easily given [his life-story] a different title, and called it *The Political Lover* after the current Political fashion of writing, but he follows altogether different principles" (Beer 2002, 12).[20] Although "The Political Lover" is emphatically *not* the title of the book, it is given as a possible alternative to "The Enamoured European," thus implicitly equalling 'Europe' with 'political history.' Admittedly, Beer digresses constantly from politics into other areas of conversation, and his novel clearly does follow different 'principles' than did the 'political novels' of Christian Weise or Johannes Riemer. But the main narrative was 'heroic,' concerned with a prince travelling to various European courts and learning about political agendas and problems of his time. The name 'Europe,' bearing as it did connotations of actuality, courts, and politics, must have seemed the right moniker for a novel that was partly factual and contained some political information, but that was not a 'political novel' or a treatise in the strictest sense.

The Foreword hints at another reason for the odd title of the book: Alexander, argues his fictitious friend and editor, has chosen the title for his life story after noticing "that a novel of the title *The Enamoured African* has recently been published. Because he saw that this little book found many admirers, he ... used the title of the enamoured European" (Beer 2002, 12).[21]

The "little book" that inspired Alexander was Gabriel de Brémond's best-seller *L'Amoureux Africain* (1671), which found "many admirers" indeed. It was reprinted three times (1675, 1676, and 1678) and translated into English (*The Fair One of Tunis*, 1674), Dutch (*Den verliefden Afrikaan*, 1677), and German (*Der Verliebte Afrikaner*, 1677).

Whether Beer knew the French original or had read the *L'Amoureux Africain* in German translation is unclear. Brémond's novel, subtitled *Nouvelle Galanterie*, is a typical example for the erotic exoticism of the French Baroque novel and was later adapted by Madame de Villedieu's *Les Nouvelles africaines* (1673). *L'Amoureux Africain* tells the story of the French nobleman Albirond, who, following his involvement in an illegal duel, is forced to leave France and to enter the "condition of a wandring Knight," as the English translator puts it: "[H]e had the opportunity of seeing the most beautiful and the greatest part of *Europe*; and with a competent proportion of wit that he was master of ..., he procur'd himself respect in all places ... and added some such passages, and adventures to the History of his Life, as were fit one day to be the subject of a Romance" (Brémond 1674, 2–3).[22] After his travels through Europe, which are only insinuated but not narrated, he enters a ship to Tunis on a whim. There he falls in love with a Christian slave, who turns out to be his French fiancée, Uranie. After many adventures, he is able to save her from his former friend Mahmet Lapsi, one of the Bassas of Tunis.

Not only did Beer change the continent from Africa to Europe—thereby writing just the 'Romance' that the French model had ostensibly deferred to the future ("one day")—but he also chose the present as his time frame, while *L'Amoureux Africain* was set in the late sixteenth century. Thus, 'Europe' in the title of Beer's novel not only referred to the European countries to which Alexander travels in the story, but was also linked to a specific time frame within which his travels are set, namely, the contemporary present. A number of instances described make it clear that the plot takes place around the time of the Treaty of Nijmegen (1678–1679), only a few years before the novel was published. Like Happel's *Toroan*, one of the first political novels to be set in the present time, Beer's 'European novel' was chiefly concerned with the current situation on the continent.

Most prominently, however, Beer transformed the more dramatic Heliodorean structure of *medias in res* and embedded retrospections and multiple subplots into an episodic narrative, in which the story moves linearly from country to country, from scene to scene. Alexander does not love, lose, and regain his one love, but falls in love sequentially, loses or leaves three of four women, and may or may not become happy with the fourth. By choosing the looser template of the Picaresque—and, incidentally, that of political journals like the *Götter-Both Mercurius*—Beer was able to integrate the various encyclopaedic discourses and conversations on recent events more easily. This didactic feature of the European novel was not only absent in the French model, but Brémond had outright rejected it: "I could here perhaps satisfie the curious," writes Brémond's narrator when Albiron first sets foot in Tunis, "by insisting upon the manners, and particular Government of this City ...; but it is not my design to mix any thing so serious, with what I only intend for a pure, and uncompounded piece of mirth. Neither do I write this for the grave Sr. *Politick Woodbee's*; the chief and only end of my writing being to entertain the amorous with a new piece of Gallantry" (Brémond 1674, 4–5).[23] The narrator refuses to give any factual information about the history, geography, or culture of Tunis. He claims he wants to be merely entertaining. Beer, on the other hand, wants to appeal especially to those "who do not cherish love stories very much" (Beer 2002, 110).[24] Lengthy accounts of cities and governments are easily intertwined with Beer's cumulative European travelogue. Of the descriptions of European cities, some are rather sketchy, like the account of Madrid, where Beer does not even bother to conceive of Spanish-sounding names, but features a local baker with the very German name Petrus Krumbhorn (Beer 2002, 22–24). Others, however, are impressively detailed, such as the report of Vienna's Stephen's Cathedral (Beer 2002, 91–92). The descriptions underline the encyclopaedic character of the novel and serve a similar purpose to the excursions in Happel's novels. They may instruct those "who wish to travel to foreign countries" (Beer 2002, 111), as the epilogue suggests, but more generally inform about the sights and features of Europe.

By eschewing a 'closed' story arc like Brémond's, *Der Verliebte Europeer* was in principle open for further travels, farces, gallant conversations, or erudite excursions. In other words, by changing the setting from Africa to Europe, Beer transforms not only the spatial and temporal setting from the remote and the long ago to the here and now. He also adjusts the narrative template in order to allow for interferences of fact and fiction. By doing so, he argues, the novel becomes more entertaining, because it loosens the "monotony of matter" (Beer 2002, 110) and holds something for everyone. "Europe" in the title of his novel connotes precisely these features, which were common in earlier fictional histories and had served as the title of other contemporary fact-fictional novels, notably Happel's *European History-Novels*.

Like the 'Asian' or 'African' novels of the time—the most important representative being Zigler von Kliphausen's *Asiatische Banise* (1689) (see Martin and Vorderstemann 2013)—the 'European novel' mixed fact and fiction, and it often dealt with matters of state and princely conduct. However, the exotic novels were mostly set in a distant time, and always in remote countries, whereas the European novels were set in the present time and on the European continent, where they were written and read. Hence, political commentaries on present princes and diplomats were much more delicate. It is no wonder, therefore, that some 'European novels' were written as *romans à clef*. The most famous example is Christian Friedrich Hunold's *Der Europäischen Höfe Liebes- und Helden-Geschichte*. This voluminous novel, based on notorious scandals of his time, tells an idealized story of August the Strong—or Gustavus, as Hunold calls him—and his love to Christiane Eberhardine of Bayreuth, named Arione von Thurabe by Hunold. The Heliodorean storyline of falling in love, separation, and reunion constitutes only the frame for a number of subplots, each of which is told by an intradiegetic narrator and presents the love story of another prince of a European state that is related in some way to August's Saxony and Poland. Like his predecessors, Hunold intertwines these subnarratives with various encyclopaedic digressions on general trivia or current events in the regions he describes. In the preface to his romance of love and deeds, he concedes that the histories ("Helden-Geschichten") "must be familiar from other historical books, because they are not invented" (Hunold 1978, 1).[25] Because they are mere facts, they run the risk of being tedious. Therefore, Hunold writes, he has provided some "diversion" ("Abwechslung") by adding love stories, so the readers will enjoy the "veiled truth" ("verdeckte Wahrheit") of the "acts of war" ("Kriegs-Thaten") as much as they would "merely fictional things" ("bloß erdichtete Sachen") (Hunold 1978, 1). *Der Europäischen Höfe Liebes- und Heldengeschichte* does indeed present extensive descriptions and histories, often taken verbatim from the *Theatrum Europaeum*; but like Happel and Beer, Hunold relates contemporary European history in the form of a fashionable love story.[26]

When Hunold wrote his "Romance of European Courts" in 1705, a number of works had already established the term 'Europe' as a commercial tool to convince the reader that the content of the novel held both something to learn and something to be entertained by. Entertainment in the gallant novel mainly meant 'erotic' fiction, while the integrated 'factual accounts' resembled the histories of the time and put forward information, encyclopaedic digressions, and political reasoning. Accordingly, as I have argued, the name of the continent hinted not only at the narrated space in these novels, but also at their hybrid referential status between fact and fiction.

Summary

German literary texts that dealt primarily with the current state of the continent and used the term 'Europe' prominently or frequently were scarce before the last third of the seventeenth century. The emergence of the 'European novel' in the 1670s and 1680s can therefore be considered something of a breakthrough for the German history of the idea of Europe. These novels were greatly indebted to contemporary news media, serial chronicles, and political journals. Seventeenth-century contemporary history helped to shape the chronotopic concept of 'Europe,' in which the continental space (the whole of a plurality of places) and the continuous present time (the whole of a plurality of recent events) were bracketed together. Referring to the time space of a period of instability, incessant wars, and ruthless ambitions, German publicists of the seventeenth century equated 'Europe' with the 'current state of Europe.' Accordingly, it was the goal of authors like Eberhard Werner Happel to integrate information previously limited to journalism into a fictional framework, combine instruction and entertainment, and further the knowledge of the political state of the continent. His *European Toroan* and the series of *European History-Novels* established a genre of political fiction on the present time, which found many successors around 1700. As the examples of Beer and Hunold show, this genre soon became self-reflective. They equated writing fiction about Europe with writing fictional histories about politics. The term 'Europe' in the titles of their novels denoted the generic roots in journalism;[27] by the same token, German fiction helped to construct a notion of Europe as a particularly eventful space of 'contemporaneity.'

Jean-Baptiste Duroselle famously synthesized the three factors that contributed most to the emergence of the (early) modern idea of 'Europe': "L'Europe face aux Turcs," "L'Europe face à l'Amerique," and "L'Europe face à elle-même" (Duroselle 1965, 75–103). Arguing from a nominalist perspective, this study has contended that from Duroselle's three factors, the last, 'Europe facing herself,' was perhaps the most crucial for the development of a German literature on Europe. It was neither the anti-Ottoman pamphlets and plays nor the travelogues and ethnographic books on Native American customs that exerted the greatest influence on the 'European novels' by Happel, Beer, Hunold, and the like. Instead, fictional constructions of Europe in the Baroque depended on the enormous success of news weeklies, periodic journals, serial histories, political broadsheets, and other 'media of contemporaneity,' which informed readers about the various events of the present happening in the various places of the continent.

Notes

1. The translations are Vives (1540) and Harsdörffer (1643). For concepts of Europe in Vives, see Margolin (1982), without mention of Eppendorff's translation; on Saint-Sorlin, see Guthmüller (2009).
2. For the distinction between a 'nominalist' and a 'realist' approach to concepts of Europe, see the Introduction to this volume.
3. Exceptions include Hanenberg (2007), Benthien (2007), and Watanabe-O'Kelly (2012). I am currently preparing a doctoral dissertation on *Concepts of Europe in Early Modern German Literature* (Detering forthcoming).
4. I am using the term 'chronotope' in a different sense than Burke (2006, 236), who means the changing varieties of understandings of 'Europe' and asks whether there "were more or fewer Europes in 1750 than there had been in 1450." See Detering (forthcoming) for an elaboration of this thesis.
5. Francus argues that reading news is useful: "Weil man dardurch in guter stiller gelegenheit / ohne gefahr / ohne müdes reisen vnd beschwerligkeit viel vnruige sachen in Franckreich / Holland / Engellant … kan erlernen." (Unless otherwise stated, all translations are mine.)
6. The title page reads: "*Relation:* Aller Fürnemmen vnd gedenckwürdigen Historien / so sich hin vnnd wider in Hoch vnnd Nieder Teutschland / auch in Franckreich / Italien / Schott vnd Engelland / Hisspanien / Hungern / Polen /

Siebenbürgen / Wallachey / Moldaw / Türckey / etc. inn diesem 1609. Jahr verlauffen vnd zutragen möchte. [Strasbourg 1609]."

7. This broadsheet is based on a Dutch model—see Paas 2002, 423–426 (= PA-376–PA-379); on images of Europe in German broadsheets, see Harms (2010).

8. The pamphlet says it will reveal the truth about European politics: "Wir wollen euch ... herfür bringen. ... Wie eins Theils Fürsten ... wieder sich selbst / Kriege ... erreget / vnd dabey wenig vff den gemeinen / alle aber vff jhren eigenen Nutz fast hitzig gedacht," *Von dem gegenwertigen Zustande* [1640], fol. A ijr-ijv. This 'oration' is based on the Latin pamphlet *De præsenti europæ statu oratio* [1640].

9. For a similar trend towards "professionalization" of literary writing in England, see Hammond (1997).

10. On Happel's *Sogenannte Europäische Geschicht-Romane*, see Scholz Williams (2014).

11. "Der Europæische TOROAN, Ist Eine kurtz-gefassete Beschreibung aller Königreiche und Länder in gantz EUROPA; Sampt ihren Regenten. ... In einem Türckischen *Roman* vorgestellet." A second edition replaces the misleading term "Turkish novel" with "Christlich-Türkischen Helden- und Liebes-Geschichte" ("Christian-Turkish Romance"), cf. Happel 1689.

12. "Im übrigen / weil ich dir die letzte Beschaffenheit unsers *Europa* vorstellen wollen / so wisse / daß es sich / Zeithero / daß ich den *Toroan* beschlossen / noch viel geändert."

13. "Ob aber dieser letzte Entwurff von *Europa* lang bestehen könne / glaube ich schwerlich / dann die *Allian*tzen sind so wunderlich / daß ich nicht glaube / daß sie zum höchsten ein Jahr bestehen können."

14. "[I]n denen verwichenen 4. oder 5. Monaten deß jetztlauffenden Jahrs haben wir solche merckwürdige Dinge und Veränderungen erlebet ..., daß es die Wichtigkeit der Materie erfordert / selbige / um der Nach Welt willen / in die Feder zu fassen."

15. Alewyn's enthusiastic judgment of Beer has been questioned by more recent scholarship (see Solbach 1994, esp. 31–49).

16. Solbach (2003, 225–226), for example, argues that the factual dialogues had "no significance for the plot, and their themes and arguments are of little significance in general." Solbach therefore "eliminates" (228) these "unorganic elements" for the sake of his analysis. While it may be true that Beer's factual excursions are not integrated into the narrative in a plausible way, they constitute quite significant parts of the text as a whole.

17. Alexander is called "der verliebte Europäer" (Beer 2002 19, 31, 48, 51, 53, and 54); and "unser Europäer" (64, 75, and 93).

18. "Vernünfftige Discurse / welche sowohl von ihm als andern gehalten worden / damit der Leser wegen einerley Materie nicht einen Eckel bekommen möchte."

19. "Der verliebte *Europeer*, Oder / Warhafftige *Liebes-Roman* / In welchen *Alexandri* Liebesgeschichte / und tapfere Helden-Thaten / womit er nicht alleine sich bey den Frauenzimmer beliebt gemacht / sondern auch in Besichtigung unterschiedliche Königreiche in Europe / dero vornehmsten Staats-Maximen angemercket / begriffen / Allem *Curio*sen Frauenzimmer / und klugen Hoff-Leuten zu sonderbaren Nutz / zusammen getragen / durch Alexandri guten Freund / welcher sonst genant wird / AMANDUS de AMANTO."

20. "Uber diß hätte auch der Autor diesem Wercke gar leicht einen andern Titel geben / und nach dem heutigen Politischen STYLO CURIÆ, den Politischen Liebhaber nennen können / aber er hat hierinnen gantz andere PRINCIPIA."

21. "Daß vor dem ein Roman / unter dem Titel des verliebten Affricaners in Druck gangen / weil er nun gesehen / daß solch Büchlein ziemlich viel Liebhaber gefunden / als hat er eben falls seinen Lebens-Lauff unter dem Titel des *verliebten Europæers* / einem guten Freunde nach und nach erzehlet."

22. The French original read: "[I]l falloit de necessité qu'il prit comme les autres, le party de Chevalier errant. Il vit sur ce piedlà, la plus belle & la plus grande partie de l'Europe & avec l'esprit raisonnable qu'il avoit, & sa maniere honéte de faire, il receut de l'honneur par tout où il pasa; il se fit des amis de tout ce qu'il rencontra de personnes bien faites, & augmenta l'Histoire de sa vie de quelques avantures propres à faire un jour un Romant" (Brémond, 4th ed. 1678, 11–12).

23. "Je pourrois contenter icy les curieux, à leur dire la maniere de ce gouvernement. ... [M]ais je n'ay pas dessein de méler rien de si serieux avec une simple galanterie. Je n' ècris pas icy pour les curieux de Politique, j'ay resolu de divertir seulement les amoureux des nouvelles galanteries" (Brémond, 4th ed. 1678, 13–14). A few pages further he muses "There is nothing more tedious, and distastful to Readers then the Descriptions of Pallaces and Gardens" (Brémond 1674, 9) / "car il n'est rien qui fatique & qui ennuye tant comme ces descriptions de Palais & de jardin" (Brémond, 4th ed., 1678, 18).

24. "[W]elche sonst nicht viel von Liebes-Büchern halten."

25. "[Sie] müssen zwar / weil sie nicht erdichtet sind / aus andern Historischen Büchern bekandt seyn."

26. Dammann (2011, 474) calls Hunold "something like a pupil of Happel." According to Dammann, Hunold's *Der Europäischen Höfe Liebes- und Helden-Geschichte* is "the most brilliant narrative modeling of contemporary events in the template of the courtly-historical novel."

27. For the thesis that the modern novel in general evolved from journalism, not from the medieval romance, see Davis 1983.

Works Cited

Alewyn, Richard. 2012. *Johann Beer: Studien zum Roman des 17. Jahrhunderts*. 2nd ed. Edited by Klaus Garber and Michael Schroeter. Heidelberg: Winter.

Anderson, Benedict. 2006. *Imagined Communities: Reflections on the Origin and Spread of Nationalism*. Revised ed. London: Verso.

Anon. 1640. *De præsenti europæ statu oratio, ad principes popvlosqve europæos*. [n.p.].

Anon. [1640]. *Von dem gegenwertigen Zustande in Europa: Eine Rede An die Fürsten vnd Völcker*. [n.p.].

Anon. [1644]. *Groß Europisch Kriegs Balet / getantzet durch die Könige vnd Potentaten Fürsten vnd Respublicken / auff dem Saal der betrübten Christenheit*. [n.p.].

Anon. [1674]. *Der Verkleidete Götter-Both Mercurius / Welcher durch Europa wandernd / einige wichtige Discoursen / Muthmassungen und Meynungen ... entdecket*. [Nuremberg: Felßecker].

Beer, Johann. 2002. *Der verliebte Europäer*. 1682. In: *Sämtliche Werke*, edited by Ferdinand van Ingen and Hans-Gert Roloff, 5–113. Vol. 10. Bern: Lang.

Behringer, Wolfgang. 2003. *Im Zeichen des Merkur: Reichspost und Kommunikationsrevolution in der Frühen Neuzeit*. Göttingen: Vandenhoeck & Ruprecht.

Benthien, Claudia. 2007. "Europeia: Mythos und Allegorie in der Frühen Neuzeit." In *Europadiskurse in der deutschen Literatur und Literaturwissenschaft*, edited by Claudia Benthien, Paul Michael Lützeler, and Anne-Marie Saint-Gille, 21–31. Bern: Lang.

Berns, Jörg Jochen. 1983. "Zeitung und Historia: Die historiographischen Konzepte der Zeitungstheoretiker im 17. Jahrhundert." *Daphnis* 12 (1): 87–110.

Bogel, Else, and Elger Blühm. 1971. *Die deutschen Zeitungen des 17. Jahrhunderts: Ein Bestandsverzeichnis mit historischen und bibliographischen Angaben*. Vol. 1. Text. Bremen: Schünemann.

Böning, Holger. 2002. *Welteroberung durch ein neues Publikum: Die deutsche Presse und der Weg zur Aufklärung – Hamburg und Altona als Beispiel*. Bremen: Lumière.

[Brémond, Gabriel de]. 1674. *The Fair One of Tunis: Or, The Generous Mistres—A New Piece of Gallantry*. London: Henry Brome.

[Brémond, Gabriel de]. 1677. *Der Verliebte Afrikaner / in einer überauß anmuthigen und gantz neuen Liebs-Geschicht*. [n.p.].

[Brémond, Gabriel de]. 1678 [1671]. *L'Amoureux Africain, Ou Nouvelle Galanterie*. Amsterdam: n.p.

Burke, Peter. 1980. "Did Europe Exist before 1700?" *History of European Ideas* 1: 21–29.

Burke, Peter. 2006. "How to Write a History of Europe: Europe, Europes, Eurasia." *European Review* 14 (2): 233–239.

[Carolus, Johannes, Ed.]. 1609. *Relation: Aller Fürnemmen vnd gedenckwürdigen Historien / so sich hin vnnd wider in Hoch vnnd Nieder Teutschland / auch in Franckreich / Italien / Schott vnd Engelland … Türckey / etc. Inn diesem 1609. Jahr verlauffen vnd zutragen möchte.* [Strasbourg: Carolus].

Dammann, Günter. 2011. "'… gutes Neues von den Europäischen Sachen': Zeitungen im Geschicht-Roman von Eberhard Werner Happel." In *Die Entstehung des Zeitungswesens im 17. Jahrhundert: Ein neues Medium und seine Folgen für das Kommunikationssystem der Frühen Neuzeit*, edited by Holger Böning and Volker Bauer, 235–269. Bremen: Lumière.

Dammann, Günter. 2012. "Fakten und Fiktionen im Roman bei Eberhard Werner Happel, Schriftsteller in Hamburg." In *Hamburg: Eine Metropolregion zwischen Früher Neuzeit und Aufklärung*, edited by Johann Anselm Steiger and Sandra Richter, 461–474. Berlin: Akademie Verlag.

Davis, Lennard J. 1983. *Factual Fictions: The Origins of the English Novel*. New York: Columbia University Press.

Detering, Nicolas. *Die Entstehung der deutschen Europa-Literatur in der Frühen Neuzeit (1590–1740)*. PhD thesis, Freiburg University.

Dethlefs, Gerd. 2004. "Schauplatz Europa: Das Theatrum Europaeum des Matthaeus Merian als Medium kritischer Öffentlichkeit." *Europa im 17. Jahrhundert: Ein politischer Mythos und seine Bilder*, edited by Klaus Bußmann and Elke Anna Werner, 149–181. Wiesbaden: Steiner.

Dooley, Brendan. 2010. Introduction. In *The Dissemination of News and the Emergence of Contemporaneity in Early Modern Europa*, edited by Brendan Dooley, 1–23. Farnham: Ashgate.

Duroselle, Jean-Baptiste. 1965. *L'idée d'Europe dans l'histoire*. Paris: Denoël.

Guthmüller, Bodo. 2009. "Zur Personifikation des Erdteils Europa in der *Comédie héroïque Europe* des Desmarets de Saint-Sorlin." In *Europa—Stier und Sternenkranz:*

Von der Union mit Zeus zum Staatenverbund, edited by Almut-Barbara Renger and Roland Alexander Ißler, 275–291. Göttingen: Vandenhoeck & Ruprecht Unipress.

Hammond, Brean. 1997. *Professional Imaginative Writing in England, 1670–1740, "Hackney for Bread."* Oxford: Clarendon Press.

Hanenberg, Peter. 2007. "Die Entdeckung und Gestaltung europäischer Identität in der deutschen Literatur der Frühen Neuzeit." In *Nation—Europa—Welt: Identitätsentwürfe vom Mittelalter bis 1800*, edited by Claudia Brinker-von der Heyde, Andreas Gardt, and Franziska Sick, 456–467. Frankfurt: Klostermann.

Happel, Eberhard Werner. 1676. *Der Europæische Toroan, Ist Eine kurtz-gefassete Beschreibung aller Königreiche und Länder in gantz Europa. … In einem Türckischen Roman vorgestellet.* … Hamburg: Nauman.

Happel, Eberhard Werner. 1685. *Der Italiänische Spinelli, Oder Sogenanter Europæischer Geschicht-Roman, Auff Das 1685.* 4 vols. Ulm: Wagner.

Happel, Eberhard Werner. 1689. *Der Erneuerte Europæische Toroan, Ist Eine kurtz-bündige Beschreibung / Aller Königreiche und Länder in gantz Europa, … In einer Christlich-Türckischen Helden- und Liebes-Geschichte leßwürdig fürgestellet; Anjetzo aber … auf Neue herauß gegeben / und durch Einführung vieler merck-würdigen Veränderungen continuirt.* … Frankfurt: Wagner.

Harms, Wolfgang. 2010. "Europa in der deutschen Bildpublizistik der Frühen Neuzeit." In *Auf dem Weg nach Europa: Deutungen, Visionen, Wirklichkeiten*, edited by Irene Dingel and Matthias Schnettger, 41–55. Göttingen: Vandenhoeck & Ruprecht.

Harsdörffer, Georg Philipp. 1643. *Japeta: Das ist Ein Heldengedicht / gesungen In dem Holsteinischen Parnasso Durch die Musam Calliope.* [Nuremberg: Endter].

Hunold, Christian Friedrich. 1978. *Der Europäischen Höfe Liebes- und Helden-Geschichte* [1705]. 2 vols. Edited by Hans Wagener. Bern: Lang.

Jouanna, Danielle. 2009. *L'Europe est née en Grèce: La naissance de l'idée d'Europe en Grèce ancienne.* Paris: Harmattan.

Kremer, Manfred K. 1984. "Nicht allein von denen Liebes-Geschichten … Anmerkungen zu Johann Beers *Der Verliebte Europaeer*." *Daphnis* 13: 409–443.

Landwehr, Achim. 2014. *Geburt der Gegenwart: Eine Geschichte der Zeit im 17. Jahrhundert.* Frankfurt: Beck.

Lentulus, Cyriacus. 1650. *Europa.* … Herborn: Corvinus.

Lercher, Laux. 1547. *Neuwe Zeitung Vom Grossen Mann / So dess Königs auß Portugals Schiffleuth haben zu wegen bracht / heißt Christian groß India / Wie er sich vermählet hat / mit einer Jungfrawen / die Christenheit. Europa genandt* … [n.p.].

Margolin, Jean-Claude. 1982. "Conscience européenne et réaction à la menace turque d'après le 'De Dissidiis Europae et bello turcico' de Vivès (1526)." In *Juan Luis Vives*, edited by August Buck, 107–141. Hamburg: Hauswedell.

Martin, Dieter, and Karin Vorderstemann, eds. 2013. *Die europäische Banise: Rezeption und Übersetzung eines barocken Bestsellers.* Boston: De Gruyter.

Paas, John Roger. 2002. *The German Political Broadsheet 1600–1700.* Vol. 7: 1633–1648. Wiesbaden: Harrassowitz.

Praun, Michael. 1663/1664?. *Relation von den Liebesneigungen Der Allerschönsten Princessin Europa. So dann von den wunderbahren Begegnüssen Ihrer mit weyland Käiser Carl dem Grossen erzeigten Fürstl. Jungen Herrn; und wie dieselbige nunmehr die beste Gelegenheit den Türcken zu bestreiten hätten.* [n.p.].

[Rusdorf, Johann Joachim?] 1629; 2nd ed. 1631. *Scena europæa personis svis instructa Sine fuco & morsu & Pvblico bono vvlgata.* [n.p.]. 2nd ed. Stralsund: Saxo.

Schmidt, Georg. 2004. "Das Reich und Europa in deutschsprachigen Flugschriften: Überlegungen zur räsonierenden Öffentlichkeit und politischen Kultur im 17. Jahrhundert." In *Europa im 17. Jahrhundert: Ein politischer Mythos und seine Bilder*, edited by Klaus Bußmann and Elke Anna Werner, 119–149. Wiesbaden: Steiner.

Schock, Flemming. 2011. *Die Text-Kunstkammer: Populäre Wissenssammlungen des Barock am Beispiel der "Relationes Curiosae" von E. W. Happel.* Cologne: Böhlau.

Scholz Williams, Gerhild. 2014. *Mediating Culture in the Seventeenth-Century German Novel: Eberhard Werner Happel.* Ann Arbor: University of Michigan Press.

Schröder, Thomas. 1995. *Die ersten Zeitungen: Textgestaltung und Nachrichten-auswahl.* Tübingen: Narr.

Schultheiß-Heinz, Sonja. 2011. "Zum Verhältnis von serieller Chronik und Zeitungs-wesen." In *Die Entstehung des Zeitungswesens im 17. Jahrhundert: Ein neues Medium und seine Folgen für das Kommunikationssystem der Frühen Neuzeit*, edited by Volker Bauer and Holger Böning, 201–211. Bremen: Lumière.

Simons, Olaf. 2001. *Marteaus Europa oder Der Roman, bevor er Literatur wurde: Eine Untersuchung des deutschen und englischen Buchangebots der Jahre 1710 bis 1720.* Amsterdam: Rodopi.

Solbach, Andreas. 1994. "Die Forschungsliteratur zu Johann Beer 1932–1992: Ein Literaturbericht." *Internationales Archiv für Sozialgeschichte der deutschen Literatur. Forschungsreferate* 3 (6): 28–91.

Solbach, Andreas. 2003. *Johann Beer: Rhetorisches Erzählen zwischen Satire und Utopie.* Tübingen: Niemeyer.

Vives, Juan Luis. 1540. "Ein Gespräch Jo. Ludouici viuis / Von der zwytracht / so vnder den Christen in Europa schwebt / vnd vom Türckischen kryeg." Translated by Heinrich von Eppendorff. In *Türckischer Keyßer Ankunfft / Kryeg und Händlung / gegen vnd wider die Christen. …* Edited and translated by Heinrich von Eppendorff. Straßburg: Schotten.

Watanabe-O'Kelly, Helen. 2012. "Fürstenbraut oder Opfer von Gewalt. Inszenie-rungen von Europa in der Frühen Neuzeit." In *Theater und Fest in Europa: Perspektiven von Identität und Gemeinschaft,* edited by Erika Fischer-Lichte, Matthias Warstat, and Anna Littmann, 228–240. Tübingen: Francke.

Weber, Johannes. 1994a. *Götter-Both Mercurius: Die Urgeschichte der politischen Zeitschrift in Deutschland.* Bremen: Temmen.

Weber, Johannes. 1994b. "'Die Novellen sind eine Eröffnung des Buchs der gantzen Welt': Die Entstehung der Zeitung im 17. Jahrhundert." In *Als die Post noch Zeitung machte: Eine Pressegeschichte*, edited by Klaus Beyrer and Martin Dallmeier, 15–25. Gießen: Anabas.

Weber, Johannes. 1997. "Deutsche Presse im Zeitalter des Barock: Zur Vorgeschichte öffentlichen politischen Räsonnements." In *Öffentlichkeit im 18. Jahrhundert*, edited by Hans-Wolf Jäger, 137–149. Göttingen: Wallstein.

Wilke, Jürgen. 1984. *Nachrichtenauswahl und Medienrealität in vier Jahrhunderten: Eine Modellstudie zur Verbindung von historischer und empirischer Publizistik-wissenschaft.* Berlin: De Gruyter.

Wrede, Martin. 2004. *Das Reich und seine Feinde. Politische Feindbilder in der reichspatriotischen Publizistik zwischen Westfälischem Frieden und siebenjähr-igem Krieg.* Mainz: Philipp von Zabern.

6 Mapping Margins in the Mediterranean

Europe, Africa, and Richard Johnson's *The Seven Champions of Christendom*

Goran Stanivukovic

In this chapter I discuss two maps produced in the early sixteenth century as a cultural frame within which I also interpret Richard Johnson's popular prose romance, *The Seven Champions of Christendom* (Part I, 1596; Part II, 1597). Johnson's romance narrates the chivalric adventures of seven knights—Saint George of England, Saint Dennis of France, Saint James of Spain, Saint Anthony of Italy, Saint Andrew of Scotland, Saint Patrick of Ireland, and Saint David of Wales—in the territories of Northern Africa, the eastern Mediterranean, and the Middle East. Their heroic progress takes place along the margin of the Mediterranean where Europe and Africa meet and intersect. The aim of this comparative analysis is to show that the notion of where Europe ended and where it began depended largely on the politics of representing the margin of the Mediterranean, as shown in the two maps and as narrated in Johnson's romance. The chapter explores the double fiction in the mapping of Europe's Mediterranean margins: the fiction of geographical representation and the fiction of literary narrative. What is common to the two maps is that each rearranges the borders between the main spaces surrounding the Mediterranean according to the power that rules the sea and its shores. In addition, both maps depict Europe as subordinate to Africa and Asia. These continents are represented as prominent in relation to Europe, with which they are connected through the Mediterranean. What brings these two maps and Johnson's fiction together is the fact that their makers fictionalized and allegorized territories along the edges of the Mediterranean and across large spaces of land in conceptually similar ways.

Prose romances of the sixteenth and seventeenth centuries were influenced by a large body of generically different texts, ranging from Heliodorus's *Aethiopica* to heroic oral literature to accounts of piracy in the Mediterranean, as Steve Mentz (2006) has demonstrated persuasively. In his and in similar accounts of cultural influences that shaped romances, however, geographical maps are not given their due place. Yet maps of the Mediterranean were a resource of representation that provided visual evidence for what romances contested and contained in their fictions of travel and geography. The maps discussed here show Europe absorbing Mediterranean Africa and Asia Minor, all as one representational space. Johnson's romance offers a fantasy version of the contact between Europe and Northern Africa in the Mediterranean, in a competing narrative to the story told in the maps. The heroic agency and victories of Johnson's knights errant in the territories of Northern Africa and in Asia Minor feature the narrative obverse of the political and representational position and power of Europe in relation to the Muslim territories of the East in the early modern maps. This engagement with the world of the East in Johnson's romance is not only a reminder that "[t]he homeland of the Western Novel is the Mediterranean, and it is a multicultural, multilingual, mixed Mediterranean" (Doody 1996, 18), but that the novel also emerges out of the conflict in the representation of political power within that Mediterranean. Doody is concerned with the novel of antiquity and its origins in the Mediterranean. But, as Mentz demonstrates, we can trace the influence of the classical novel from the Mediterranean on prose romances throughout the sixteenth and seventeenth centuries. This influence is evident in the construction of character type, geographical and pastoral settings, sea voyage, and erotic stories.

When the seven Christian knights in Johnson's popular prose romance look back at the battleground where they have defeated an army of Muslim warriors, and when they see "the murthered Infidels like scattered corne overspred the fields of *Hungary*" (Part I, 9),[1] the writer uses the fields of Hungary as a hyperbole to convey the idea of the champions' total victory over their enemy defeated at the African shore of the Mediterranean. Their utterance refers to the plains in eastern Europe, the battleground where Christian Europe fought the persistent Ottoman attempts to conquer the European continent. When Johnson's fiction invokes Hungary against the background of his knights' victories in the Ottoman Africa of the Mediterranean, it symbolically superimposes the victory over Muslims in the fiction of the Mediterranean over the defeat of the Christians by the Ottomans in Hungary. The comparison of defeated infidels with scattered corn emphasizes the importance of the defeat of the Muslim foe against the background of Christian bounty.

Geography in romances is either arbitrary or invented, featuring as exotic the space where actions occur that violate verisimilitude and decorum. Physical space in Johnson's romance is imagined against the background of the ideological stance that defined Anglo-Mediterranean politics in the last decade of the 1590s. As Jennifer Fellows has stated, "The world outside England [in Johnson's romance] is a largely amorphous arena for the assertion of Christian, and especially English Christian, superiority" (2003, xvii). Yet, as I argue in this chapter, sometimes that fictional geography can be influenced by real places. Late medieval and early modern geography is also a historical and political, not just physical, geography. Therefore possible meanings of invented, arbitrarily placed, and real geographical locales are determined by the external circumstances that motivated the production of geographical maps and fictions that drew on them. Thus, when the narrator in Johnson's romance makes retribution the justification for the killing of Muslims by the seven knights coming from "true anointed Nations" (Part I, 90)—Scotland, England, Wales, Ireland, France, Spain, and Italy— the context for what initially appears to be an error in reference to Hungary, starts to make sense. Namely, when the narrator presses upon the reader that "no doubt but the invincible Armie of the Pagans, had ruinated the borders of *Europe*" (Part I, 91, emphasis in original), the line that separates the geographical location of the actual Hungary in the east-central part of Continental Europe and the African coast of the Mediterranean becomes blurred. Since the historical frame for the clash between the seven Christian champions and the Muslim warriors is also nourished by anti-Islamic senti- ments that imbue romance writing, the line along which this cross-religious conflict is kept alive in literature, stretching from Hungary to the shores of Mediterranean Africa, also marks the boundary between the world of central European Christianity and the Ottoman Islamic rule that creeps into Europe. The juxtaposition of Hungary for the Mediterranean suits contem- porary historical realities that underpin this discursive articulation in imag- inative literature and that would make sense to Johnson writing at a time when the historical events that determined Hungary's position in relation to the Ottoman empire were still within living memory.

After the Ottoman army of Sultan Süleyman the Magnificent defeated the forces of the Hungarian king in the battle of Mohács in 1526, the border between the Ottoman empire in Europe and Christian Europe in the north was established. Less than two decades after this battle, in 1541, Hungary was officially partitioned between the Habsburgs and the Ottomans. By the middle of the sixteenth century, Hungary had become the symbol for the defence of the border separating Christian Europe and the Ottoman empire. Thus Hungary became Europe's easternmost geographical location that pre- vented the Ottomans from invading the rest of Europe. The fall of Hungary to the Ottomans would have endangered the security and stability of Europe within its Christian borders. This is why Hungary remains an important location in prose romances and in other early modern writing that mentions it. "The borders of *Europe*," which the narrator tells us have just been secured by the knights' defeat in the Muslim Mediterranean Africa imagined as Hungary, have now been imaginatively redrawn, bringing the margin of Europe to the shores of Mediterranean Africa. In this interplay between historical and imaginary margins, separating and bringing together the two rivalling worlds, Johnson's narrative shows an awareness of the importance borders play in shaping the story of Christians and Muslims in his romance. This geographical margin and conceptual edge becomes a political and representational factor in the cultural definition of the Mediterranean.

The significance of this edge is the subject of discussion in some of the most influential studies of the Mediterranean. From Fernand Braudel's (1985) history of the interaction between peoples living around the shores of the Mediterranean to the account of political contact between the societies inhabiting the sea's littoral in David Abulafia's (2012) history of the sea, the edge has been used to define the Mediterranean as a subject of analysis. Both Braudel and Abulafia pay more attention to the history of port cities, coastal towns, and islands than to the hinterlands on which the edge depended for its political and economic stability. Reading these detailed histories, one can see that the edge, the shores of the Mediterranean, played a central role in the perception of power in different parts of the Mediterranean over time. Cartographers who depicted the Mediterranean for the purposes of travel, navigation, and trade, be they Muslim or Christian, demarcated this sea by the actual geography of its shores, that is, by its margin.

Mapping the Ottoman Mediterranean in cartography and textualizing it in romances were corresponding narrative activities, performed in different yet culturally related forms, each reflecting the cultural and historical moment, the circumstances, and agents involved in the production of maps and fictions. Jerry Brotton has recently observed that "[c]entres, boundaries and all the other paraphernalia included in any map of the world are defined as much by 'world views' as they are by the mapmaker's physical observation of the earth, which is never made from a neutral cultural standpoint anyway" (2012, 6). In the sixteenth and seventeenth centuries, both maps and romances were also grounded in experience recorded in travel accounts, which, like fictions, mixed visual experience with fanciful fictions. In *La Méditerranée: Espace et l'histoire*, Braudel restates the point that Mediterranean travels had their historical basis in the long history of trade in the sea and their cultural origins in the sea wanderings of Ulysses in the *Odyssey* (1985, 61).[2] The maps produced in the era preceding the period of the great sixteenth-century cartographers like Abraham Ortelius reveal the growing sophistication in charting navigational routes with the impulse to fill the blank spaces beyond the margin with fantastical presentations of the landscape and flora that existed in the territories that lay beyond the Mediterranean. Fanciful though these representations are, they reveal the aspirations of those who claim political power and achieve political goals in competition with the opponent. Most often that power would come from a wealthy patron who commissioned a cartographer to produce a map for him.

One of my main goals in this chapter, then, is to recover the idea of early modern Europe as part of the larger world of the Mediterranean and to show how both Europe and the worlds beyond its margins were imagined, understood, interpreted, and reconceptualized in early modern fiction and cartographic representation. In order to achieve this goal, I employ what recent critics recommend as a more rigorous version of a "nuanced and subtle" historicism "founded on employing cultural structures from within the period" (Healy and Healy 2009, 3). The interaction between mapping and fictionalizing the Mediterranean brings together two concrete manifestations of such cultural structures that demonstrate how the early modern period comprehended Europe.

Early modern maps, as Richard Helgerson has argued, "enabled and inspired Europe's vast overseas expansion and ... spread the new knowledge that resulted from that expansion" (2001, 241). Yet before European powers embarked on their colonial projects, early sixteenth-century maps produced visual stories about the margins of the Mediterranean, stories that registered differences and hierarchies between geographical parts and national, ethnic, and racial groups. By juxtaposing maps of the Mediterranean, produced for Christian and Muslim patrons, and romance writing, we can see how the margin becomes a politically charged entity, a border shifted by political interests and ideological aspirations; and how in turn, this fluid status of the margin determines who holds power over the Mediterranean and the strategically important trading routes beyond it. As the examples of the two maps I examine show, to rewrite and transform the margin is to avoid being treated as marginal in the battle for hegemony in the Mediterranean.

The West–East Margin of the Mediterranean

The margin of the Mediterranean is not a fixed, geographical notion. At different times writers, historiographers, and cartographers determined this margin by the shifting line that showed either the advancement or the withdrawal of the Ottoman rule in Europe. In a way, the flexible lines that demarcated different parts of the early modern Mediterranean reflected the physical characteristic of this sea in both symbolical and real terms. Just as "the physical features of the [Mediterranean] certainly cannot be taken for granted" (Abulafia 2012, xxvii) because of the forces of nature that shaped it, so the political and geographical characteristics of the Mediterranean as they are presented in maps cannot be taken for granted because in these maps the Mediterranean features as the zone where the interests of the European Christian states and the Ottomans constantly clashed. These political, religious, and, in the sixteenth century, increasingly commercial interests, shaped the flexible dynamics of the centre and the margin that represented the way in which the relationship between the continents that circle the Mediterranean—Europe, Africa, and Asia Minor—was comprehended in the early modern period. Geographical maps of the late medieval and early Renaissance periods traced the historical fluidity of the margin, and romance literature has registered this fluidity in a similar way, dilating the relationship of the margin and the world beyond it. Thus, both maps and romances participated in the construction of the West–East margin within the Mediterranean. Literary romances were informed by cartographic representations of the sea revealing what those who ordered the maps thought and believed in and aspired to, and showing the extent to which the Mediterranean was an entity of manifold historical and representational construction and transformation initiated by writers, cartographers, and rulers.

Maps inform romance narratives but neither literally nor actually. When we discuss romances and maps together, as I do, we should take into consideration what I call the double fiction within this comparative methodology. This double fiction is created by a romance author's imagination just as it reveals the shape of known, or real, geography. It creates a perspective that allows critics studying this double traffic of cultural influence—from maps to fictions and vice versa—to consider as twofold the space, the actual territory, which is at the heart of the critic's analysis. So the narrative space of romances is relative or topological space. In contrast, the real or geographical space is topographic or absolute space.[3] It is in the interweaving of these two planes of representations, geographic (visual) and literary (textual), that the discourses of margin will develop, in relation to Europe and Northern (Ottoman) Africa. This creates the dual fiction of the Mediterranean, created by both fictional narrative and cultural stories told in maps. These kinds of pictorial and textual representations, in turn, show that both mapmakers and romance writers thought about space, and the power relationships that shape it, in their presentations of Europe and Africa. Crowding the margins of the Mediterranean with images and heroic narratives, mapmakers and romance writers, respectively, advanced arguments about the status of the sea's edges in the larger historical context of the worlds they glorified.

In the maps and literary fictions of the early modern period, edges of the Mediterranean are demarcated less geographically and more historically, temporally, and in terms of ethnic and racial belonging. Whether those edges exist in the fiction of geographical representation in maps or the routes on which knights errant travel from West to East, those edges mark the territories that are not too different from the spaces of cultural identification that register "the ambivalence of the nation as a narrative strategy" (Bhabha 1990, 292). In modern times, Bhabha suggests, movements towards and gatherings "on the edge of 'foreign' cultures" (292), which characterized the postcolonial experience of the once colonized when they moved from former colonial places into the spaces of former empires, have redefined the meaning of what a frontier of language, culture, and nation is, and where that frontier lies. The ambivalence of the meaning of the edge between ethnically and racially different and opposing worlds, however, started to be imagined and conceptually formulated in the premodern world, precisely in the maps and fictions describing the frontier between the West and the East. In these representations of the two worlds that meet and historically overlap, the edge is not a physical barrier but a trace of a complex strategy of visual or rhetorical representation of ideological (mostly religious), cultural, military, and diplomatic power claimed by those authoring the registration, be they mapmakers on behalf of a Christian patron or authors of English romances writing for their male and female readership in the West. The edge, the seashore, is, therefore, a cultural territory of contested meaning because it captures the ambivalence in conceptualizing ethnic and national signification as coherent in the Mediterranean. Imagined in such a way, the edge represents less a demarcation of Christian Europe from the Muslim world, and more a concept that reminds us of the multitudinous ways in which the Christian and the Muslim worlds contested over the European space before the time of national borders. This flexible, ambiguous, fuzzy edge of the Mediterranean is, therefore, the best reminder of Peter Burke's claim that "Europe is not so much a place as an idea" (1990, 21).

Mapping the Margin of the Mediterranean

A version of the historical reconceptualization of the dynamic relationship between the centre and the margin as shown in the cartographic representation of the Mediterranean can be found in a map belonging to the tradition of the so-called Catalan world maps. It was produced in 1525, probably using an earlier version, by the well-known Italian maker of navigational maps Jacopo Russo for Mansa Musa, the ruler of Mali. At the time of the map's production, Mali was one of the most powerful Muslim kingdoms in Saharan Africa. The map is a striking illustration of both the Muslim idea of domination of the Mediterranean and of how central that idea was for the representation of Europe and Africa. The Catalan world maps, produced on Majorca from the 1370s onwards, presented historical, political, and geographical views of the world. As such, they started to replace the medieval *mappaemundi*, which combined a biblical worldview with geographical knowledge. Later on, from the 1450s onwards, more detailed versions of Catalan maps were created in Venice. The Mansa Musa map (Fig. 6.1) belongs to this Italian tradition of the Catalan map cartography.

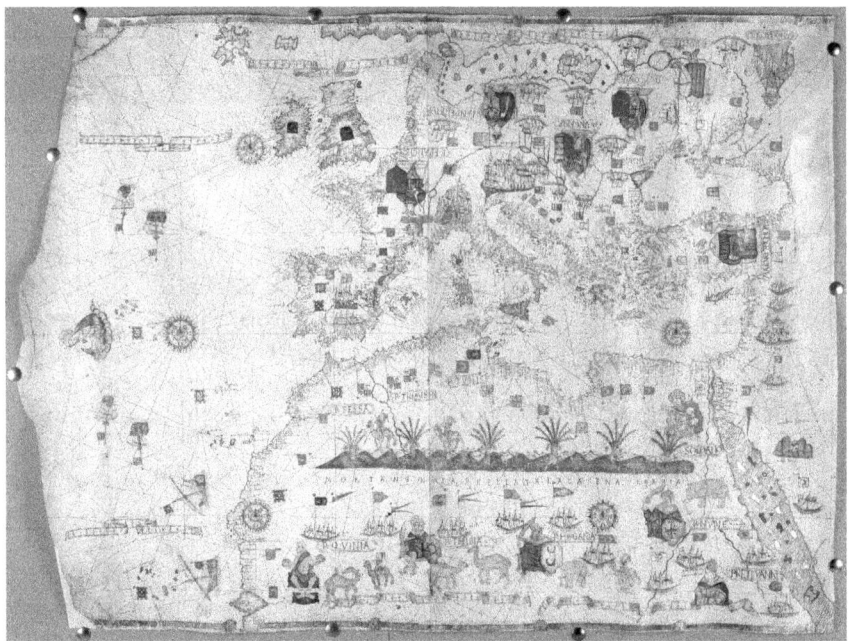

Figure 6.1 The Mansa Musa Map, c. 1525, Nautical chart of the Mediterranean by Jacopo Russo. © The British Library Board, Add. MS 31318B, vellum.

The Mansa Musa map is an example of cartography that shows the extent to which geography and fiction tell a story whose reach is beyond the purpose of a specific map. This map, intended for navigation, represents a record of how the early modern Muslim world saw itself in relation to Europe and where it wielded its political power against Europe. In the northwestern corner of Ottoman Africa, above the line of palm trees and the Atlas Mountains represented as a series of hills coloured green, appear the names of real kingdoms like Fesse (i.e., Fez, standing for modern Morocco) and Tunis. In the bottom line, below the Atlas Mountains, where Saharan Africa starts, we find the kingdoms of Quinia, Thibia, Hogania, Nubia, and Pretivanni. To the right of the Atlas Mountains, in Egypt ("Egiptus"), the figure of the Turkish sultan ("Soldan") is shown seated, which was a common practice in Catalan navigational maps (Astengo 2007, 203). In the location of Constantinople (Istanbul), there is a vignette of the Great Turk ("Magno Turcho") overlooking the Mediterranean Sea. The Great Turk is positioned in a straight line directly opposite the image of the West, represented in the figure of the Virgin Mary,[4] far in the Atlantic Ocean, suggesting that the West's power extends beyond the bounds of the Mediterranean ruled by Muslims. Between Egypt and Constantinople lies "Judea," dominated by the built-up city of Jerusalem. The landmass of Ottoman Africa nudges into the sea, pushing Europe further north in the region where the Western powers, England, France, and the Flemish lands, which had not yet emerged as opponents to the Ottomans in the Mediterranean, are presented as small and without any distinct visual characteristics. They are marginalized and moved close to the blank, thus insignificant, margin at the top of the map.

The lands distinguished by the detail of artistic execution, however, tell their own story. Namely, it was common for navigational charts produced in the tradition of Catalan cartography to include the place-names alongside the shores. These place-names were crucial to sailors, helping them navigate along the shores. What was important in drawing these place-names, according to Astengo, was "not the choice of place-names or their correct spelling but rather their ordering in an exact sequence along the coast" (2007, 204). But place-names included in the interior were more arbitrary in name and sequence, since they were of little use for sailing. These place-names could have been invented either by Russo, the cartographer directly involved in the intellectual labour of conceptualizing and producing this map, or by his assistants who actually drew details in the map.[5]

This is where the story of the Munsa Map could be said to start. The place-names in the interior fill in the blank space of the Sahara Desert that stretches south of the Mediterranean coast of Africa. Place-names like Pretivanni, Trimish, and Hogania, which dot the Saharan territory, sound like the places of fictional lands from chivalric romances of the early modern period, set in the same geographical sweep of lands—except that romances often reverse the process of geographical representation by also invoking real places, even when those fictions rearrange them ambiguously in the textual geography in their narratives. It could be said that their names, which sound Christian because they were invented by Christians, have the purpose to create an appearance of ruling over Christian territory and thus to appeal to the ruler of Mali, given his territorial ambitions. The discrepancy between the approach of the Italian mapmakers and early modern romance writers to the relationship between the Christian and non-Christian worlds of the Mediterranean is that the maps produced for a non-Christian market represent the Muslim as the ruler of Christian lands, whereas prose romances offer fictions of Christian victories over and rule in the very same lands that the mapmakers depict as controlled by Muslims. There is, then, a competition for representation, depending on who the recipient of the document is: a non-Christian ruler in Africa or a Christian reader in Europe, respectively. Like this map, which connects real with fictional places within the image of the Mediterranean, prose romances also bring together specific and invented geography. What becomes obvious when reading romances of the 1590s is that their writers tend to locate the narratives of their fictions increasingly in the eastern Mediterranean, reflecting the growing political, diplomatic, and commercial engagement of northwestern Europe with the Ottoman empire, which dominated the eastern Mediterranean. The action in the anonymous romance *Palmendos* (1589) takes place in "Europe and the Mediterranean sea, verie neere the Isle of Delphos" (n.p.); and the anonymous *Palmerin d'Oliva* (1597) is set in Phrygia (Asia Minor), "Durraco" (Dürres in Albania), and Constantinople; and Johnson's *The Seven Champions* is set in Tunis, Alexandria, Egypt, Jerusalem, Libya, Persia, Ormuz (the Strait of Hormuz), Constantinople, and Syria. When real lands become fictional spaces in prose romances, as is the case in these examples, these lands do not lose the sociopolitical significance they played in the actual politics of contacts and conflicts between Christians and Muslims. Rather, the presence of these places within prose romances indicate that reclaiming the Mediterranean's Christian margins, now lost to Muslims, is what chivalric agency in these fictions is about. In both instances—the Mansa Musa map and Johnson's romance—the heaping up of place-names has the rhetorical effect of repetition, affirming the claim of ownership. The rhetoric of claiming power over the East, by turning lands of the East into places where Christian knights defeat their Islamic enemy, represents a way in which the early modern world imagined its victory over Muslims in territories that were increasingly becoming of strategic commercial importance to the West's growing mercantile empire in the Mediterranean and the world that lay beyond it.

The Mansa Musa map tells the story of the peoples of Africa as well. The figures on the African territory are presented as light-skinned, matching their European counterparts in the images of royal figures standing for France, Hungary, Poland, Germany, Russia, and the Great Tartary on the Black Sea. Claiming the sea means claiming also the race of the European Muslim rival. Through a reverse racial conversion, the cartographer makes Muslim Africans look like fair-skinned Europeans, engaging in a process of racial and ethnic assimilation and appropriation. By representing Africans as fair-skinned people, the Mansa Musa map claims European sovereignty and power beyond geography and political realities. It makes Mediterranean Africa a European space. Yet this representation of Africans as fair-skinned in turn also subverts 'whiteness' as 'European,' as well as the binary in which 'European' implies 'whiteness' and 'African' connotes 'dark-skinned.' If domination, as order, is identified with whiteness, then Africa could be said to have become European without being ruled by 'Europeans' in a geographical sense. In turn, then, this politics of the representation of skin colour in relation to geography troubles an essentialized notion of what it means to be European, if the Muslim Africans can become European because their white skin is not a racial marker, but a sign of their status as rulers.

Looking at early modern Europe from the perspective of this symbolical interplay of race, one can say that the Mansa Musa map turns the European and African coasts of the Mediterranean into interchangeable worlds; that the Christian and the Muslim Mediterranean is one world. This visual representation of the Mediterranean as a space of interconnected powers, races, and religions (or races *as* religions) illustrates Fernand Braudel's claim that the Mediterranean is not "the preserve of any one power" (1975, 17). The Mansa Musa map shows that the balance of, and rivalry between, powers in the Mediterranean extends real politics to the level of representation where each power can claim dominance and advantage over its rival in terms and signs that reflect that power's idea of, or aspiration to, the actual dominance in the Mediterranean. Yet the map also signifies the relationship between the West and the East that goes beyond Braudel's historical map, suggesting that the margin between the West and the East was understood to be fluid. While Braudel's primary focus is the western and the northern Mediterranean, dominated by Venice, as a space of intertwined diplomatic interests, the Mansa Musa map draws our attention to the fact that the Mediterranean Europe of the early modern world was equally determined by the tensions and contacts alongside what Andrew C. Hess (1978) calls "the forgotten frontier," namely, the frontier between the north of Africa and the south of Europe. Hess's interest is primarily the Ibero-African frontier, but the Mansa Musa map shows that this frontier, important for any attempt to answer the question whether Europe existed before the eighteenth century,[6] extended alongside the entire coast of North Africa and that it covered the whole southern coast of Europe in the Mediterranean.

The Mansa Musa map captures the history of Muslim political aspirations in the Mediterranean and in relation to Europe. Nowhere is the power dynamic between Christians and Muslims in these maps more vividly captured than in the conceptualization of the ways in which the ideas of unity and disunity are represented within the Mediterranean. While "the modern nations of Europe," according to Richard Helgerson, "had, for all their differences from both antiquity and the middle ages, to be represented as either ancient or medieval, either Greek or Goth" (1994, 23), the notion of Europe as a geographical unity with clearly marked borders between Christian and Muslim worlds did not exist. Yet unity within the Mansa Musa empire of North Africa is embodied in the shape and image of North Africa as a territory that bursts into the Mediterranean and determines it while marginalizing the rest of Europe. Thus the Mansa Musa map is a reminder of how dominant North Africa was and how present-day writing about the Mediterranean has for a long time favoured explaining and fictionalizing the relationship between the East and the West while leaving the contact between the north and the south of the Mediterranean relatively unexamined. This interest in the Mediterranean of the south of Europe, especially of Spain and Italy, in the Mansa Musa map is symbolized by the prominence given to this region and in the density of visual detail. This pictorial density draws attention to both political investment and knowledge interest in the south, where the memory of Muslim rule, which ended when the last Moors of Granada were defeated in 1492, was still alive when Jacopo Russo would have worked on his map for the ruler of Mali.

Treating Europe as a subject of representation in the depiction of the Muslim power in the Mediterranean, the Mansa Musa map makes Europe not the core but the periphery of the Mediterranean world. Early modern maps are evidence of the "demonstration of power and authority" (Sanford 2002, 12), and this map represents one cartographic version of what we could describe as the difference between the periphery of Europe in relation to Africa based on the fluidity of frontiers in spatial sense, and the conceptual unity of Europe based on religion. While towards the end of the sixteenth century the term, as Peter Burke suggests, and therefore the notion of Europe "was coming in, the more traditional concept of 'Christendom' was slow to go out" (1990, 27). The two notions coexisted and interconnected for a while in the early modern period, revealing one aspect of the extent to which the period did not recognize a single, essentialized notion of Europe. What we then see in the Mansa Musa map is how this slowly emerging concept of Europe based on territory and boundaries is also being troubled by the symbolical exchange of racial representations of white Christians and black Africans in the map itself. The shifting boundary between Europe and Africa is also evident in the representation of the Atlas mountain range emphasized out of proportion, suggesting a divide within Africa. This divide makes Mediterranean Africa at once African and European, leaving the rest of the empire of the ruler of Mali, the ruler of a country consisting mostly of desert, to a different world that stands outside the Mediterranean Euro-African politics of representation in this map. Therefore, the Mediterranean represents the defining point of what Europe stands for both spatially and racially (and religiously) in this early modern presentation, where Europe features as a conceptual 'other' in relation to the dominant Muslim identity given to the shared territory of the Mediterranean.

Early modern maps capture the complex relations of political and ideological power between the lands they represent in the Mediterranean.

The Mansa Musa map is one of the navigational charts that remind us of the uncertain position the Europeans of the early sixteenth century held in what today we might call global dominance. James G. Harper addresses this problem:

> The Europeans, who students and even scholars tend to instinctively regard as conquerors and colonizers, actually occupied a much more ambiguous position in the premodern and early modern periods. By no means assured of their dominance in the world, Renaissance and Baroque Europeans anxiously watched the steady progress of a powerful enemy Other, which had colonized the territories of the now-defunct Byzantine Empire and was colonizing large parts of the Venetian and Holy Roman empires.
>
> (Harper 2011, 7)

Colonization is not the explicit topic of the Mansa Musa map; nor is it the prime focus of narrative in Johnson's romance. Colonialism and empire, as concepts, were relatively 'unfamiliar' topics in the early modern period, and they did not start to imply what Armitage calls a "spatial dimension" (2001, 103), that is, claiming foreign territories through assimilation. What the geography of the Mansa Musa map captures, in fact, are political, ethnic, and religious rivalries and power dynamics between the Christian and the Muslim worlds of the Mediterranean in the precolonial world of the sixteenth century. Fictions that came out of that political situation, like Johnson's romance, capture the world at the point when reconquering the Muslim Mediterranean was wrapped in the nostalgia for waning chivalry in Elizabethan England and religious rivalry, while also preoccupied with claiming territories and mining resources. They are narratives of merchant kingdoms, of territories imagined to be available for profit-making commerce between geographically connected worlds in the future. The Crusades and the fall of Muslim Jerusalem to the crusading armies in the eleventh century marked a turning point in the reconceptualization of the Mediterranean as a zone of cross-religious conflict and of the Western ambitions to reclaim the old Christian territories lost to Muslim rule before the Crusades. It is out of this contact between the East and West that the prose romances of the sixteenth century arose. The maps examined here participate in telling the same cultural story as the literary narratives explored.

The Mediterranean and the Empire of Trade

I now want to discuss the 1550 "Map of the World" by Pierre Desceliers (Fig. 6.2), made on vellum, placing Africa in the centre of the world and emphasizing the presentation of Europe and Asia as a continuous stretch of land.

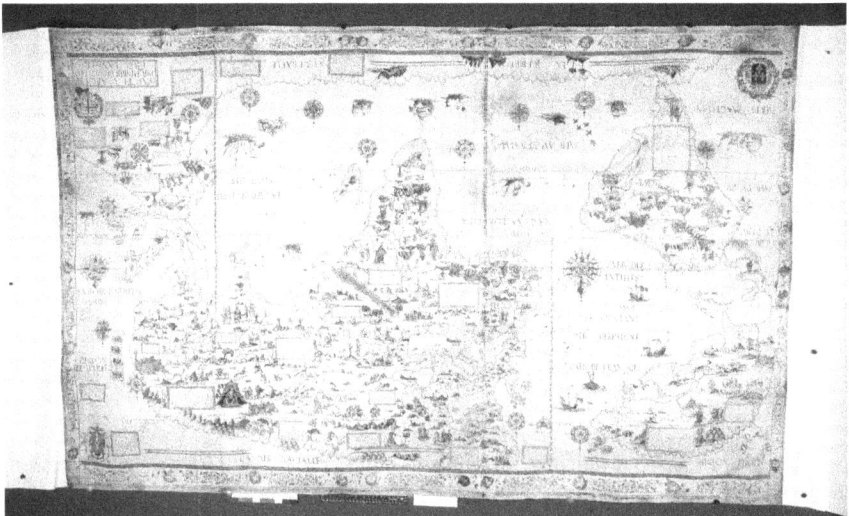

Figure 6.2 Pierre Desceliers, "Map of the World," Arques, 1550. © The British Library Board, Add. MS 24065, Vellum.

In its illuminated borders, this map shows "fantastic features of people, flora and fauna" (Sloan 2007, 15) of the territories it represents. The difference between Europe and Asia is naturalized through such representations, and in this depiction that difference is elided. This representation registers the fact that "[a]ll boundaries that separate Europe and Asia are to some extent arbitrary and liable to change according to political and military events" (Murrin 2014, 187). This kind of representation correlates with romance geography presented as continuous, since both maps and romances belong to the time before firm borders between different lands came into being. The continuous geography between Europe and Asia explains why it was possible for romance writers to imagine their knights' travels from the West to the Middle East and beyond as one uninterrupted, if arduous, heroic journey.

This aspect of presentation is a version of an earlier idea about how the two continents were conceptualized as one land, as Murrin has recently argued: "Around the middle of the thirteenth century Europe discovered that it was but a peninsula of Asia" (2014, 9). As Johnson's *The Seven Champions* shows, this understanding of Europe and Asia as a continuous landmass explains why the knights errant could wander without encountering geographical obstacles between the West and the East. It also explains why Johnson could imagine the territories beyond the Strait of Hormuz, in the Persian Gulf, as the natural extension for trade in the eastern Mediterranean.

Desceliers's map privileges Muslim Africa and Asia over the Christian Mediterranean and Europe, making the non-Christian world its centre, while relegating the Christian world to the margins. Pierre Desceliers belonged to the group of mapmakers working in Dieppe who "from the 1530s depicted French and Portuguese discoveries" in maps that were "influenced by contemporary Portuguese charts." The official website of the British Library goes on to describe this map as being "highly unusual in its dual orientation; north of the equator texts and figures are inverted, suggesting that it was specifically designed to be spread out and viewed around a large table." The Red Sea is demarcated as a water link that brings Asia closer to Europe. The power of representation follows a specific historical situation of the world in which Desceliers produced this map.

The Red Sea, which is vividly coloured red, follows the tradition in this kind of charts "of emphasizing coastlines with different colors [which] served to indicate different historical regions," which in this case "symbolize[s] the Jews' passage out of Egypt" (Astengo 2007, 202). Yet, the mapmaker's primary goal was not to record historical knowledge as much as to chart the territories whose natural resources could be exploited and from which commodity goods could be obtained through trade and exchange, which is evident in the texts that accompany the map. Desceliers's map of the world not only represents the landmasses and seas of the world as geographical spaces but also presents these territories and waterways in such a way to indicate a streamlined passage of trade and to facilitate commercial contacts between East and West. This historical feature of the map, however, is complemented with political meaning, which brings the map closer to the concerns of Johnson's prose romance. Namely, many of the texts that accompany the map describe the world beyond Europe, the East, as abounding with precious stones and spices. These texts also refer to the barbarous native peoples of the territories in the East, imagining them as pagan peoples represented as dog-headed cannibals and sun worshippers. This textual framing of the spatial representations of the world helps us understand Desceliers's map in the context of the early modern discourse of imperial expansion and the West's plans for acquiring resources overseas. It is in this imperial spirit that we should also read the knights' progress from the North African coast of the Mediterranean, via Egypt, Syria, the Arabian Peninsula, to the Strait of Hormuz in the Persian Gulf, where Johnson's knights errant fight the Persians.

As a water route that connected the Indian Ocean with the Arabian Peninsula and the eastern Mediterranean cultural sphere, the Persian Gulf was coveted in the sixteenth century by many a Mediterranean power trading in the East. As such, the Persian Gulf became one of the most frequent battlegrounds between early modern Christians themselves, especially the northern Europeans and the Portuguese at Hormuz, and between Christians and Persians. It is not surprising, then, that Johnson allegorizes the heroic and revenge-driven journey of his knights in the direction of Hormuz. In the context of European investment in the Persian Gulf as a commercial artery leading to the lucrative source of commodities in Asia, imagining Europe and Asia as one continuous sweep of land and sea in Desceliers's map would have also made sense to a romance writer setting his narrative in the eastern Mediterranean.

Johnson's romance fictionalizes the knights' travels as prudent agency, that is, as actions that lead to creating fictional scenarios for other routes leading to profit from the imperial expansion to the East. This symbolic inter-action between different agents battling for power in the territory deeply invested with political and commercial significance for Europe is a reminder that both Desceliers's map and Johnson's romance are striking examples of how national interests of the Western countries make domestic concerns also international preoccupations of romance.[7] Further, reading Johnson's romance with this map in the critical background shows Europe's secondary status as an economic power in relation to the East and its inadequacy as such a power, when it is represented as a geographical appendix to Asia.

Romancing the Margin in North Africa

Spatial and symbolic presentation of political power in the Mansa Musa and the Pierre Desceliers maps are reversed in the fantasies of Johnson's romance, in the narratives involving knights' adventures in the Ottoman regencies of Libya, Tunisia, and Egypt. Constance Relihan has argued that the "linkage between geography, gender, and fictional narrative" in romances is visible in "the attempt to violate geographic fact" (2004, 77). Leaving gender aside on this occasion, one could argue, *pace* Relihan, that the linkage between geography and fiction is an attempt not so much to relativize or violate geo-graphic fact, but to enhance the meaning and symbolism of geographic fact. Fictionalizing Ottoman Africa enables readers to read it as both political geography and ethnography, and as chivalric fiction framed by the religious sentiments that underpin romances. Fictional and geographical represen-tations of Africa, for instance in the Mansa Musa map, as a territory that incorporates southern Europe as well in one conceptual space in which race and religion can be at least symbolically exchanged, make both Europe and Africa a 'chronotope,' as Peter Burke suggests, or a "a time–space package" (2006, 236) that captures the cultural history of Europe shaped by competing and complementing forces, of language, history, and religion. These cultural forces, in turn, determine what we understand Europe to be along the various, and often porous, dividing lines created by those forces in the first place. The European chronotope of the early modern period is characterized less by a divide between the northern and southern, European and African, shores of the Mediterranean; and also less by the historical and cultural dif-ferences that distinguish the constituent parts of Christian Europe. Rather, the European chronotope is increasingly determined by the extent and depth of the interconnectivity of the histories, religions, and ethnicities coexisting alongside each other in the geographical territories that did not correspond to a strict demarcation between the East and the West alongside religious, racial, and cultural lines. Such an understanding of chronotope illuminates early modern geographic and fictional representation of Africa and Europe as a shared entity brought together by the Mediterranean. It also captures this early modern space as a narrative that speaks about the idea of 'a coherent world' within a narrative work that predates the emergence of the novel as a literary form.[8]

Like other English writing about North Africa and the Levant characterized by an "intense religious polarization" (Maclean and Matar 2011, 8), such as travelogues, religious, and mercantile writing, romance narratives are driven by the holy war discourse. The Mansa Musa and Pierre Desceliers maps became cartographic symbols that visually embodied the cause for the Christian fantasy over a Muslim invasion of Europe. In discussing Johnson's romance against the two maps, we can see how the limits of geographic representations and the limits of romance storytelling are expanded because each medium dilates the meaning of shared representations. When the narrator in Johnson's romance tells his readers that "the Provinces of *Affrica* and *Asia*, had mustered up their forces to the invasion of *Europe*" (Part I, 74, emphasis in original) at which point "all Christian Kings, at the intreaty of the Champions, appointed mighty armies of well approved Souldiers, both by sea and land, to intercept the Infidels wicked intention" (Part I, 74), he fictionalizes what the two maps present visually: the centre of the Mediterranean. This quotation makes it clear that Europe and Africa are represented as antagonists, which is the position frequently claimed by the narrator in Johnson's romance. Only a few pages before, the readers are told that the

> Noble and adventurous Champion *Saint George* ... arrived in the Territories of *Barberie*, in which Countrie he purposed for a time to remaine, and to seeke for some noble atchievement, whereby his fame might be increased and his honored name ring through all the Kingdomes of the world. (Part I, 70, emphasis in original)

Barbary land, which was the name Christians often used to refer to Muslim Northern Africa in the early modern period, is the rival against which the Christian knight will prove his valour and might.

Johnson's focus on the world beyond Europe liberates knightly agency by giving it a license to act in ways that at home would appear as lacking in virtue and honour, as in the acts of unleashed violence. Yet knightly violence, as Edmund Spenser's epic romance *The Faerie Queene* (1987 [1590/1596]) shows page after page, provides the narrative frame for the allegory of affirming Christian valour and advantage over the opponent of the false religion. When the Redcrosse knight representing "[t]he true *Saint George*" (I, ii, 1) defeats the "faithlesse Sarazin" Sansfoy (II, 1, 6), Spenser's text celebrates the victory over the combined enemy of Catholicism and Islam. Like Spenser's epic romance, Johnson's prose romance fictionalizes what Michel Foucault calls "the great pilgrimages into the beyond" of the

Crusades, a movement intended to bring to life "what happened when [the] nobility's attention was fully concentrated on the next world" (2003, 154). In "the next world," margins are neither fixed nor defined. They are the boundaries of allegorical fictions of political and religious dominance of one world over another.

The idea of the Crusades in North Africa representing a kind of spiritual quest for another life in another world carries before itself also the notion of the errant knight as the symbolical herald of a new Christian government and of a new space for expanding that government's commercial aspirations and entrepreneurial ambitions. Just as Saint George, the champion of England from Johnson's romance, is entrusted "by the whole consent of Christendome" (Part I, 83) to rally other knights to become his fellow soldiers and "chiefe assistants in all attempts that appertained either to the benefit of Christendome, or the furtherance of their fortunate proceedings" (Part I, 83), Saint George is also confronted with an Arabian merchant-king as an obstacle to be tackled.

At this point in the narrative, as indeed throughout *The Seven Champions*, Johnson casts England as the leader of Europe. The role given to England in this representation and the power symbolically assigned to Saint George as the leader of the cohort of Christian knights representing Europe mix imaginary self-aggrandizement with the persistence of "crusading narrative" (Manion 2014, 212) in early modern literature. Specifically, this reliance on crusading narratives in Johnson's prose romance can also be associated with political motivations engendered by crusading. This motivation turns the West's anxieties over the growing Muslim conquests of Europe into a fantasy of counterconquest; of defeating the Muslim armies in their own territories of Northern Africa and clearing the paths through those territories for potential mercantile endeavours. Lee Manion has argued that "crusading literature represented military campaigns as well as individual crusading" (2014, 212). Johnson's fiction is an example of a prose romance that blends these two kinds of representation in one narrative, as knights errant, both as a group and as individual warriors, wield victories over their Northern African foes for political and personal reasons. Against the historical background of the Christian military failure to recover the loss of the old lands of Christianity for the West, once those lands fell to Muslim conquerors, Johnson's romance challenges the idea of Europe as a defeated margin in Northern Africa and creates a literary fantasy of it as still a winning power symbolically represented in the lands and places of Western Christianity from whence Johnson's champions come. The knight errant of romance produces a cultural order that is European in its scope and symbolical reach, and is presented as superior to the Muslim world. In this sense, real mercantile politics governs fiction's attempt to imagine the Mediterranean as the zone where chivalric agency is put to its most difficult tests.

The old world of Christianity fallen to Muslims is reclaimed for Christianity through the knight's chivalric victories over Muslims, represented as Saracens, Moors, and Turks, and allegorized as dragons and monsters, but also, in Johnson's fiction, in their defeat of cannibals, lions, and tigers (Part I, 34), those dangerous creatures from the world beyond the boundaries of the European Christian rule. Presented in *The Seven Champions* as desolate and destroyed by non-Christian barbarians who now inhabit them, these lands also function as the starting point for more lucrative commercial enterprises which the Christian West is launching within and beyond the eastern Mediterranean at the time. Competing for representational power in two media—cartography and romance—that proliferated in the early modern period, the maps and Johnson's romance illustrate the shifting idea of centre and margin within the multiracial world of the Mediterranean.

The seven champions fight "Saracens"[9] equipped with "the Arms of *Mahomet*" (Part I, 139, emphasis in original), in the territories along the coast of the Mediterranean held by Muslims, stretching between Jerusalem and Constantinople. This party of knights confirms Jennifer R. Goodman's point that "within the confines of Europe, late medieval chivalry was an international preoccupation" (1998, 23). Chivalry became an obsession of romance writing through which national boundaries were extended symbolically, not only because of the transnational group of knights but also because of their activities in the Mediterranean. Generations of writers, Goodman asserts, wrote about chivalric adventures "in their own time" (1998, 22), appropriating late medieval chivalric narratives to political and historical conditions of later periods. Johnson's romance would animate the most vehement of patriotic sentiments because it would have been read against the period's anxieties over the Muslim invasion of Europe, which fuelled anti-Islamic sentiments across northwest Europe. The knights' heroic adventures would have reminded Johnson's readers that in the wild lands of the "Saracens," the most important heroic goal was the champions' revenge of "Europes fatall overthrow" (Part I, 139), that is, the fall of Europe to Muslim rule in the East. It is through this chivalric mission, in fact, that Johnson's romance displaces western European anxieties over the further incursion of Muslims to Europe.

Johnson often uses the narrative trope of the protagonists' own passion for telling the stories of the knights errant and their heroic victories over Muslims to reinforce the moral intention of his own narrative:

> In the Easterne Parts of the world the fame and valiant deedes of the Champions of Christendome was noised, with their honorable victories, heroicall actes, and feates of armes, naming them the mirrours of nobilitie, and the types of bright honour. (Part II, 247)

The narrator projects on the East the patriotic affect and political support given to the knights' military violence as he would have imagined it to be the case at home, too. In the spirit of Elizabethan patriotism, in which Johnson wrote *The Seven Champions*, the English knight, Saint George, is elected the champions' leader, leaving the other six champions to be "chiefe assistants in all attempts that appertained either to the benefit of Christendome, or the furtherance of their fortunate proceedings" (Part I, 83). At this point, Johnson's romance both extends and itself participates in the formulation, not of, what Michel Foucault argues is "the discourse of sovereignty" (2003, 69) in postmedieval writing of chivalry, but of "a discourse about races, about confrontation between races, about race struggle that goes on within nations and within laws" (69). The discourse about the confrontation of races frequently runs through the pages of Johnson's fiction. For example, in the episode in which Saint James, the champion of Spain, who is banished from Jerusalem, plans how to get a glimpse of his beloved lady Celestine, daughter of the king of Jerusalem, the disguise of skin colour turns from a mere stratagem of the plot and narrative into a more specific construction of race. Saint James decides to paint his body black and heads to town:

> So gathering certaine blackberies from the trees, he coloured his body all ouer like a Blackamoore: But yet considering that hys speech would discouer him, intended likewise to continue dumbe all the time of his residence in *Ierusalem*: … But when the King [of Jerusalem] behelde his countenance, which seemed of the naturall colour of the Moore, hee little mistrusted him to be the Christian Champion whome before he greetly enuied, but accounted him one of the brauest *Iudean* Knights that euer his eye behelde. (Part I, 34–35, emphasis in original)

Soon after his encounter with the King, Saint James will reveal his identity, not to the King but to Celestine, the King's daughter and the champion's beloved. He will dance with her a Morisco dance in a masque staged at the King's court, and at an opportune moment, the knight will show her the diamond ring which she gave him before his departure. The point of revelation is also the moment of the lovers' fleeing the court and fury of the King. Race, for Johnson as well as for his characters, is cultural and religious as well as a matter of skin colour. The artificial construction of race in this instance only shows that in Johnson's playfulness with race and in his attempt to erase racial difference only fair-skinned characters have the privilege to construct identities. In restricting this play with skin colour to a fair-skinned Christian knight, the narrative of Johnson's fiction also assigns racial, political, and religious power to Christians. In early modern fictional writing as well as in cartography, the representation of race became one of the key features of comprehending the difference between Europe and the territories that extended along its Mediterranean margins.

The juxtaposition of the two maps with Johnson's romance shows that at approximately the same time, within the span of several decades, a battle of representation was being fought for the margin that defined the boundary between the Muslim and the Christian world of the Mediterranean, that world beyond the known and the familiar in relation to Elizabethan England. If the Mansa Musa and Pierre Desceliers maps decentralize Europe from the Mediterranean, by putting Muslim Africa in the centre of the Mediterranean world, Johnson's fiction attempts to restore Christian Europe to the centre of the Mediterranean, into, that is, the contested margin and its representation.

The Welsh champion, Saint David, addresses the importance of the margin between Europe and Africa in terms that make this margin the main motive that drives the knightly revenge. As a pretext for their mission in Africa, the knights take the alleged deaths of seven daughters of a Sicilian merchant. In order to revenge this murder, Saint David and his fellow knights seek aid from "all the Kingdomes from the furthest part of *Prester Johns* Dominions to the borders of the red Seas" (Part I, 82, emphasis in original). In both maps, the Red Sea is represented as the line that brings together the worlds of Africa, Europe, and Asia into one strategically crucial point on the world map. Given its enormous importance for the growth of European wealth through Eastern trade, the Red Sea could be said to mark yet another margin of Europe before its territory bleeds into the East. That push further in the East, in Johnson and in the maps, suggests that the European political strategy in the late sixteenth century, to extend its claim on new territories for commerce, acquired force in visual and textual representations of both Europe and the East at that time. It is in this spirit that Saint George encourages his fellow champions:

> You men of *Europe* ... & my country men, whose Conquering fortunes never yet hath feared the enemies of Christ: you see we have forsook our Native Lands, and committed our destinies to the Queene of chaunce, not to fight in any unjust quarrel ... but to prevent the invasion of Christendome, the ruines of Europe, and the intended overthrow of all Christian Provinces. (Part I, 86, emphasis in original)

Europe is understood to refer only to the lands of Western Christianity and as a space whose stability is threatened by the incursion of non-Christians. The lack of space for non-Christians in the Europe of Johnson's romance conveys the notion of Europe as a territory based on Christian exclusivity, territory protected by the power of Christian armies. Thus the conceptual framework for this rallying of Christian troops is conquest, and cultural and religious preservation, as ways of preserving Europe by fighting the enemy, the potential threat to "all Christian Provinces," beyond Christian borders. Defence becomes a precondition for conquest, and conquest, as Foucault argues, became one of the main preoccupations of nobility from the postmedieval chivalric world, nobility whose "attention was fully concentrated on the next world" (2003, 154).

The attempt to bring Europe, Mediterranean Africa, and Asia together under Christian rule is articulated in Saint George's request that non-Christian nations become subordinate to Christian powers, made when he invites the "three Kingdomes of *Barbary, Moroco & India*, [to] sweare true alleagance to all annointed Nations" (Part I, 92, emphasis in original). At this point, Johnson's romance fictionalizes a precolonial sentiment, reminding us that "the English went to the Mediterranean to trade and pillage, not to seize and settle" (MacLean and Matar 2011, 7). Since trade and pillage depend on movement from one place to another, it is not surprising that the prose romance, whose narrative emphasises movement, became a suitable literary medium to imagine the proportion and destinations in precolonial fantasies. Geographical maps also shaped the period's view of Europe's struggle for a position of power in the Mediterranean.

The margin between the European and African Mediterranean is made apparent by the difference in the quality and matter of description, which suddenly shifts from stylized Christian paradise to the rough landscape of heroic battle. The change in the linguistic register correlates with the crossing of the margin between Europe and Africa, as the narrator says:

> When they [the seven knights] crossed the seas, the silver waves seemed to lye as smoothe as christal ice, and the Dolphins to daunce above the waters, as a signe of a prosperous journey. In travelling by land, the wayes seemed so short and easie, and the chirping melody of birdes made them such musique as they passed, that in a short season they arrived beyond the borders of Christendome, and had entred the confines of *Africa*.
>
> There they forced instead of downie beds nightly to rest their wearie limes upon heapes of sun burnt mosse: and in sted of silken curtens and curious canopies, they had the clowdes of heaven to cover them. Now their naked legs and bare feet, that had wont to stride the stately steede, and to trample in fields of Pagans blood, were forced to clime the craggie mountains, and to endure the torments of pricking briers, as they travayled through the desert places and comforthlesse solitarie wildernesses. (Part II, 157, emphasis in original)

The difference in the description, from echoing the apparently mellifluous melodies of Europe, imagined as the world defined by ease and comfort, to zooming in on the barren wilderness of Africa, fictionalized as an inhospitable landscape under a gloomy sky, shows how literary style evokes the contrast between the joy of Christianity and the danger of both Islam and the world of pagan rites, at the point in the narrative when the knights errant "arrived beyond the borders of Christendome, and had entred the confines of *Africa*" (Part I, 157, emphasis in original). In this respect, Johnson's romance narrates the reversal of representation of the non-Christian Africa from the Mansa Musa map, where Africa is presented as a verdant landscaped territory of bustling small kingdoms, and where Europe features as just a sweep of place-names on a neutral background.

But the difference between Europe and Africa achieved through the shift in the styles of the description of landscape sets the romance apart from the representation of Africa and Europe in Pierre Desceliers's map, where the two worlds are depicted as lush and green. The attention to flora and fauna shared between these two worlds erases the political and religious line that divides Europe and Africa, reflecting, in fact, more accurately the idea of the Mediterranean as a shared, multiethnic and multireligious place. The margin between the places that is marked rhetorically in Johnson and pictorially in the Mansa Musa map has been displaced in the Desceliers map, which privileges a Euro-Asian and Euro-African identity of the Mediterranean.

Johnson's fiction is one of the many 1590s romances where the ideology of neo-chivalric ethos is engaged in a much larger cultural project of claiming victories of the West over the East. This romance tradition grew at a time when the new social elite of gentlemen and merchants took over the space of representation from the "traditional martial nobility" (Wilson-Lee 2010, 483) of late medieval and early Tudor romances. Since the mid-sixteenth century, the urban and mercantile elite in England became associated, as Wilson-Lee argues, with the "leading edge of the Reformation movement" (2010, 483). In that post-Reformation struggle, "[g]lorifying a hierarchy based on regional power bases and military service was no longer simply a reinforcement of a perceived status quo: it could now also be a partisan affiliation in an undecided struggle" (Wilson-Lee 2010, 483). This partisan struggle acquired different forms in the fictions that started to flourish as the result of England's presence and politics in the Mediterranean. The focus was now on the reemergence of the chivalric ethos as a way by which the new class of urban and noble men expressed their valour, in adventures that may yield practical advantage to Elizabethan England, and in overseas travel. As part of that "undecided struggle," the effort to define the margins of the Christian world and to push those borders as far to the East as possible became a way of asserting oneself in the protoglobalized world. And in the early modern period, the global world was that of the multiethnic Mediterranean, still dominated by the Ottomans in the second half of the sixteenth century. Therefore, the question that Tony Judt asks, "How many Europes are there?" (1996, 45), referring to the dividing lines between the North and the South, the East and the West, within the modern European Union, is a question whose origins go back to the early modern period, and further in the past, as he contends. Yet when Judt maintains that "the eastern boundaries of the European continent are fuzzy, shading into western Asia across a broad and topographically indefinite terrain; but elsewhere its limits are clear enough" (1996, 45), it is hard not to hear, on the one hand, the voice of the Westerner charting the boundaries of where Europe starts, where it stops and how far is stretches.[10] On the other hand, it is uncannily certain that Judt's speculation about the elusive boundary between Europe and the East was also a concern of early cartographers.

Like the West, the Europe that emerges in the two maps discussed in this chapter is "demonstrably an imaginary entity" (Chakrabarty 2000, 43). It appears like a province across the sea from Northern Africa, a province whose boundary is not only porous and fluid but also determined by its Muslim counterpart in the Mediterranean. Seen this way, the early modern Europe of these maps and of Johnson's romance, a literary text whose author reclaims the African territories of the Mediterranean lost to the Ottomans, also represents, to echo Chakrabarty, a provincialized project in the sense that this text refers to the history of Europe before this history became fully formulated in the Enlightenment. The Europe in these two early modern documents also captures a history of representation belonging neither to 'Europeans' nor specifically to Christians or the West in this instance, but to others—the Muslims of Africa and the Mediterranean. Pierre Desceliers's map of the world, showing Europe, Northern Africa, and Asia as a joint landmass that spans the globe from East to West as one uninterrupted territory, represents an attempt to understand not just the notion of a fluid boundary between Europe and the East, but more broadly the very understanding of Europe's place on the world map in relation to other territories at a time before boundaries fully came into being. This map suggests that there are as many Europes as there are representations of it and as there are literary texts and geographical maps that produce such representations. Johnson's romance and the two maps from the same period reveal the ways in which the chronotope of the European margin is conceptualized in documents that capture competing politics in print and in the mapping of the Mediterranean. The effect of representing margins in Johnson's romance is to suggest that the margin of Europe has to be fought for in Northern Africa in order to defend Christianity, which the early modern world saw threatened by the Muslim forces of the East. In the maps, however, the margin between Europe and Africa shifts to the advantage of the non-Christian world, making Europe not something that is defended against the world beyond it, but a space subsumed by the political power of non-Christian Africa. The effect of such a representation of the European margin is that Europe emerges not as a fully formed political entity in the Mediterranean but as a complex meeting point of Christian and Islamic worlds. It becomes a space where history and representation have struggled for dominance for a long time.

Notes

1. I have silently changed "v" for "u," "i" for "j," and "y" for "i" in all quotations from early modern documents.
2. Das (2011, 1) makes a similar point about the crossover between travel literature and fiction writing in the early modern period.
3. I am grateful to Robert McCalla from the Department of Geography at Saint Mary's University for his help with this formulation. I also thank Jason Grek-Martin for his conversation about these maps.

4. According to Astengo (2007, 202), the image of the Virgin Mary inserted in navigational maps was one of the characteristics of Rossi's mapmaking.
5. Astengo (2007, 186) distinguishes between the roles of the chief cartographer, involved in the labour of creating the map, and his helpers, who drew details in the map.
6. Here, I echo Peter Burke's (1990) question asked in the title of his essay "Did Europe Exist before 1700?"
7. Fuchs's phrase "domesticating romance" (2014, 45) captures this process of merging domestic with international concerns in romance writing. This is most evident in romances of the East in which knights and merchants seem to swap roles, at the conceptual and symbolic levels.
8. I explore this point in detail in Stanivukovic (2011).
9. Johnson follows his period's custom in referring, derogatorily, to Muslims as Saracens.
10. Judt's estimation of European boundaries appears to be only based on geography. Yet as has been evident throughout the history of Europe, stretching from early modern to present times, where Europe stops and where it begins has often been the argument based on geopolitics as well.

Works Cited

Abulafia, David. 2012. *The Great Sea: A Human History of the Mediterranean.* London: Penguin.
Anon. 1597. *Palmerin d'Oliva.* Translated by Anthony Munday. London: B. Alsop and T. Fawcett.
Anon. 1589. *The Honorable, pleasant and rare conceited Historie of Palmendos.* London: J. C. for Simon Waterson.
Armitage, David. 2001. "Literature and Empire." In *The Oxford History of the British Empire*, volume *The Origins of Empire*, edited by Nicholas Canny, 99–123. Oxford: Oxford University Press.
Astengo, Corradino. 2007. "The Renaissance Chart Tradition in the Mediterranean." In *The History of Cartography*, Vol. 3, *Cartography in the European Renaissance*, edited by David Woodward, 174–262. Chicago: University of Chicago Press.
Bhabha, Homi. 1990. "DissemiNation: Time, Narrative, and the Margins of the Modern World." In *Nation and Narrative*, edited by Homi Bhabha, 291–322. Abingdon: Routledge.
Braudel, Fernand. 1975. *The Mediterranean and the Mediterranean World in the Age of Philip II.* Translated by Siân Reynolds. 2 vols. London: Fontana.
Braudel, Fernand. 1985. *La Méditerranée: l'espace et l'histoire.* Paris: Flammarion.
British Library. 2015. www.bl.uk/mapviews/desceliers. Accessed January 12, 2015.
Brotton, Jerry. 2012. *A History of the World in 12 Maps.* London: Allen Lane.
Burke, Peter. 1990. "Did Europe Exist Before 1700?" *History of European Ideas* 1: 21–29.
Burke, Peter. 2006. "How to Write a History of Europe: Europe, Europes, Euroasia." *European Review* 14 (2): 233–239.
Chakrabarty, Dipesh. 2000. *Provincializing Europe: Postcolonial Thought and Historical Difference.* Princeton, NJ: Princeton University Press.
Das, Nandini. 2001. Introduction. Special Issue "Travel and Prose Fiction in Early Modern England." *Yearbook of English Studies* 41 (1): 1–4.

Desceliers, Pierre. 1550. "Map of the World." BL MS Add. 24065.

Doody, Margaret Anne. 1996. *The True Story of the Novel.* New Brunswick, NJ: Rutgers University Press.

Fellows, Jennifer. 2003. Introduction. In *The Seven Champions of Christendom* by Richard Johnson, edited by Jennifer Fellows, xiii–xxxi. Aldershot: Ashgate.

Foucault, Michel. 2003. *Society Must Be Defended.* Translated by David Macey. New York: Picador.

Fuchs, Barbara. 2014. *The Poetics of Piracy: Emulating Spain in English Literature.* Philadelphia: University of Pennsylvania Press.

Goodman, Jennifer R. 1998. *Chivalry and Exploration, 1298–1630.* Woodbridge: Boydell and Brewer.

Harper, James G. 2011. Introduction. In *The Turk and Islam in the Western Eye, 1450–1750*, edited by James G. Harper, 1–18. Farnham: Ashgate.

Healy, Margaret, and Thomas Healy. 2009. Introduction. In *Renaissance Transformations: The Making of English Writing 1500–1650*, edited by Margaret Healy and Thomas Healy, 1–11. Edinburgh: Edinburgh University Press.

Helgerson, Richard. 1994. *Forms of Nationhood: The Elizabethan Writing of England.* Chicago: University of Chicago Press.

Helgerson, Richard. 2001. "The Folly of Maps and Modernity." In *Literature, Mapping, and the Politics of Space in Early Modern Britain*, edited by Andrew Gordon and Bernhard Klein, 241–262. Cambridge: Cambridge University Press.

Hess, Andrew C. 1978. *The Forgotten Frontier: A History of the Sixteenth-Century Ibero-African Frontier.* Chicago: University of Chicago Press.

Johnson, Richard. 1596/1597–2003. *The Seven Champions of Christendom.* Edited by Jennifer Fellows. Aldershot: Ashgate.

Judt, Tony. 1996. *A Grand Illusion? An Essay on Europe.* New York: Hill and Wang.

MacLean, Gerald, and Nabil Matar. 2011. *Britain and the Islamic World, 1558–1713.* Oxford: Oxford University Press.

Manion, Lee. 2014. *Narrating the Crusades: Loss and Recovery in Medieval and Early Modern English Literature.* Cambridge: Cambridge University Press.

Mentz, Steve. 2006. *Romance for Sale in Early Modern England: The Rise of Prose Fiction.* Aldershot: Ashgate.

Murrin, Michael. 2014. *Trade and Romance.* Chicago, IL: University of Chicago Press.

Relihan, Constance. 2004. *Cosmographical Glasses: Geographic Discourse, Gender, and Elizabethan Fiction.* Kent, OH: Kent State University Press.

Russo, Jacopo. c. 1525. "The Mansa Musa Map." BL MS Add. 31318B.

Sanford, Rhonda Lemke. 2002. *Maps and Memory in Early Modern England.* New York: Palgrave-Macmillan.

Sloan, Kim. 2007. *A New World: England's First View of America.* London: British Museum Press.

Spenser, Edmund. 1590/1596–1987. *The Faerie Queene.* Edited by Thomas P. Roche. London: Penguin.

Stanivukovic, Goran. 2011. "The Prenovel: Theory and the Archive." In *Narrative Developments from Chaucer to Defoe*, edited by Gerd Bayer and Ebbe Klitgård, 178–198. New York: Routledge.

Wilson-Lee, Edward. 2010. "Romance and Resistance: Narratives of Chivalry in Mid-Tudor England." *Renaissance Studies* 24 (4): 483–495.

Part III
Values

7 Imperial Violence and the Limits of Tolerance
Reading Luther with Las Casas

Nina Berman

At the same time that Spain and Portugal were devising practices of conquest in the New World, areas of East Central Europe were faced with invasions from the Ottoman empire. The hostilities between Ottoman and European troops escalated in the early sixteenth century, with substantial terror inflicted upon the populations of East Central Europe. Meanwhile, reports about the atrocities committed by Europeans during the conquest of the Americas began to surface in Europe. This chapter considers these two hostile interactions, one taking place in the Caribbean and in Central and South America, and the other in East Central Europe, in order to ask questions about how these distinct engagements with other cultures and empires shaped European approaches to cultural and religious difference. In particular, the focus of this investigation turns to sixteenth-century discussions regarding the deployment of state violence, in one case for the purpose of defence, in the other as part of a conquest with presumably humanitarian dimensions. What happens when we read Martin Luther's (1483–1546) treatises about war against the Ottoman invaders in the early sixteenth century alongside a corpus of texts that is widely considered as articulating the first critique of genocide, namely, the writings of Bartolomé de Las Casas (1484–1566)? How does the critique of the violence inflicted on the indigenous populations of the newly 'discovered' Americas resonate with accounts of the Ottoman treatment of conquered European peoples? How do the arguments against state violence that were voiced by the Catholic priest compare to those in support of state violence that were brought forth by the advocate of Reformation? What insights can be gained from this kind of comparative reading, especially with regard to Europe's views of its Others?

Whereas the significance of Las Casas's writings and activism for critiquing and redefining imperial power in the context of conquest has been widely discussed, the relevance of Luther's writings to understanding their historical context has been viewed primarily in terms of their impact on internal European affairs. This chapter relates Luther's writings about the Ottomans to the larger imperial project and shows how Luther's views of the Ottomans and of war against them also speak to contemporary concerns regarding the role of the state vis-à-vis the non-European Other more broadly, in this foundational moment of imperial conquest. I suggest that the seemingly profoundly distinct positions articulated by Luther and Las Casas exemplify interrelated paradigms that continue to define basic Western attitudes toward cultural and religious difference.

The idea of a 'European' sense of identification is implicit, rather than explicit, in the debates reviewed here. State and Church struggled for domination throughout the Middle Ages (the *communitas Christiana* was never uncontested),[1] and the positions articulated by Luther and Las Casas document a moment in which the Christian matrix of belonging was beginning to be relegated to a secondary position vis-à-vis the imperial state. Part of the experience of European secular and religious elites at the time was an awareness of conquest, colonization, and the possibilities of empire; as critics from Tzvetan Todorov and Mary Louise Pratt to Anthony Pagden and Edward Said have pointed out, in the process of engaging with the non-European world, Europeans developed *concepts of self and other*. In contrast to, for example (the early) Said, I would like to emphasize that these concepts were developed in relation to and interaction with *practices and the materiality of imperial rule*; that is, discourses did not necessarily (though they did sometimes) produce practices and materiality (Berman 2011, especially 1–22). While the concepts of self and other that emerged out of Europe's encounter with the rest of the world did not explicitly articulate a 'European' identity, the shared experience of various actors who were, in one way or another, involved in or positioned themselves toward conquest and colonization contributed to creating various *ideas (in discourse) and practices of Europeanness over time*. The texts by Luther and Las Casas were part of this process of generating concepts and shaping practices that defined Europe's stance toward non-European others in the early modern period and beyond.

Luther

In order to assess the significance of Luther's writings about the Ottoman Turks and his views about state violence, in their historical moment and beyond, a look at the larger political and military situation in early modern Europe is instructive. The fall of Constantinople in 1453 was clearly an awakening for Europe: calls for a crusade against the Muslims, which had abated since the end of the medieval Crusades, were renewed. While the *Reconquista* had ended Muslim rule in Spain in 1492, increasingly the Ottomans attacked European Christianity on its own territory. Europe continued to be divided, and those powers whose territories were not immediately affected—namely, Britain and France—showed the least concern. Changes were also brought on by the discovery of the New World, which boosted the self-esteem of the powers involved in this enterprise at the time, particularly Spain and Portugal. The rise of the Spanish empire affected power constellations in Europe: after 1516, the Habsburg dynastic connection with the Spanish empire resulted in a political axis of the Holy Roman

Empire and Spain, whereas France, caught geographically in the middle between their spheres of influence, developed a tense relationship with these powers that further precluded a unified front against the Ottomans.

The Ottoman expansion continued with renewed vigor under Selim I, who conquered Syria and Egypt in 1517. His son, Suleiman the Magnificent, took power in 1520 and continued the conquest. In 1521 he invaded Hungary and Serbia. In 1526 the Ottomans waged another large-scale operation in the area, defeating the Hungarian army in the battle of Mohács (during which King Louis II Jagellon was killed) and pillaging Buda. The Hungarian defeat and the death of the king had major repercussions: the Hungarians elected János Zápolya as king, challenging the dynastic politics that had united Hungarian and Habsburg rule, and secured economic stability in the area.[2] One month later, however, another group of Hungarian noblemen elected Ferdinand of Habsburg as king. Both laid claim to the Hungarian crown, a fact that enabled the Ottoman sultan to find a collaborator in Zápolya. Zápolya accepted the sovereignty of the sultan, and Hungary became a tributary of the Ottoman empire. This alliance was further strengthened in 1535, when France, which was formally allied with the Ottomans after 1536, recognized Zápolya as the legitimate king of Hungary.[3] Hungary was from then on divided into three areas: Transylvania (Siebenbürgen), which had become Protestant by the 1550s and had secured independent status; the middle part of the country, which was a tributary of the Ottomans; and the western part, which belonged to the Habsburg empire.[4] Apart from France and parts of Hungary, other states also entered into alliances with the Ottomans, such as the Venetians, who signed separate peace treaties with the Ottomans in 1540 and 1573. The Ottomans were able to maintain their presence in central Europe until the end of the seventeenth century, when in 1699 they lost Hungary in the Peace Treaty of Karlowitz. Clearly, throughout this period, Europe did not engage with the Ottomans as a unified block, in spite of the substantial suffering that the Ottomans inflicted on large parts of Europe and its Christian populations.

The encounter with the Ottomans was traumatizing, and the images of violence that circulated in Europe were grounded in actual atrocities committed by the invading army. The focus on Ottoman atrocities was a prominent topic in times of direct military confrontation. A text by Peter Stern von Labach from 1530, for example, reports on the sieges of Ofen and Vienna and clearly functions to render a tale of the heroic resistance of the Viennese and their survival in the face of several weeks of shelling and burning, from September 24 to October 14, 1529. The strength of the Ottoman army has been estimated at over a quarter-million people, with about 80,000 to 120,000 troops. No supporting army came to the assistance of the Viennese, but the Ottomans did not succeed in taking the city. Yet, by the time the Ottomans finally retreated, in part owing to the early onset of winter and the lack of food sources from the areas they had laid waste, tens of thousands of soldiers and civilians had been killed or wounded. Women, children, and many of the notables and well-off were captured by the Turks after fleeing Vienna. Grisly descriptions give a sense of the brutality of the battles: heads of captured Viennese on pikes; children cut out of their mother's wombs, thrown away, or impaled; and virgins, whose bodies were lying in the streets, raped to death ("Warhafftige handlung"). These kinds of descriptions became standard topoi incorporated into countless reports about battles with the Ottomans that circulated across Europe in different languages.[5] Carl Göllner's (1961/1968) two-volume compilation of sixteenth-century documents about the Ottoman invasions records 2,460 prints, 1,000 of which were written in German; these reports would be read throughout Europe in the sixteenth and seventeenth centuries. The Saidian paradigm of *Orientalism* would have us treat such images of cruel Ottomans as European fabrications. But how does the image of Ottoman atrocities rendered in these accounts fare in light of comparative historical evidence?

According to available European and Ottoman sources, the Ottoman army was feared because of the widespread destruction it inflicted on local populations, settlements, and agricultural land. The first and most gruesome phase of devastation was brought about by unsalaried troops of volunteers and by contingents of enlisted raiders. These units preceded and collaborated with the salaried and more disciplined regular troops and "mount[ed] punitive expeditions outside periods of formal warfare" (Imber 2002, 265). Numerous German-language writings of the era expressed fear of these troops, which often invaded in large numbers, the volunteers alone making up at least 20 per cent of the Ottoman army (Fodor 2000, 263). The unsalaried troops lived off the booty they pillaged and were thus especially ambitious in their actions. The enlisted raiders' income also came mostly from booty (Imber 2002, 261; Nicolle 1983, 14). In addition to the loot made from plundering and selling individuals into slavery, the volunteers were often remunerated for their actions with prebends, monetary rewards, and other forms of compensation (Murphey 1999, 160–163). To prove the successful slaughter of the enemy, heads were cut off and presented to the army leaders, who then set the reward for the accomplishment. Impaled heads were displayed in public places and became grisly symbols of Ottoman warfare. These practices are confirmed by historical sources written by both German and Ottoman authors of the period.[6] Descriptions of war are rendered, for example, in the chronicle of Aşıkpaşazade, who covers events of the fifteenth century, and Oruç, who reports about expeditions carried out under the leadership of Sultan Bayezid I (1481–1512). The portrayal of brutal violence certainly functions as proof of military strength, tangibly so in descriptions that boast, for example, about high towers made of the heads of enemies (Kreutel 1978, 70; also Kreutel 1959).

The atrocities committed by the Ottoman army sent waves of fear through central European areas, even though, as Göllner points out, we have to recognise that the Ottoman atrocities did not differ from practices common to warfare generally at the time (Göllner 1978, 24). Descriptions by Franz Christoph Graf von Khevenhüller (1420–1462) (also spelled Khevenhiller), who created a monumental work of historiography with his twelve-volume *Annales Ferdinandei*, confirm that severing the heads of enemies was also practiced by Habsburg military. Especially grisly is the account of the fate of French mercenaries who had rebelled against their Habsburg employer. The captured French troops were slowly killed through an extended process of various unspeakable torture methods. The heinous atrocities included the roasting of mutineers, whose bodies were then fed to their fellow mutineers (1722, 2256–2257).

Accounts of this kind certainly put the portrayals of Ottoman atrocities in perspective; war was fought brutally on both sides. Even if many of the widely circulated reports from the front were recycled and not based on firsthand information, the image of the Ottomans as cruel and reckless soldiers needs to be acknowledged as based in reality. The number of casualties was high; according to some estimates, approximately 100,000 civilians lost their lives during the First Siege of Vienna, when large regions were burned and looted (Gutkas 1984, 106). The unceasing invasions of the Ottomans throughout the fifteenth, sixteenth, and seventeenth centuries led to depopulation in some areas. The cruelty of the volunteer troops, raiders, and other army units was a frequent topos: they plundered and destroyed villages, burned the fields, killed scores of soldiers and civilian men, captured women and children, and sold captives into slavery (Buchmann 1999, 87–89; Kreutel 1982, 242–243). At times the local population was saved so that they might become future subjects who would pay taxes (Kreutel 1982, 224). In the course of the sixteenth century, new weapons came into use, and guns and mines increased the number of casualties even more (Imber 2002, 267–275; Ágoston 1999, 125–126).

Ottoman military terror was generally followed by an offer of peace in exchange for tribute under relatively lenient conditions. The local population was allowed to retain the legal and administrative structures of its society (although differences existed with regard to the specific status of the territory), and those not converting to Islam had to pay an additional tax in return for attaining "the status of *ahl al-zimma*, i.e., protected subjects of the Muslim state in accordance with Islamic Law."[7] This manner of proceeding, which amounts to a kind of shock-and-awe strategy by the Ottomans, was successful; as mentioned earlier, the Ottomans annexed large territories over the course of a few centuries in Europe, North Africa, and Asia Minor, and many Christians converted to Islam. In Europe the Ottomans solidified their influence by pursuing "an active diplomacy ..., everywhere supporting forces opposed to the papacy and the Habsburgs, such as the Calvinists in France, Hungary and the Netherlands, the Moriscos in Spain and the rising national monarchies in France and England" (Inalcik 1994, 21).

How did Europeans, who, as we have seen, were not unified, articulate their resistance to the Ottoman empire? European accounts from the period express the fear of Ottoman military might, though this fear was mixed with admiration. A host of attitudes about the Ottomans was voiced in publications across Europe, on a spectrum described by Hans Joachim Kissling (1964) as ranging from "Türkenfurcht" (fear of the Turks) to "Türkenhoffnung" (hope for the Turk). Some humanist thinkers, especially in Italy, came to see the Turks as 'barbarians,' which, as Nancy Bisaha argues, "provided one more avenue for conceptualizing the Turks via ancient sources" and allowed the humanists to dehumanize the Ottomans and to express their own sense of cultural superiority (Bisaha 2004, 75). Other attempts at understanding the Ottoman invaders included seeing them more neutrally as powerful political adversaries or even favorably as admirable opponents. John of Segovia (?–1458) and Nicholas Cusanus (1401–1464) engaged with the Ottomans on a theological level and took a scholarly stance toward Islam. Bisaha explains that "both believed that the key to solving the problems posed by Islam lay in the study of textual sources—namely the Qur'an" (2004, 144). But attitudes were certainly influenced by the geopolitical location of writers of any kind, and specific political, economic, religious, and other ideological factors determined the view of the Ottomans. One of the central issues was the question of who should lead the war against the Ottomans, the pope (as in the case of the Crusades) or the emperor? That is, was the war against the Ottomans a holy war in the tradition of the Crusades, or was it a secular war that should be led by the forces of empire?

This discussion became crucial in German territories, which, unlike France or England, had been directly affected by the Ottoman invasions. Until the events in Hungary, German leaders had not perceived the Ottomans as a threat to their own territory. The situation changed with the battle of Mohács; the Hungarian defeat made German (particularly Habsburg) territories much more vulnerable to Ottoman conquest and, indeed, ultimately led to the First Siege of Vienna in 1529. The conflicts with the Ottoman empire were discussed in many areas of cultural production. Theologians and authors of fiction commented on the hostilities and used the threat of Ottoman invasion to articulate a wide range of positions. Secular and religious leaders debated their political and military options (Göllner 1978, 26; Mertens 1997). The topic was prevalent in all kinds of popular and highbrow genres of cultural expression (Berman 2011, 78–97).

The question of who should lead the war was taken up centrally by theologians, and here the writings of Luther are key, if only because they articulated and brought about a fundamental shift in the way state violence was legitimized. Luther was one of the most prominent voices in the public call for unity against the Ottomans. His views differed substantially from those of other European humanists, such as Segovia and Cusanus, but were in line with those of thinkers such as the Italians Petrarch, Salutati, and Leonardo Dati (Bisaha 2004, 161–166). His opinions were discussed in both Protestant and Catholic churches and came to influence political and religious events across and beyond German territories. Luther's writings about the Ottomans shed light on the new role of the state in leading wars, particularly against non-European and religious others, and contains arguments that various thinkers also used to legitimatize colonial wars against non-Christian populations.

The position Luther articulated in several texts from 1529, before and after the First Siege of Vienna, differed substantially from his earlier positions. In December 1518, for example, Luther had stated that the pope was a greater menace than the Turks and was unwilling to support a call for war against the Ottomans. In the following years Luther insisted that the Turks were fought best by undergoing introspection and repentance and by leading a life in the spirit of Christianity (Mau 1983, 647–648). In particular, Luther fought renewed calls for a crusade against the Ottomans and the connected practice of selling indulgences. Even after Mohács, he continued to see the Ottoman invasions as God's punishment for the dismal state of Christianity and he refrained from calling for war against the Turks. His views were not only contrary to those of both secular and religious leaders, but also largely out of touch with public opinion.[8] The general fear of renewed Ottoman intervention finally motivated Luther to speak out publicly. This move occurred, however, under pressure from the Protestant princes and cities, which used the conflict with the Ottomans to extract concessions from the emperor in return for their military support. It should be pointed out that independence from Rome extended beyond the religious dimension and also entailed political and economic benefits (Schmidt 1999, 100–111). In this conflict between Protestant rulers and the Habsburg emperor and his allies, Luther's writings played a central role.

Luther worked on "Vom Kriege wider die Türken" (On War Against the Turks) between fall 1528 and spring 1529. The text was printed in April 1529, only a few months before the First Siege of Vienna began and at a moment when the Second Diet of Spires was in session, deliberating, among other questions, resistance to the Ottomans.[9] Luther's "Vom Kriege" needs to be understood in the immediate context of impending danger. The theologian pursues two main trajectories in this text: first, he details his new position with regard to taking up arms against the Ottomans; second, he uses his condemnation of the Turks to attack the papacy. He acknowledges that he had indeed preached against fighting the Turks but that he had gained new insight "about temporal authority" that implicitly justifies his altered position (1909, 108–109). Luther's revised understanding of the difference between temporal and spiritual authority—he had first elaborated on these concepts in "Von weltlicher Obrigkeit" (On Temporal Authority, 1523)—figures prominently in this argument. He sharply attacks the notion of a holy war and argues that the war against the Turks must be led by the emperor. Luther blames Islam for attempting to spread its teachings not through preaching but, rather, by the sword. He recounts practices of the Ottoman army, such as selling captives into slavery and the murder of civilians, which as we have seen did correspond to historical events. Luther discounts reports that under Ottoman rule Christians have the option to keep their faith and argues that Christians are forced, instead, to comply with definite restrictions.

Those instances of Christian captives who "become altogether Turkish" pose a particular problem for Luther (1909, 121). Here the theologian is addressing the situation of a large number of converts. According to Pál Fodor, up to 30 per cent of volunteers in the sixteenth-century Ottoman army can be identified as first-generation renegades, which also "tallies with the ratios experienced within the Ottoman forces of the border areas" (2000, 262–263).[10] These renegades and those Christians who fared relatively well under Ottoman rule concerned Luther greatly. Only through deceit and violence, the theologian claims, are these people kept in a confused state in Ottoman lands (121). Those who voluntarily join the Turks, says Luther, become complicit in the Turks' actions. His ultimate verdict about Turkish religion and customs is unequivocal condemnation, for "the Turk is the irate rod of our Lord God and the slave of the angry devil" (1909, 116). In his discussion the only rival to the Turks' purported evilness is the pope, who, he claims, is "the antichrist, just like the Turk is the living devil" (126). Such comparisons pervade the text and culminate in the conclusion that one has to fight the pope just as much as one has to fight the Turks. Regardless of the pressing historical situation, which explains the urgency of the polemic, we have to acknowledge its ideological purport. Luther's main target is the pope: strengthening the role of the emperor by arguing that only the worldly leader is entitled to lead the army against the Ottomans is primarily aimed at disqualifying the pope. His critique of Islam and the Turks is indeed an attack on religious and cultural difference but simultaneously provides Luther with ammunition in his struggle against the papacy.

Luther's second text from 1529, "Heerpredigt wider den Türken" (Military Sermon Against the Turk), in which he calls for war against the Turks, was written within months after the publication of "Vom Kriege."[11] The immediate cause propelling Luther to write once again about the topic was the fact that the Ottomans had invaded German lands and laid siege to Vienna. In "Heerpredigt," Luther sets out to highlight religious dimensions of the conflict with the Turks. In order to prove his point that the Turks continue to be a threat, he picks up the apocalyptic tone he had introduced at the end of "Vom Kriege" and invokes the prophecies in the seventh chapter of the book of Daniel (1909, 143–144, 148). Luther's exegesis of biblical passages consistently associates the Ottoman empire's invasions with the Apocalypse. Accordingly, Luther exhorts his fellow Germans to follow his instructions regarding proper behavior in light of the impending end of the world. He repeats what had been the central argument in his previous publication: that the Turks should be fought, first of all, spiritually by Germans behaving like good Christians and by accepting the leadership of the temporal ruler with regard to the military struggle. That the war was not to be fought as a crusade and in the name of Christ comes as a surprise after the detailed association of the Turkish threat with the prophecies of the Bible. This tension, which may be perceived as an internal contradiction, begins to make sense when considered in light of Luther's conflict with the pope: he has to reject the notion of a crusade in order to continue his defiance of papal orders. He justifies his choice of the emperor as the only legitimate leader of a war against the Turks by referring to Romans 13:1 and Titus 3:1, the biblical passages that (in Luther's interpretation) demand obedience to the temporal ruler, who is appointed by God.

In light of these concepts, war against the Turks is legitimate. As Luther states, a Christian fighting under the leadership of the emperor should not worry about spilling innocent blood among the Turks, as the Turks are the archenemy of Christianity. And, if a Christian should die at the hands of the Turks, what better fate can happen to the believer than to become a martyr, to die an "honest holy death" (1909, 175)? Again, we can detect dissonance within Luther's view of the role of the temporal ruler as leader of the military campaign against the Turks. In spite of his appeals to secular leadership, the idea of dying a martyr's death resonates with crusading rhetoric. In fact, this idea figures centrally in Luther's elaboration; over several pages Luther details the advantages and importance of martyrdom (174–180). Even if war against the Turks is not a crusade, it remains a holy war, a war understood in religious terms, because Luther's notion of temporal government is solidly placed within sacred history. Luther's "Heerpredigt" (1529) restates several of the arguments made in "Vom Kriege," but here the emphasis lies in the eschatological dimension of the conflict with the Turks. In spite of the fact that individual European powers (such as Hungary, Venice, and France) had entered into alliances with the Muslim invaders and that the Ottoman army included Christian soldiers and renegades, Luther stages the conflict as one between Christians and Muslims in religious and even apocalyptic tones.[12] As he did in the first text, Luther draws comparisons between the Turks and Jews as a means of amplifying the gravity of the blasphemous behaviour he exposes (186). Using the tools of polemic and propaganda, he ignores or reinterprets conflicting evidence and simplifies the situation by rendering the struggle as one between good and evil, even if reality were more complicated and events defied easy categorization. Luther's discourse distorts not only Ottoman society and Islam but also the actions of European religious and political leaders.[13]

This analysis of Luther's support of war against the Ottomans highlights the ways in which the rise of the Reformation movement, the development of national consciousness (particularly through Luther's use of the German language), and the conflicts with the Ottoman empire were related. Acknowledging this nexus, historian Stephen Fischer-Galati argues that the Ottoman invasions were the main factor bringing forth the success of the Reformation movement (1959, 117; see also Fischer-Galati 1956). The conflict with the Ottoman empire had a significant impact on developments within Germany. The First Siege of Vienna produced a large corpus of texts, as did the Second Siege later on, and was formative in shaping both information and clichés about the events.[14] The image of the cruel invading Ottoman army became crucially tied to Germany's, and, in the larger context, Europe's self-image. Opposing viewpoints developed in Europe as well: Erasmus of Rotterdam (1466–1536), for example, as a "strong proponent of Christian nonviolence ... challenged contemporary European notions of holy war and the Infidel" (Bisaha 2004, 74). Erasmus changed some of his views after the First Siege of Vienna; nevertheless, in his *Consultatio de bello Turcis inferendo* (1530), "Erasmus did not cease in his attacks on crusade and his calls for more charitable views of the Turks" (Bisaha 2004, 175). Generally, however, Luther was more representative of the dominant attitudes being voiced in Germany and variously across Europe.

Luther's sermons were based on existing sources about Islam and the Ottomans, and had a formative function for subsequent texts about the Ottomans.[15] His discussion of converts and renegades; his interpretation of commendable aspects of Ottoman culture as ruses of the devil; his description of Turkish atrocities; his view of the Turk as Satan; the great importance of biblical prophecies in his analysis; the refutation of specific aspects of Islam—these and other topoi were picked up in scores of texts published throughout the sixteenth and seventeenth centuries. Luther's writings were at once part of the discourse on the Ottomans and also played a crucial role in its further development.[16] But his views about the use of state violence against a people distinguished by cultural and religious difference resonate with other events of the period. These include Luther's advocacy of the killing of non-Christians, his support for war led by the emperor rather than the pope, and his ruthless condemnation of cultural difference built on principles that were becoming central to imperial and colonial ideology. Considering the contemporaneity of violent events in the Americas and in Europe, in particular the fact that the conquest of the New World took place while the Old World was being threatened by the Ottoman empire, allows us a broader perspective on the larger significance of Lutheran war propaganda and his views regarding the complex relationship between state power and religious power.

Luther's support for the emperor has often been seen as revolutionary, especially because he argues for a separation of state and church powers through what later became known as the Two Kingdoms Doctrine. But in the context of the Reformation this separation of powers was primarily a ploy designed to disempower the pope and ensure the support of the emperor for the Protestant movement. Luther knew whose support he was seeking; Charles V was the most powerful European ruler of the time. And clearly, as the conquest of the Americas shows, it was now the emperor, not the pope, who claimed the role of protector of Christianity. The Christian mission had not disappeared from the ideological framework bolstering expansion; in fact, it functioned as the central belief system justifying imperial expansion and was often—but not in the texts discussed here—articulated using the notion of 'just war.' Luther was less of a visionary than a pragmatic politician writing in full awareness of the power dynamics of the moment. This dimension of Luther's arguments comes to the fore more clearly when we turn to the writings and activism of Las Casas.

Bartholomé De Las Casas

Bartholomé de Las Casas, the Dominican friar who became an outspoken critic of imperial violence against American Indians, had originally been enlisted in support of the conquest. Born in 1484 (as early as 1474 according to some, by now generally disputed, accounts) (Rand Parish 1976), he is reported to have experienced one of his early childhood encounters with the New World in his hometown of Seville:

> Bartolomé de las Casas witnessed the enthusiastic parades in Seville to commemorate the return of Christopher Columbus from his first voyage of discovery in 1493. On that occasion, Columbus displayed the seven brightly decorated Indians he brought back with him from the New World, along with some gorgeously colored parrots, painted native masks, several curiosities, and a small sample of gold. ... The Columbus display was a highly successful recruiting technique for the second voyage, attracting as it did three male members of the Las Casas family and many of those who would later achieve great fame in the New World.
> (Knight 2003, xvii)

Seville became crucial to trade with the New World: the city's inland port was the only location facilitating legal trade with the New World, which was administered through the *Casa de Contratación* (the Spanish government agency that controlled exploration and colonialism).

Seville's proximity to the kingdom of Granada is also relevant to situating Las Casas, as Granada was the last Muslim stronghold on the Iberian Peninsula between 1252 and 1492. Seville itself had been captured by Castilian forces in 1248. The wrath of Reconquista forces, as we know, was not directed only against Muslims; it also affected Jews. In 1391, large-scale pogroms occurred in Seville, and the staging of various forms of *autos da fé* (Inquisition tribunals that at times included public burnings) and forced conversions followed. All synagogues were closed and later converted to churches. The fact that the Spanish Inquisition, founded in 1478, operated entirely under the auspices of the royal sovereign, is notable. After various pieces of legislation regulated the status of Muslims and Jews in distinct ways, Jews were expelled from Spain in 1492 (*Alhabra Decree*), as were Muslims in 1502 (dates differ for the various regions of the Iberian Peninsula), unless they chose to convert. Conversions became a survival strategy, but distrust of converts led to further discriminatory actions. At the beginning of the seventeenth century, the Moriscos, the Muslims converts to Christianity, were expelled from Spain.

Benzion Netanyahu (1995) has argued that the history of European racism begins there and then, when conversion alone no longer erased the markers of difference, which became located in culture, histories, and bodies. While Netanyahu's views have been the subject of controversy, they seem especially sensible when apprehending the role of the Inquisition in the conquest of the Americas and as a paradigm for Europe's approach to cultural and religious difference in the context of colonization (conversion does not guarantee equality!) and with regard to minorities within Europe, more generally.

Members of the Las Casas family may or may not have belonged to this group of *conversos*, but, as Lawrence Clayton suggests, "Las Casas almost certainly also witnessed the deportation of the Jews earlier in 1492" (2012, 12), along with other manifestations of the Reconquista. Awareness of the difficulties of conversion and exclusionist policies, the Inquisition, and more generally exposure to the religious, cultural, and racial politics of post-Reconquista Spain most certainly formed the background against which the positions articulated by Las Casas would be developed later.

After years of study, Las Casas left for Hispaniola in 1502, at the age of 18, accompanying his father, who had been allotted an *encomienda*—that is, a number of Native Americans who were supposed to be 'protected' and instructed in Christianity, but who were, in return, required to work for their protectors. This system of de facto slavery provided ample opportunity for abuse. Over time, the younger Las Casas worked as a "lay teacher of religious doctrine," but he also held *encomiendas* in Hispaniola and Cuba, and was thus initially involved not only as a member of the clergy (probably ordained between 1507 and 1510) and later as a Dominican friar (1522) but also as a settler and even soldier, and thus as an economic and military agent of the conquest (Knight 2003, xix). He travelled widely in the region, including to other islands of the Caribbean, Mexico, Guatemala, Nicaragua, Venezuela, and Peru, and witnessed the atrocities that were committed throughout the colonies first-hand. Gradually, Las Casas turned from "astounded eyewitness" to fierce critic of the methods employed by the Spanish conquistadors (Clayton 2012, 45). The views Las Casas expounded in his writings were not unique, and he was clearly influenced by critical voices within the Catholic Church, such as the Dominican Friar Father Antonio Montesino (c. 1475–1545).[17] After 1515, Las Casas began his quest to raise public consciousness about the situation of American Indians. He wrote treatises, pleaded in court, argued before audiences, and, in 1516, was appointed 'Protector of the Indians' by Cardinal Francisco Jiménez de Cisneros. Following failed attempts at, among other things, creating a peaceful colony, and while in search of further ways to sway public opinion, he turned to writing histories of the events he had seen unfold in front of his eyes. While Luther was drumming up support for the emperor, arguing vehemently against the pope, and lobbying passionately for war against non-Europeans to be led by the state, Las Casas, for his part, brandished the atrocities resulting from state-condoned violence inflicted upon non-Europeans in his missives directed at the same emperor, Charles V.

One of these texts, the *Account, Much Abbreviated, of the Destruction of the Indies* (*Brevísima relación de la destrucción de las Indias*, 1542, published 1552), was particularly effective in documenting the horrors of conquest and attracting attention to the issue. Scholarship on Las Casas's writings about the genocide of the American Indians has addressed their significance in terms of political and legal theory and their religious dimensions, and tackled specific issues related to colonization and imperialism, such as the image of American Indians, colonial ideology, Las Casas's changing positions on slavery, and the trajectory that links Las Casas to present-day forms of humanitarian intervention. My investigation seeks primarily to establish a link between Las Casas's and Luther's views regarding the use of state violence against non-European others, in order to demonstrate that the two positions, which seem polar opposites at first sight, are both integral to a larger approach toward the non-European and non-Christian other.

If we turn to the first few pages of the *Account, Much Abbreviated*, the parallels to European images of Ottoman atrocities are striking: conquering Christians have enslaved the local population; they enrich themselves beyond belief; and they commit acts of heinous cruelty. Regarding violence in Hispaniola, today's Haiti and the Dominican Republic, Las Casas writes:

> The Christian ... would enter into the villages and spare not children, or old people, or pregnant women, or women with suckling babes, but would open the woman's belly and hack the babe to pieces, as though they were butchering lambs shut up in their pen. They would lay wagers who might slice open the belly of a man with one strike of their blade, or cut off a man's head with one swift motion of their pike, or spill out his entrails. ... They would erect long gibbets, but no higher than that a man's feet might dangle just above the ground, and bind thirteen of the Indians at one time, in honour and reverence, they said, of Our Redeemer and the twelve Apostles, and put firewood around it and burn the Indians alive. Others, they would tie or bind their bodies all about with dry straw, and set fire to the straw and burn them that way. Others, and all those they desired to let live, they would cut off both their hands but leave them hanging by the skin. (1552/2003, 9)

This description of cruel terrorization of the civilian population could have been taken right out of one of the contemporary accounts of Ottoman atrocities: infanticide, disembowelling, and decapitation were part of the repertoire of Ottoman soldiers. But, as discussed earlier, those were the practices of warfare at the time, and the descriptions of both Ottoman and European wartime atrocities illustrate this disheartening assessment. The scope and scale of Spanish violence in the Americas, however, was genocidal:

> On the Island of Hispaniola, of the above three millions souls that we once saw, today there be no more than two hundred of those native peoples remaining. The Island of Cuba is almost as long as from

Valladolid to Rome; today it is almost devoid of population. The Island of San Juan and that of Jamaica, large and well-favoured and lovely islands both, have been laid waste. On the Isles of the Lucayos [Bahamas] ... where there were once above five hundred thousand souls, today there is not a living creature.

(Las Casas 1552/2003, 6–7)

While the validity of the actual figures is disputed (and similar figures are reported in the account for numerous areas), Las Casas clearly articulates the devastating effect of European colonizing methods.[18] Depopulation of some areas in Europe had been registered as an effect of the Ottoman invasions, but Spanish violence took on unprecedented dimensions (Buchmann 1999, 87–89).

Las Casas describes the colonizers as "Spaniards" but more often also as "Christians," in this way accentuating the monstrosity of their "unchristian" acts in contrast to notions of Christianity he believes ought to be promoted. Phrases such as "[t]hose, calling themselves Christians," "these Christians," "one evil Christian," "the Christian tyrants," and, even more generally, "a Christian" underline the tension between the purported goal of a Christianising mission and the reality of inhumane practices against the Native Americans (Las Casas 1552/2003, 7, 8, 46). Las Casas also rails against the Germans who had been given the Province of Venezuela (which they called Klein-Venedig, Little Venice) in 1528:

These men [the Germans] entered into those lands, then with more, I do think, incomparable cruelty than any of the other tyrants that we have spoken of, and more unreasonably and furiously than the most bloodthirsty tigers and ravening wolves and lions. ... They have murdered and utterly hacked to pieces large and diverse nations, devastated many tongues and left no one to speak them. ... And above four and five million souls of those innocent generations (I do believe) they have murdered and destroyed and cast into hell by foreign and divers and new forms of cruel iniquity and impiety. (1552/2003, 65)

The extremely tyrannical and cruel rule of the Welsers, the Augsburg-based family of bankers and merchants who had been given the territory by Charles V in return for their financial support of the emperor, led to their loss of the colony in 1556 (Schmitt 2008; de Behrens and de Venturini 1977).

Las Casas contrasts the inhumanity of the conquistadors with his own view of the native population: he envisions American Indians as humans who are perfectly fit to become Christians. They are "a simple people, altogether without subtility, malice, or duplicity, excellent in obedience"; they are "among the most cleanliest and most unoccupied of the inhabitants of the earth, and of a lively understanding, very apt and tractable for all fair doctrine, excellently fit to receive our holy Catholic faith" (1552/2003, 5–6).

Las Casas even makes an effort to explain local resistance as a reaction against the tremendous cruelty experienced: "And when the Indians saw that even with so much humility and offerings and patience and suffering they still could not break or soften such inhumane and bestial hearts ... they agreed to meet and to join together and to die in war, taking vengeance as best they could upon such cruel and hellish enemies" (1552/2003, 39).

In 1542, Las Casas's advocacy on behalf of Amerindians took on a decidedly public turn, when he

> made his arguments day in and day out through the winter and spring of 1542 before the special council in Valladolid. Las Casas's *modus operandi* was to overwhelm his hearers with evidence in almost numbing detail. ... Las Casas's hearers sat on for hour after hour, week after week, as the story of brutality, greed, and injustice almost overwhelmed their senses. Las Casas read for days on end.
>
> (Clayton 2012, 277)

His public exhortations and indictments had an effect. On November 20, 1542, Charles V approved and signed the New Laws. The key points of the legislation addressed the following issues:

> (1) The dignity of the Indians as subjects of the Crown; (2) The elimination of Indian slavery; (3) Provisions for the extinction of the *encomienda* as a principal form of exploiting the Indian as labor and vassal; (4) Prohibiting further wars of conquest; (5) Strict and detailed laws and decrees for the enforcement of all the above.
>
> (Clayton 2012, 282; see also Clayton's footnote 42)

While these laws marked a significant change at the time, Las Casas was not content and continued his advocacy on behalf of Amerindians. In hindsight, we know that these laws did not end colonial violence and impunity; in fact, colonial and imperial violence had just begun. Daniel Castro emphasizes the de facto ineffectiveness of Las Casas's endeavour and argues that Las Casas was an integral part of the establishment of imperial power (Castro 2007). Indeed, while the New Laws marked a milestone in the debate regarding Europe's relationship to non-European and non-Christian peoples, the practices of conquest continued to be fraught with contradictions.

Scholarship on Las Casas is thus controversial and includes positions ranging from praise to sharp criticism of the friar. Las Casas's plea for recognition of the humanity of Native Americans contains, as Enrique Dussel (2013, 178) enthusiastically suggests, "a modern and surprisingly critical position." Dussel identifies six key aspects that distinguish Las Casas's position: the idea that all human beings have a "universal claim of truth"; the importance of recognizing in conflict situations that the other culture also presents claims to universal truth; the possibility of accepting the dissent of the Other; acknowledgment that the Other has an obligation to observe these dissenting principles; the irrationality and ethically unjust nature of forced acceptance of the truth of the Other (i.e., forced conversion); and his proposition that reasoning and ethical examples are the only acceptable ways to demonstrate a claim to universal truth (Dussel 2013, 178–179). But against this positive view, Las Casas encountered an increase in the number of his critics and the force of their arguments. Cristián Roa-de-la-Carrera, for example, argues that Las Casas was less of an idealistic defender of indigenous peoples than a rigorous intellectual in the service of empire. He rests his analysis mainly on the fact that Las Casas's writings contributed to the reification of the concept of the Indian as an anthropological category in the service of colonization (Roa-de-la-Carrera 2010). Even more compellingly, Daniel Castro (2007, 182) warns against the celebration of Las Casas, who never questions the legitimacy of the Christian mission: "While the colonizers advocated and preferred military conquest, the Dominican consistently called for the peaceful evangelization and colonization of the natives."

For our purposes, the most relevant critique of Las Casas is articulated by Daniel Brunstetter (2010). Brunstetter evokes Anthony Pagden, who has tied the development of human rights in the West to the encounter with cultural difference in the New World. Pagden deserves to be quoted at length:

> It is undeniable that, at present, the "international community" derives its values from a version of a liberal consensus which is, in essence, a secularized transvaluation of the Christian ethic, at least as it applies to the concept of rights. ... The history of rights, of *iura*, and in particular of those rights which were to become "human rights," is doubly embarrassing for their culturally sensitive defendants in that such rights were not only a creation of the Roman legal tradition but were developed in the form we understand it today, in the context of imperial legislative practices, and have remained closely associated with *imperial* expansion and its consequences until at least the late nineteenth century. Some plausible account of the evolving relationship between rights and the development of the European empires might, perhaps, provide a better position from which to evaluate why we continue to believe that "our" values are necessarily conterminous with those of the human race as a whole, and whether we are justified in so doing.
>
> (Pagden 2003, 173)

Brunstetter (2010, 421) pursues the relevance of these thoughts with regard to Las Casas and shows that "Las Casas' claims about the humanity of the Indians delimit a tension-laden view of the human that sheds light on the friction between universalism and alterity and thus the place of inequality in the liberal thread of Modernity." While Las Casas argues for the acknowledgement of the humanity of the Other and even his right to resist, the ultimate goal remains conversion, the potential of the Other to become like and part of the Self. Las Casas grounds his recognition of humanity in religion, which "he sees as the universal criterion of humanity—recognizing the existence of God" (Brunstetter 2010, 424). The contradiction inherent in Las Casas's argumentation—the right of the Indians, as Brunstetter says (2010, 425), "to choose their way of life" in contrast to Las Casas's belief in the superiority of the Christian religion—reflects a tension that was constitutive of the European approach to the Other emerging at the time. This duality also distinguishes the tensions contained in the universalist claim of human rights, a codex of rights that is grounded in very specific European (liberal, modern) notions of rights and self.

Brunstetter supports his argument most forcefully by referring to another key text written by Las Casas, *In Defense of the Indians* (1552; *Apologética historia summaria de las gentes destas Indias*), the document containing the arguments he employed in his dispute with Juan Ginés de Sepúlveda in what has become known as the Valladolid Debate of 1550–1551. This text evokes the Ottoman Turks, in particular, as an example of a people who consciously refuse to accept the Christian message. Brunstetter argues that Las Casas's "passing comments on the Turks and the Indians who refuse assimilation provide some indication of the limits he places on tolerating the Other that move beyond his initial and oft-heralded defense of the Indians" (2010, 413). Here, the evidence is already established: Turks and Moors, "the truly barbaric scum of the nations" (Las Casas 1552/1974, 47), will not convert.[19] Las Casas draws on popular strategies of vilifying the Turks and other Muslims: "The Turks and the Arabs … are an effeminate and luxury-loving people, given to every sort of sexual immorality. The Turks, in particular, do not consider impure and horrible vices worthy of punishment" (1552/1974, 51). In Las Casas's condemnation of the Turks lies the key evidence that significantly qualifies his support of Amerindians: acceptance of the Other is conditional and limited; it is based on the potential for conversion. If the Other refuses to accept our values, the limits of tolerance have been reached. In addition to cases of self-defence, Las Casas has no qualms about advocating violence against pagans, such as the Turks, Moors, and Saracens, "if they are maliciously, knowingly, and insultingly blasphemous toward Christ, the saints, or the Christian religion by speaking out of hatred and contempt for Christian truth" or if they "hinder the spread of the faith deliberately."[20]

We thus encounter in Las Casas's writings a profound tension; on the one hand, he advocates the recognition of American Indians as humans with rights to their own culture and even resistance. On the other hand, rights and tolerance are tied to the potential for conversion, and once the goals of conversion are thwarted, a hostile reaction betrays the limits of tolerance.

Luther and Las Casas

Reading Luther alongside Las Casas enables us to recognize a historical moment in which imperial violence against culturally and religiously different individuals and groups of peoples was theorized and redefined. At first reading, the contrast between the positions advocated by Luther and Las Casas could not be greater. While Luther argues for the use of state force in the context of an invasion, Las Casas argues against the use of state violence in the context of conquest. While Las Casas suggests that it is possible to view Amerindians on their own terms, Luther is not interested in considering Turks or Muslims or Jews as equal human beings. Luther's vilification of Turks as satanic and evil occludes any space of shared humanity; in contrast, Las Casas's defence of Native Americans theorizes the rights of non-European and non-Christian peoples vis-à-vis their invaders. While Las Casas does not give up on the Christianizing mission per se, the shift toward the recognition of a right to differential 'universal truths' seems fundamental. Luther could not be positioned farther from this kind of approach to cultural and religious difference. But the contrast between the two thinkers diminishes when we factor in the comments Las Casas made about Turks and other Muslims. The Ottoman Turks, reflecting the very real challenge they posed to Europe at the time, were not peaceful and meek like the Amerindians who appear in the accounts of the Spanish priest. Not only had they attacked Christian territory, but they had proven their disinterest in conversion to Christianity for centuries. Thus war against the Ottomans, unlike the war against Native Americans, was justified for Las Casas.

By addressing his ideas about how to engage with the Other to Charles V, the sovereign of the state, Las Casas paid tribute to the unquestioned role that imperial power had attained. While Luther was advocating the primacy of state power, the situation in the New World already reflected what he desired. As state power was clearly in charge of the conquest, an appeal to the pope would not have had the potential to bring about the kind of reforms that Las Casas envisioned. Yet state power was not secular; it had appropriated the ideological agenda of the Church, drawing on the ideological power and facilitating the goals of the Christian mission vis-à-vis the conquered Other through the state apparatus, including the Inquisition.

Both Luther and Las Casas appealed to the emperor, then the sovereign who would decide when and in what way the state would use violence. Placing Luther in the context of Europe's imperial expansion allows us to comprehend his writings as not so much visionary, but strategic interventions in his quest for state support for the Reformation. Las Casas struggled to achieve his missionary goal amidst the genocidal violence that deprived him of subjects who could be converted. Only the state, as the guarantor of the Christian mission, had the power to create the conditions necessary for conversion. Luther and Las Casas articulate distinct views on how to engage with the Other, ranging from tolerance to unconditional rejection. As distinct as their approaches are, however, both categorize the Other in relation to the idea of Christian salvation. They agree with regard to their disdain for Turks (Arabs, Moors, Saracens), which speaks to European enmity toward Islam over the *longue durée*.

Let me complicate the analysis of this multilayered situation by adding a final point. While Luther and Las Casas agreed with regard to their view of Turks and other Muslims, this apparent unity does not account for the spectrum of European *realpolitik* at the time. After all, the French, among others, were allied with the Ottomans against the Habsburg-Spanish axis (the political framework in which both Luther and Las Casas operated). This fact highlights even further that religious identity—the *communitas Christiana*—did not provide the unifying matrix for European powers in the early modern period (and, as suggested earlier, it had never been uncontested). Rather, political and economic interests, be they motivated by conquest or various alliances, determined the relationships between *distinct* European and non-European powers. But in the course of the next two centuries, as more and more European powers joined the colonial enterprise, conquest and colonization indeed became a unifying mode that determined Europe's relationship to the rest of the world. The texts by Luther and Las Casas highlight the ways in which these new ideas and practices about the use of imperial power and the changing role of Christianity were articulated at an early stage in this process.

Notes

1. In the German context, the Walk to Canossa, the Investiture Controversy, the Concordat of Worms, and the controversy between Emperor Frederick II and Pope Gregory IX over Frederick's participation in a crusade exemplify the power struggle between the Church and imperial power. The wars that were waged during the Middle Ages against heretical movements across Europe also defy the idea of a unified Christianity.
2. In a similar way the dynastic alliance between Habsburg and Bohemian rulers had also stabilized the region (see Gutkas 1984, 100). See also Fischer-Galati (1959) and Fodor and Dávid (2000).
3. One of the most eminent Ottoman sources covering the events of the period is Mustafa Celalzade's *Tabakat ül-Memalik*; see Kappert (1981) for a facsimile edition, with introduction, German-language summary, and notes.
4. Szakály (1985, 40). Regarding the treaties between Transylvania, Hungary, and the Ottomans, see Papp (2003).
5. For a summary of the events of 1529, see Düriegl (1979); for additional examples of gruesome Ottoman warfare practices, see Sutter Fichtner (2008), especially 42–58.
6. Walter Sturminger (1968) juxtaposes both German-language and Ottoman sources. See also von Hammer (1834), who wrote the earliest history of the Ottomans in the German language by drawing on Turkish sources. Sutter Fichtner (2008, 41) also states that European imagery of the Ottomans was "confirmed by contemporary Ottoman publicists themselves."
7. Inalcik (1994, 14); on military strategies and weapons of the Ottomans, see Yücel (1979).

8. The humanist Johann Cuspinian wrote: "Laßt euch nicht wankend machen durch die nichtige Versuchung eines gewissen jemand, der behauptet, gegen die Türken zu kämpfen heiße gegen Gott zu kämpfen" ("Do not allow yourself to waiver as a result of the futile tempation of a certain somebody who claims that to fight against the Turks would mean to fight against God"; Mau 1983, 649). See also Schillinger (2001, 41–42).

9. Regarding the genesis of Luther's essay and the history of reprints, see the introduction to "Vom Kriege wider die Türken" in Cohrs and Goetze (1909, 81–106).

10. Even as late as 1844, two-fifths of the inhabitants of the Ottoman empire were Christians and other non-Muslims, with higher figures for earlier periods, especially in European areas (Koç 2000, 545).

11. For the textual history of the essay, see the introduction to "Heerpredigt wider den Türken" in Cohrs and Goetze (1909, 149–159).

12. In this regard, my discussion challenges Bernard Lewis's argument that "Islamic religion was no longer feared as a serious rival" (1993, 73).

13. Ottoman sources often present the war by resorting to religious terminology; that is, the attempt to erase the internal complexities is also a trait of Ottoman commentators.

14. Heinrich Kábdebo (1876) lists 135 textual and visual representations of the first Siege and 341 such sources for the Second Siege of Vienna. The references include material composed in various European languages; the bibliography is followed by an appendix listing 71 coins referring to the sieges.

15. For a broader discussion of religious arguments voiced in pamphlets, broadsheets, single-leaf woodcuts, and book sections, see Kaufmann (2008).

16. For a more detailed discussion of Luther's writings, see Berman (2005); see also Adam Francisco's *Martin Luther and Islam* (2007), which approaches Luther's writings on Islam primarily from a theological perspective.

17. Clayton (2012, 56–62, 272–277) discusses Montesino and other clerics and scholars who held views similar to those articulated by Las Casas.

18. Knight (2003, xlii–xliv) summarizes the scholarly discussion of figures regarding population density and the impact of conquest.

19. Tzvetan Todorov, whose nuanced discussion of Las Casas precedes Brunstetter and other critics by decades, wrote: "[W]e may note in passing that Las Casas never shows the slightest tenderness toward the Muslims" (1984, 166).

20. Las Casas (1552/1974, 165, 168; see also 183–184). Daniel R. Brunstetter and Dana Zartner (2011, 749) turn to Las Casas in an essay about the relevance of the Valladolid Debate with regard to the concept of *jus ad bellum*. The authors argue that Las Casas's positions with regard to just war have to be acknowledged as a considerable improvement in their historical context, especially in terms of his warning against wars that are "draped in moral universals and humanitarian imperatives."

Works Cited

Ágoston, Gábor. 1999. "Ottoman Warfare in Europe, 1453–1826." *European Warfare, 1453–1815*, edited by Jeremy Black, 118–144. New York: St. Martin's Press.

Berman, Nina. 2005. "Ottoman Shock-and-Awe and the Rise of Protestantism: Luther's Reactions to the Ottoman Invasions of the Early Sixteenth Century."

Reassessing Orientalism in German Studies. Ed. Friederike Eigler. Special issue, *Seminar* 41 (3): 226–245.

Berman, Nina. 2011. *German Literature on the Middle East: Discourses and Practices, 1000–1989.* Ann Arbor: University of Michigan Press.

Bisaha, Nancy. 2004. *Creating East and West: Renaissance Humanists and the Ottoman Turks.* Philadelphia: University of Pennsylvania Press.

Brunstetter, Daniel R. 2010. "Sepúlveda, Las Casas, and the Other: Exploring the Tension between Moral Universalism and Alterity." *The Review of Politics* 72: 409–435.

Brunstetter, Daniel R., and Dana Zartner. 2011. "Just War against Barbarians: Revisiting the Valladolid Debates between Sepúlveda and Las Casas." *Political Studies* 59: 733–752.

Buchmann, Bertrand Michael. 1999. *Österreich und das Osmanische Reich: Eine bilaterale Geschichte.* Vienna: WUV-Universitätsverlag.

Castro, Daniel. 2007. *Another Face of Empire: Bartolomé de Las Casas, Indigenous Rights, and Ecclesiastical Imperialism.* Durham, NC: Duke University Press.

Clayton, Lawrence A. 2012. *Bartolomé de las Casas: A Biography.* New York: Cambridge University Press.

Cohrs, F., and A. Goetze. 1909. Introduction to "Vom Kriege wider die Türken." *D. Martin Luthers Werke: Kritische Gesamtausgabe.* Vol. 30.2, 81–106. Weimar: Hermann Böhlaus Nachfolger.

de Behrens, Marianela Ponce, and Letizia Vaccari de Venturini. 1977. *Los Welser.* Caracas: Academia Nacional de la Historia.

Düriegl, Günter. 1979. "Die erste Türkenbelagerung." *Wien 1529: Die erste Türkenbelagerung*, edited by Günter Düriegl, 7–33. Vienna: Böhlau.

Dussel, Enrique. 2013. "Las Casas, Vitoria and Suarez, 1514–1617." Translated by James Terry. *Human Rights from a Third World Perspective: Critique, History, and International Law*, edited by José-Manuel Barreto, 172–207. Newcastle upon Tyne: Cambridge Scholars.

Fischer-Galati, Stephen A. 1956. "Ottoman Imperialism and the Religious Peace of Nürnberg." *Archiv für Reformationsgeschichte* 47 (2): 160–180.

Fischer-Galati, Stephen A. 1959. *Ottoman Imperialism and German Protestantism, 1521–1555.* Cambridge, MA: Harvard University Press.

Fodor, Pál. 2000. "Making a Living on the Frontiers: Volunteers in the Sixteenth-Century Ottoman Army." *Ottomans, Hungarians, and Habsburgs in Central Europe: The Military Confines in the Era of Ottoman Conquest*, edited by Géza Dávid and Pál Fodor, 229–263. Leiden: Brill.

Fodor, Pál, and Géza Dávid, eds. 2000. *Ottomans, Hungarians, and Habsburgs in Central Europe: The Military Confines in the Era of Ottoman Conquest.* Leiden: Brill.

Francisco, Adam S. 2007. *Martin Luther and Islam: A Study in Sixteenth-Century Polemics and Apologetics.* Leiden: Brill.

Göllner, Carl. 1961/1968. *Turcica: Die europäischen Türkendrucke des XVI. Jahrhunderts.* Vols. 1 & 2. Bucharest: Editura Academiei.

Göllner, Carl. 1978. *Turcica III: Die Türkenfrage in der öffentlichen Meinung Europas im 16. Jahrhundert.* Bucharest: Editura Academiei.

Gutkas, Karl. 1984. *Geschichte Niederösterreichs.* Munich: Oldenbourg.

Imber, Colin. 2002. *The Ottoman Empire, 1300–1650.* New York: Palgrave Macmillan.

Inalcik, Halil, ed. 1994. *An Economic and Social History of the Ottoman Empire,
1300–1914.* Vol. 1. Cambridge: Cambridge University Press.
Kábdebo, Heinrich. 1876. *Bibliographie zur Geschichte der beiden Türkenbelagerungen
Wien's.* Vienna: Faesy and Frick.
Kappert, Petra. 1981. *Geschichte Sultan Süleyman Kanunis von 1520 bis 1557.*
Wiesbaden: Franz Steiner.
Kaufmann, Thomas. 2008. *"Türckenbüchlein": Zur christlichen Wahrnehmung
"türkischer Religion" in Spätmittelalter und Reformation.* Göttingen: Vandenhoeck
& Ruprecht.
Kissling, Hans Joachim. 1964. "Türkenfurcht und Türkenhoffnung im 15./16.
Jahrhundert: Zur Geschichte eines 'Komplexes'." *Südost-Forschungen* 23: 1–18.
Knight, Franklin W. 2003. "Introduction." Bartolomé de las Casas. *An Account,
Much Abbreviated, of the Destruction of the Indies.* Trans. Andrew Hurley.
Edited by Franklin W. Knight, xi–l. Indianapolis, IN: Hackett.
Koç, Yunus. 2000. "The Structure of the Population of the Ottoman Empire
(1300–1900)." *The Great Ottoman-Turkish Civilization,* edited by Kemal Çiçek,
Ercüment Kuran, Nejat Güyünç, and İlber Ortaylı, 531–548. Vol. 2. Ankara:
Semih Ofset.
Kreutel, Richard F., ed. and trans. 1959. *Vom Hirtenzelt zur hohen Pforte: Frühzeit
und Aufstieg des Osmanenreiches nach der Chronik ›Denkwürdigkeiten und
Zeitläufe des Hauses 'Osman‹ vom Derwisch Ahmed, genannt 'Aşik-Paşa-Sohn.*
Graz: Styria.
Kreutel, Richard F., ed. and trans. 1978. *Der fromme Sultan Bayezid: Die Geschichte
seiner Herrschaft (1481–1512) nach den altosmanischen Chroniken des Oruç
und des Anonymus Hanivaldanus.* Graz: Styria.
Kreutel, Richard F., ed. and trans. 1982. *Kara Mustafa vor Wien: 1683 aus der Sicht
türkischer Quellen.* Rev. ed., ed. Karl Teply. Graz: Styria.
Las Casas, Bartolomé de. 1552/1974. *In Defense of the Indians.* Trans., ed., and
annotated by Stafford Poole. DeKalb: Northern Illinois University Press.
Las Casas, Bartolomé de. 1552/2003. *An Account, Much Abbreviated, of the
Destruction of the Indies.* Trans. Andrew Hurley. Ed. Franklin W. Knight. Indi-
anapolis, IN: Hackett.
Lewis, Bernard. 1993. *Islam and the West.* New York: Oxford University Press.
Luther, Martin. 1529/1909. "Heerpredigt wider den Türken." *D. Martin Luthers
Werke: Kritische Gesamtausgabe.* Vol. 30.2, 160–197. Weimar: Hermann Böhlaus
Nachfolger.
Luther, Martin. 1529/1909. "Vom Kriege wider die Türken." *D. Martin Luthers
Werke: Kritische Gesamtausgabe.* Vol. 30.2, 107–148. Weimar: Hermann Böhlaus
Nachfolger.
Mau, Rudolf. 1983. "Luthers Stellung zu den Türken." *Leben und Werk Martin
Luthers von 1526 bis 1546: Festgabe zu seinem 500. Geburtstag.* Vol. 2. Edited by
Helmar Junghans, 647–662, 957–966. Göttingen: Vandenhoeck und Ruprecht.
Mertens, Dieter. 1997. "'Europa, id est patria, domus propria, sedes nostra …': Zu
Funktionen und Überlieferung lateinischer Türkenreden im 15. Jahrhundert."
Europa und die osmanische Expansion im ausgehenden Mittelalter, edited by
Franz-Reiner Erkens, 39–57. Berlin: Dunker and Humblot.
Murphey, Rhoads. 1999. *Ottoman Warfare, 1500–1700.* New Brunswick, NJ:
Rutgers University Press.

Netanyahu, Benzion. 1995. *The Origins of the Inquisition in Fifteenth Century Spain*. New York: Random House.

Nicolle, David. 1983. *Armies of the Ottoman Turks, 1300–1774*. Oxford: Osprey.

Pagden, Anthony. 2003. "Human Rights, Natural Rights, and Europe's Imperial Legacy." *Political Theory* 31 (2): 171–199.

Papp, Sándor. 2003. *Die Verleihungs-, Bekräftigungs- und Vertragsurkunden der Osmanen für Ungarn und Siebenbürgen: Eine quellenkritische Untersuchung*. Vienna: Verlag der Österreichischen Akademie der Wissenschaften.

Pratt, Mary Louise. 1992. *Imperial Eyes: Travel Writing and Transculturation*. London: Routledge.

Rand Parish, Helen, with Harold E. Weidman, S.J. 1976. "The Correct Birthdate of Bartolomé de las Casas." *Hispanic American Historical Review* 56 (3): 385–403.

Roa-de-la-Carrera, Cristián. 2010. "El 'Indio' como categoría antropológica en la *Apologética Historia Sumaria* de Fray Bartolomé de las Casas." *Confluencia* 25 (2): 81–93.

Said, Edward. 1978. *Orientalism*. New York: Pantheon Books.

Schillinger, Jean. 2001. "Le Saint-Empire face à la menace ottoman (1526–1568)." *Luther et la Réforme, 1525–1555: Le temps de la consolidation religieuse et politique*, edited by Jean-Paul Cahn and Gérard Schneilin, 33–47. Paris: Éditions du Temps.

Schmidt, Georg. 1999. *Geschichte des Alten Reiches: Staat und Nation in der Frühen Neuzeit, 1495–1806*. Munich: Beck.

Schmitt, Eberhard. 2008. *Die Welser in Venezuela, 1529–1546*. Braunschweig: Archiv.

Sturminger, Walter. 1968. *Die Türken vor Wien in Augenzeugenberichten*. Düsseldorf: Rauch.

Sutter Fichtner, Paula. 2008. *Terror and Toleration: The Habsburg Empire Confronts Islam, 1526–1850*. London: Reaction Books.

Szakály, Ferenc. 1985. "Der Wandel Ungarns in der Türkenzeit." *Habsburgisch-osmanische Beziehungen: Beihefte zur Wiener Zeitschrift für die Kunde des Morgenlandes*. Vol. 13. Ed. Andreas Tietze, 35–54. Vienna: Verlag des Verbandes der wissenschaftlichen Gesellschaften Österreichs.

Todorov, Tzvetan. 1984. *The Conquest of America: The Question of the Other*. Translated by Richard Howard. New York: HarperPerennial.

von Hammer, Joseph. 1834. *Geschichte des Osmanischen Reiches*. Vol. 2. Pest: Hartleben.

von Khevenhiller, Franz Christoph Graf. 1722. *Annalium Ferdinandeorum*. Vol. 5. Leipzig: Moritz Georg Weidmann.

"Warhafftige handlung / wie vnd welcher massen der Tuerck die Stat Ofen vnd Wien belegert / Erstlich durch Koen. Mayt. zu Hungern und Behem / u. Kriegs Secretari / Herrn Peter Stern von Labach kuertzlich begriffen vnd beschrieben / Nachfolgend durch Nicolaum Meldeman / Bürger zu Nuernberg / mit merer anzeigung / was von tag zu tag sich zugetragen hat / aus angeben deren / so von anfang mit vnd dabei gewesen sind / gemehrt vnd erlengert / im Jahr 1530." No. 1 in 4 Hist. Turc. 712, Göttingen. This volume of Turcica includes 56 broadsheets in quarto format. The first printing dates from 1530, the last from 1717.

Yücel, Ünsal. 1979. "Türkische Kriegführung und Waffen." *Wien 1529: Die erste Türkenbelagerung*, edited by Günter Düriegl, 107–121. Vienna: Böhlau.

8 Saxon Agonistes
Reconstructing and Deconstructing Identities in Milton's *History of Britain*

Willy Maley

In the preface to his *Novum Organum* (1620), Francis Bacon (1561–1626) compares time to a river "which has brought down to us things light and puffed up, while those … weighty and solid have sunk" (Rossi 1996, 40). One such weighty object is John Milton's *History of Britain* (1670). At 95,000 words the longest prose work Milton published in his lifetime, encompassing over a thousand years from founding myths through the Roman invasion and occupation to the Norman Conquest, the *History of Britain* is a formidable text. Its title was drawn out by a subtitle: "That part especially now call'd ENGLAND. From the first traditional beginning continued to the Norman Conquest. Collected out of the Ancientest and Best Authors thereof." The word 'ENGLAND' on the title page is a good half-size taller than 'BRITAIN.' Moreover, the running header throughout reads: "The History of England." Its six books deal, respectively, with pre-Roman history from Brutus to the coming of Caesar, Roman conquest and colonization, post-Roman Britain and the coming of the Saxons, Saxon hegemony, the invasions of the Danes, and finally the coming of the Normans. One of the most significant works on British history, this remarkable text has implications for our understanding of the act of writing a national history that is always also a European and world history. It bears witness to the ways in which a great poet embarked upon a patriotic journey, found little to celebrate along the way, and ended by appealing to foreign writings, lessons learned, and shared wisdom as the answer to establishing liberty.

I first encountered *The History of Britain* as a PhD student working on Edmund Spenser and Ireland 30 years ago. Intrigued that Milton had written a British history, I expected it to enrich my understanding of Spenser, since I knew Milton had read that author's *A View of the Present State of Ireland*, first published in 1633. I found that Milton's narrative, despite his commitment in *The Second Defense of the English People* (1654) to undertake "a history of the nation from its remotest origin; intending to bring it down, if I could, in one unbroken thread to our own times," ends abruptly at 1066 (*CPW* 8: 137). The exception is the so-called "Digression," a 2,500-word posthumously published section of Book III—*Mr John Milton's Character of the Long Parliament and Assembly of Divines in 1641* (1681)—that links the fifth and seventeenth centuries, as the Britons' failure to choose liberty after the Romans becomes the failure of Milton's contemporaries to sustain their commitment to the English republic. In each case, political backsliding—inviting in the Saxons and submitting to another colonization, and permitting a restored monarchy to supplant the short-lived commonwealth—saw a chance of freedom spurned. Arguments around the dating of the "Digression"—estimates vary from 1649 (Dzelzainis 2008; von Maltzahn 1993) to 1659–1660 (Morrill 1994; Woolrych 1993)—divert attention from the *History* as a whole. Milton's elaborate reworking of European origin myths in the context of a radical reshaping of the British state can be seen as the high point, or tipping point, of ideas about early modern nation-formation.

Milton's *History of Britain* aids our understanding of early modern Europe beyond its allegorical implications or the direct analogy between seventeenth-century political crisis and fifth-century postcolonial hiatus drawn in the "Digression." The *History* remains a rich resource for understanding early modern European nationalisms, informed by anticolonialism, humanism, and republicanism. Milton's history is grounded in Britain's complex interaction with the Continent. The basis for English national identity is not European descent but a biblical narrative originating outside Europe. Milton's story has intercontinental origins and ends in an appeal that transcends nationalist histories. Milton opens with "the Flood, and the dispersing of Nations, as they journey'd leisurely from the East" (8), and closes by asserting that "as Wine and Oyl are Imported to us from abroad: so must ripe Understanding, and many civil Vertues, be imported into our minds from Foreign Writings, and examples of best Ages" (1681, 10). Milton's constant refrain is that the repeated cycles of invasion and occupation that beset Britain favoured ruling elites, with the clergy and monarchy key beneficiaries in an unsettled state.

Having sacrificed his sight writing in defence of the English people in the 1650s, only to see the hated monarchy restored, Milton, writing to his German friend Peter Heimbach on August 15, 1666, four years prior to the publication of the *History of Britain*, complained that England, "[a]fter captivating me with her fair-sounding name, has almost left me without a country" (Zagorin 1992, 123). Yet Milton had made it his mission to memorialize the achievements of his country, even as he acknowledged the enormity of the task. In the conclusion to his *Second Defense of the English People* (1654), Milton, defending the killing of the king as "one of the heroic actions of my countrymen," asked, "who could do justice to all the great actions of an entire people?" (*CPW* 8: 252–253). But what if their actions fell short of greatness? Milton did not extend his narrative "in one unbroken thread to our own times" (*CPW* 8: 137). What we have runs from Brutus to William the Conqueror. Moreover, Milton found "little to cheer in Saxon history and culture" (von Maltzahn 1991, 197). If in the anticlerical tracts of the 1640s, the major republican texts of 1649, and the two *Defenses* of the 1650s, Milton appealed to ancient English liberties to spur his contemporaries into heroic action, in the *History* he searches in vain for the seeds of liberty.

Milton alluded in one of his earliest prose works, *The Reason of Church Government* (1642), to the task of nation writing:

> that what the greatest and choycest wits of Athens, Rome, or modern Italy, and those Hebrews of old did for their country, I ... might doe for mine: not caring to be once nam'd abroad ... but content with these British Ilands as my world, whose fortune hath hitherto bin, that if the Athenians ... made their small deeds great and renowned by their eloquent writers, England hath had her noble atchievments made small by the unskilfull handling of monks and mechanicks.
>
> (*CPW* 1: 811–812)

Milton's own excavations into British history undermined his patriotic purpose. His research altered his intention. In his commonplace book in the late 1630s Milton declared that his history would have as one of its targets the 'Norman Yoke,' a familiar source of resentment in the seventeenth century (Hill 1958): "Alfred turn'd the old laws into english. ... I would he liv'd now to rid us of this norman gibbrish" (*CPW* 1: 424). According to Matthew McCrady, "Milton's negative attitude towards the pre-Saxon British people, as well as his attitude towards the Anglo-Saxons themselves, for whom he saves his sharpest barbs, can best be explained as a critique of a popular seventeenth-century notion called the Norman Yoke theory" (McCrady 1999, 31). After the Reformation, "the Norman Conquest took on added significance as ecclesiastical historians looked to discover the origins of the Roman tyranny over the English Church" (von Maltzahn 1991, 185). Since Milton found tyranny in the English Church in his own time, his anticlericalism stopped him from sharing in celebrations of ancient Saxon liberty.

Milton's refusal to sign up to the myth of a Saxon Golden Age before the Norman Yoke makes his *History* appear unpatriotic. Critics have agonized over Milton's approach to his country's past, one that finds few redeeming features. Gary Hamilton remarks of Milton's enterprise: "If Samson is Milton's fantasy of having made a difference in the world, the *History* shows the author himself ... tugging at the pillars" (Hamilton 1990, 253). Most Miltonists find the *History* disappointing, but some dissenting voices find comedy and irony in the invective. Milton's contemporaries harked back to a golden age prior to the Norman Conquest. Conversely, Milton felt himself and his country to be struggling under a double yoke, Saxon and Norman, and his dismantling of English—and British—history put him out of step with most of his contemporaries.

In writing the *History*, Milton went against the grain of established authorities. William Camden's *Remains Concerning Britain* and Richard Verstegan's *A Restitution of Decayed Intelligence*, both published in 1605, located English origins in the Saxon period. In *Of Reformation* (1641) Milton speaks sarcastically of "*Camden*, who cannot but love Bishops, as well as old coins, and his much lamented Monasteries for antiquities sake" (Milton 1641, 17). According to Graham Parry, "uniquely among seventeenth-century writers, Milton did not want to write a history that was patriotic and hopeful" (Parry 1996, 246). Why should patriotism and hope be yoked together? Milton refused to accept evidence that vindicated bishops and kings. His sceptical stance towards sources is salutary. He regarded the writings of "monks and mechanicks" with suspicion bordering on contempt. It has been suggested that the *History of Britain* "may tell us more of the seventeenth century than it does of pre-Conquest England" (Fogle 1965, 17). In fact, I will suggest that it may tell us more about the twenty-first century than the seventeenth.

Milton's *History* reminds us of a persistent paradox of modern Britain, namely, that an imperial monarchy and former world power remains deeply Eurosceptic, both insular and expansionist. Despite his anti-Catholic stance, Milton acknowledges that the origins of civility—of 'history' as such—lie with Rome, and he concludes by proposing "Foreign Writings" (Milton 1681, 10) as key to future liberation. By contrast, Milton's depiction of key figures in the formation of Britain, mythical and actual, is scathing. He undermines the icons and idols of Saxonist and British mythmakers: Brutus, Boadicea, Arthur, and Harold.

Critics are deeply divided on Milton's status as an historian. Some are sympathetic. For one critic, Milton's *History* "is a work of learning and originality, worthy to be remembered in any account of the development of historical writing in England" (Firth 1938, 61). For another, "[t]he critical, sceptical spirit dominates the *History of Britain* from beginning to end" (French 1935, 472). This assessment contrasts sharply with Graham Parry's claim that Milton gets caught up in myth:

> By ignoring Camden and Selden's studies of ancient British society, Milton forfeits the right to be considered a serious historian by his educated readers. Milton's sources are all the medieval chroniclers who, by the 1640s, were suspect or discredited as reporters of the earliest times. He makes no use of contemporary scholarship about British antiquity ... but uses instead Geoffrey of Monmouth, Henry of Huntingdon, Matthew of Westminster, and Holinshed.
>
> (Parry 1996, 240)

Some admirers redeem the text by calling it a 'poetical history.' Andrew Escobedo sees Milton working at "the delicate border between history and poetry": "As a national historian Milton wants to free himself of the falseness of poetry but also regrets giving up poetry's inventiveness" (Escobedo 2004, 200). Spenser in his letter to Raleigh and Sidney in his *Apology for Poetry* privilege poetry above history, and their arguments render Milton more poetic than historical. For Spenser, "a Poet thrusteth into the middest, even where it most concerneth him" (Spenser 1590–1596/2007, 716–717). The "Digression" shows Milton doing exactly this. Sidney envisages the historian "better acquainted with a thousand years ago than with the present age … curious for antiquities and inquisitive of novelties" (Sidney 1595/2002, 89). Milton's wariness about sources and insistence on applying accrued wisdom to the present show him to be in tune with Sidney's argument.

David Underdown upbraids Milton's *History* for its aversion to *realpolitik*, maintaining that "we encounter a Milton more at home in the Latin culture of the intellectuals than in the muddy waters of political reality" (Underdown 1994, 212). For Milton, Latin is a basis for European identity, the universal language of learning in which to address an elite audience, but also a language out of which his own engagement with English emerges, in which he conveys to continental readers the particularities of his nation. He is more at home in the "muddy waters of political reality" than Underdown allows, and nowhere more so than in his insistence that the Norman Yoke was neither the first nor last imposition of tyranny upon his nation.

One editor of the *History* hails it as "the most unified, condensed, and continuous narrative of pre-Conquest England that had yet appeared" (Fogle 1971, xlviii), while another critic directs would-be readers to the epic poetry that bookends the British history: "For the infinitely richer and more deeply pondered reflections of his experience of defeat, one reads between the lines of his great epics" (Woolrych 1986, 246). And while some accept Milton's historical analogies—"Britons, Saxons, Milton's contemporaries: the continuities in the national character had been established in the Digression" (Von Maltzahn 1991, 189)—others are confused as to whose side the poet-historian is on:

> Milton will refer to Anglo-Saxon history as "our own Annals" in comparison with "Danish History" … by then, the "Britans" have devolved into the "Welch." Milton concludes his *History* by gesturing to "misery and thraldom to those our ancestors"—here clearly referring to the Saxons—at the hands of the Normans. … Exactly whose history is being portrayed remains a central problem of definition throughout Milton's work.
>
> (Jenkins 1999, 314)

According to Graham Parry, Gildas, the sixth-century author Milton admires most, is crucial to Milton's pessimistic perspective in his own account of the post-Roman period:

> So completely did Milton commit himself to Gildas's dark perspective on the Britons that he lost sight of the fact that the Britons of the fifth

century had really no connection to the English of the seventeenth century whom he was so eager to castigate. ... The Britons had been reduced so effectively by the Saxons, and driven into a corner of the island, into Wales, that they could be largely ignored in the analysis of English characters and institutions. Our true progenitors in all things that mattered—language, religion, institutions, and government— were the Saxons.

(Parry 1996, 242–243)

Parry's own critical view, in which Wales is "a corner of the island," is less convincing than Milton's more nuanced perspective. If, as Ivan Roots suggests, "[t]he *History* is not a source likely to be cited as authoritative in any modern survey of pre-Conquest England" (Roots 1994, 114), then that is unfortunate, given the rise of racialized theories of Anglo-Saxonism in the nineteenth century (Baldwin 1943; Horsman 1976; Reynolds 1985). Moreover, to see Milton's *History* as confined to 'pre-Conquest England' is to take a limited view of the poet's project. John Shawcross tells us that "the nineteenth century saw Milton as a significant historian, one who cast aside the theories of the past in order to reexamine the past through his own point of view, but at the same time as an imperfect historian, one whose attention to the demands of history and to details was at best temporary" (Shawcross 1974, 342–343). My own view is that Milton's vision is more far-reaching, making his critique of national origins pressingly relevant today, precisely because the most profound patriotism lies in taking a hard look at the past of one's own nation, warts and all. Indeed, Cromwell's famous request to be painted "warts and all" is how Milton came to see British history—not pretty to look at, but better viewed in all its gory glory than glossed over by fakery and flattery (Knoppers 2000, 80).

Arguably the most decisive site of conflict in the *History* is Milton's attitude to sources and in particular his attitude to Saxons. Nicholas von Maltzahn puts it thus:

The final three books of the *History* cover the period from the Saxon invasions to the Norman Conquest. They have often disappointed students of Milton. Early, the Whig readers of the *History* found these books curiously silent on the subject of Saxon glories. Whigs hoped for more on those Saxon institutions of Law and Parliament which might be invoked against royalist historical claims. But Milton had failed to present any account of the ancient constitution that might satisfy their emerging interpretation of history.

(von Maltzahn 1991, 166)

Milton failed to conform to developing historiographical practices or to provide patriotic milestones that could be seized on to plot a future. Rather, he found a way forward, as we shall see, outside of history.

Milton's anti-Saxonism, like his anti-antiquarianism—both amounted to the same thing—makes him an anomaly. Critics express relief that Milton's chosen topic for his epic poem was the Fall and not the epic failures of his once beloved but now tarnished Britain: "As an expression of patriotism, he started but never completed *The History of Britain*, a deadly compendium of factoids, and I for one am grateful that he was distracted by another project" (Von Sneidern 2005, 18). Yet to suggest Milton's *History* is "a deadly compendium of factoids" is a restricted view, and surprising coming from a critic preoccupied with colonial themes. David Armitage calls Milton a "poet against empire," viewing *Paradise Lost* as "an epic of empire" that tells "the story of Satan's colonization of the New World" (Armitage 1995, 216). There is evidence of Milton's anti-imperialist stance in his *History*, where successive invasions and occupations are viewed as obstacles to civility, but two qualifying comments must be made in this regard. The first is that Milton's anticolonial rhetoric does not extend to Rome, which remains a positive example of a civilizing colonial experience: "of the *Romans* we have cause not to say much worse, than that they beate us into som civilitie; likely else to have continu'd longer in a barbarous and savage manner of life" (60). The second related point is that for Milton the real enemy is incivility, "whether forren or native," which is why civil broils attract his anger as much as invasions: "For looke how much right the King of *Spaine* hath to govern us at all, so much right hath the King of *England* to govern us tyrannically" (Milton 1649, 19).

Milton dealt harshly with the ancient Britons, who, having failed to be fully civilized by the Romans, promptly lapsed into luxury and license with their departure, but if the Britons were "Progenitors not to be glori'd in" (60), the Saxons were worse. Nicholas von Maltzahn remarks that Milton's "reliance on published sources and use of Latin translations for all medieval annals, histories, and laws argues his unfamiliarity with the language of some of their originals" (von Maltzahn 1991, 195). Yet Milton's unfamiliarity with the original language of his sources did not prevent him from being critical. Milton's *History* may be derivative, but it is also iconoclastic.

In the third book of the *History*, Milton famously pairs the fifth and seventeenth centuries. The Britons, between Roman exit and Saxon entry, enjoy a brief breathing space but abuse the peace they have. Besieged, they invite in the Saxons, putting the fox in charge of the henhouse:

> Wherein by advice of all it was determin'd, that the *Saxons* be invited into *Britan* against the *Scots* and *Picts*. ... The *Saxons* were a barbarous and heathen Nation, famous for nothing else but robberies and cruelties done to all thir Neighbours both by Sea and Land; in particular to this Iland, witness that military force which the *Roman* Emperors maintain'd heer purposely against them, under a special Commander, whose title, as is found, on good record, was Count of the *Saxon* shoar in *Britan*. (129)

Milton views the Saxons from a Roman perspective, not from the vantage point of his own contemporaries, those English antiquarians who sought a positive post-Roman—and postcolonial—image of the past. Milton's genealogy ties the Saxons to the Scythians who Spenser claimed were the source of Irish barbarism (Hadfield 1993), and whom Christopher Marlowe depicted in the foreboding figure of:

> the Scythian Tamburlaine
> Threat'ning the world with high astounding terms
> And scourging kingdoms with his conquering sword.
> (Cunningham and Henson 1998, 41)

According to Milton, the Saxons "were a people thought by good Writers, to be descended of the *Sacæ*, a kind of *Scythian* in the North of *Asia*, thence call'd *Sacasons*, or Sons of *Sacæ*, who with a Flood of other Northern Nations came into *Europe*, toward the declining of the *Roman* Empire" (129). It is here that Milton makes the comparison between the coming of the Saxons and the inability of his contemporaries to seize their own liberty:

> Such guests as these the *Britans* resolve now to send for, and entreat into thir houses and possessions, at whose very name heertofore they trembl'd afar off. So much do men through impatience count ever that the heaviest which they bear at present, and to remove the evil which they suffer, care not to pull on a greater: as if variety and change in evil also were acceptable. Or whether it be that men in the despair of better, imagine fondly a kind of refuge from one misery to another. (130)

No sooner were the Saxons in the door than they allied themselves with the marauding Picts and Scots against whom they were supposed to be defending the Britons. In due course, the Saxons are at "continual War either with *English, Welch, Picts,* or *Scots*" (165), and soon lording it "over all the fowr *British* Nations, *Angles, Britans, Picts* and *Scots*, exerciseing Regal Authority" (182). Indeed, the Saxons prove a scourge for the Romanized Britons, who in this scenario are the English, or Angles, as opposed to their British brethren, the Welsh, or their Northern neighbours, the Picts: "[The Saxons] on the other side making League with the *Picts* and *Scots*, and issuing out of *Kent*, wasted without resistance almost the whole Land eev'n to the Western Sea, with such a horrid devastation, that Towns and Colonies overturn'd, Priests and People slain, Temples and Palaces, what with Fire and Sword lay altogether heaped in one mixt ruin" (134).

Milton's criticism of the Saxons extends to the supposed Arthur of the Britons who fought them: "But who *Arthur* was, and whether ever any such reign'd in *Britan*, hath bin doubted heertofore, and may again with good reason" (144). Milton not only doubts Arthur's existence but in an interesting amendment to an earlier comment about the Britons being fighters at home rather than abroad, he adds: "Surely *Artur* much better had made War in old *Saxony*, to repress thir flowing hither, than to have won Kingdoms as far as *Russia*, scarce able heer to defend his own" (148). This amendment is interesting because Milton here points out that foreign wars without purpose are as damaging as civil wars. Arthur should have taken the struggle to the Saxons.

Milton sums up the Saxon reign in the most unflattering terms:

> Thir actions we read of, were most commonly Wars, but for what cause wag'd, or by what Counsells carried on, no care was had to let us know: wherby thir strength and violence we understand, of their wisdom, reason, or justice little or nothing, the rest superstition and monastical affectation; Kings one after another leaving thir Kingly Charge, to run thir heads fondly into a Monk's Cowle. (202)

Here, Milton's anticlericalism goes in step with his antimonarchism. The clergy and the monarchy are to blame for the lack of good governance that leads to dissolution. The skirmishes that scarred the Saxon period leave Milton cold: "such bickerings to recount, met oft'n in these our Writers, what more worth is it than to Chronicle the Warrs of Kites, or Crows, flocking and fighting in the Air?" (217). Two bald men fighting over a comb, that sums up the supposed Saxon Golden Age in Milton's eyes. Even a much-vaunted union fails to bring with it peace and plenty, "the lesser Kingdoms revolting from the *West-Saxon* yoke" (223), so that the country is once more open to invasion, and expectations of "the flourishing of all Estates and Degrees" (222) are dashed. The reign of King Egbert promised peace and unity,

> but far the contrary fell out soon after, Invasion, Spoil, Desolation, slaughter of many, slavery of the rest, by the forcible landing of a fierce Nation; *Danes* commonly call'd, and somtimes *Dacians*, by others, the same with *Normans*; as barbarous as the Saxons themselves were at first reputed, and much more; for the Saxons first invited came hither to dwell; these unsent for, unprovok'd, came only to destroy. But if the *Saxons*, as is above related, came most of them from Jutland and *Anglen*, a part of *Denmark*, as *Danish* writers affirm, and that *Danes* and *Normans* are the same; then in this Invasion, *Danes* drove out *Danes*, thir own Posterity. And *Normans* afterwards, none but Ancienter *Normans*. (222–223)

Here, Milton deconstructs 'British' history by drawing attention to the complex pattern of invasions and occupations that mark it, which emanate from those very parts of Europe in which earlier waves of invasion and occupation originated. Milton's jeremiad against his own nation—rooted in his understanding of the cyclical nature of history and the tendency for misgoverned nations to fall into decline and become prey to invasion and occupation—is founded in anger at its dependence upon despots, domestic and foreign:

> But when God hath decreed servitude on a sinful Nation, fitted by thir own Vices for no condition but servile, all Estates of Government are alike unable to avoid it. God had purpos'd to punish our instrumental punishers, though now Christians, by other Heathen, according to his Divine retaliation; Invasion for invasion, spoil for spoil, destruction for destruction. The *Saxons* were now full as wicked as the *Britans* were at thir arrival, brok'n with luxury and sloth, either secular or superstitious; for laying aside the exercise of Arms, and the study of all vertuous Knowledge, som betook them to over-worldly or vicious Practice, others to Religious Idleness and Solitude, which brought forth nothing but vain and delusive Visions. (223–224)

The Saxon Yoke precedes the Norman Yoke, and just as the benighted Britons erred in inviting in their Saxon conquerors, so the slothful Saxons deserved their comeuppance at the hands of their Norman conquerors. This is the state of affairs when Harold sits on the throne, on the eve of the Norman Conquest. After a brief rehearsal of Harold's alleged qualities, curtly dismissed as mere manipulation—"so good an actor is ambition" (347)—Milton leaves us with a vision of England in a state of dissolution:

> Whence it came to pass, that carried on with fury and rashness more than any true fortitude or skill of War, they gave to *William* their Conquerour so easie a Conquest. ... If these were the Causes of such Misery and Thraldom to those our Ancestors, with what better close can be Concluded, than here in fit season to remember this Age in the midst of her Security, to fear from like Vices without amendment the Revolution of like Calamities. (357)

As in the fifth century when the Romans left and the Saxons entered, so in the eleventh century the Norman Yoke supplants the Saxon one. Another chance of freedom lost to an invader. Will the Britons of the seventeenth century likewise let their chance of liberty slip by? As Matthew Binney observes, after reading Milton's accounts of the rise and fall of nations, "it becomes clearer why in *Paradise Lost* Milton places much more stress upon governance of the self, rather than the state. Although Milton traces a hierarchy within nature, its influence is circumscribed extensively by people's critical capacity to reason and the laws of nature" (Binney 2010, 45). A nation's self-determination depends on its inhabitants' level of self-governance. This is why in *Areopagitica* (1644) Milton cited Spenser's Knight of Temperance in the Bower of Bliss episode of *The Faerie Queene* Book II as a model of self-restraint. Milton's verdict on Guyon could stand sentry over the *History of Britain*:

> Since therefore the knowledge and survay of vice is in this world so necessary to the constituting of human vertue, and the scanning of error to the confirmation of truth, how can we more safely, and with lesse danger scout into the regions of sin and falsity then by reading all manner of tracts, and hearing all manner of reason?
>
> (Milton 1644, 13)

For Milton, "all manner of tracts" means native histories that tell tough home truths as well as "Foreign Writings" offering lessons in civility, more valuable than those unworthy historians whose "inbred vanity" and "fond zeal of praising thir Nations above truth" means they fail to educate and inform their readers (121). The Britons toiled under "the *Roman* yoke" (89), but when the Romans departed, they "shrunk more wretchedly under the burden of their own Libertie, than before under a Foren Yoke" (118). Later, the "unexpected riddance of the *Danish* Yoke" (324) merely ushers in the Norman invasion and yet another "Yoke of an Out-landish Conquerour" (356). For Milton, the series of yokes Britain struggles under proves her unfitness for self-rule until she learns the true lessons of liberty, where the only yoke worth wearing is humility, "the yoke of Christ" (168).

Milton's insistence upon a warts-and-all approach to national history is evident in *Areopagitica*, where censorship is depicted as a serious infringement of rights, "more then if som enemy at sea should stop up all our hav'ns and ports, and creeks, it hinders and retards the importation of our richest Marchandize, Truth" (Milton 1644, 29). Milton goes on to say that although

> we are to send our thanks and vows to heav'n, louder then most of Nations, for that great measure of truth which we enjoy, especially in those main points between us and the Pope ... he who thinks we are to pitch our tent here, and have attain'd the utmost prospect of reformation, that the mortall glasse wherein we contemplate, can shew us, till we come to *beatific* vision, that man by this very opinion declares, that he is yet farre short of Truth. (1644, 29)

The "mortall glasse" must show the warts, and that entails the importation of truth.

For David Loewenstein, "[t]he final books of *Paradise Lost* would of course integrate history, epic, and tragedy; but in its own way so does the *History of Britain*, which begins, like an epic story, with the myth of Brutus and then charts a tragic pattern of failed deliverances in national history, with numerous references to the troubles of Milton's own age" (1990, 82).

Loewenstein points to Milton's sense of history as a pattern of successive falls and false dawns: "'that confused Anarchy' of the Britons following the Roman departure may be compared to 'the late commotions' of the 1640s" (1990, 87).

In the "Digression," Milton meditates on the nature of liberty—not a native plant it seems:

> For *Britain*, to speak a truth not often spoken, as it is a Land fruitful enough of Men stout and courageous in War, so is it naturally not over-fertile of Men able to govern justly and prudently in Peace … Civility, Prudence, love of the Publick good … are to this Soyl in a manner Outlandish. … For the Sun which we want, ripens Wits as well as Fruits; and as Wine and Oyl are Imported to us from abroad: so must ripe Understanding, and many civil Vertues, be imported into our minds from Foreign Writings, and examples of best Ages, we shall else miscarry still, and come short in the attempts of any great Enterprise. (1681, 10–11)

If military invasion brings bondage, then literary invasion brings benefits. This is a peculiar statement, as Hugh Jenkins notes:

> In Book III, and in "The Digression," Milton drastically revises the concept of the "foren yoke." Milton creates a potentially deconstructive paradox: the Britons' natural love of liberty can only be strengthened by foreign ideas about civility, which are essential to maintaining that liberty. (1999, 315)

Foreign books will free the people from foreign yokes and domestic tyranny. If Milton's faith in native wit falters in the *History*, then he certainly believed foreign books would supplement any deficiency. Milton is unsympathetic to the Saxons but is an admirer of the classics and of the humanist project in its classical form. Native culture needs access to material from beyond its borders in order to improve. Milton recognizes the need for European engagement as a prerequisite for future development.

If it ended there, with Milton urging his compatriots to read foreign writings to improve their chances of securing liberty that would be good and well. But there's more. In a "foreign book," a volume of his posthumously published lectures, Michel Foucault says something pertinent to Milton. Foucault begins by restating the Saxonist line:

> Saxon right was described as being both the primal and the historically authentic … right of the Saxon people, who elected their leaders, had their own judges, and recognized the power of the king only in time of war; he was recognized as a wartime leader, and not as a king who exercised an absolute and unchecked sovereignty over the social

body. Saxon right was, then, a historical figure, and attempts were made—through research into the ancient history of right—to establish it in a historically accurate form. (2003, 106)

Then Foucault does something more Miltonic by proceeding to unpack and unpick the process of difference and repetition that characterizes this history:

> The Norman regime is a regime of pillage and exaction, and it is the outcome of war, and what do we find beneath that regime? In historical terms, we find Saxon laws. But weren't the Saxon laws themselves the outcome of a war, a form of pillage and exaction? Ultimately, wasn't the Saxon regime itself a regime of domination, just like the Norman regime? And shouldn't we therefore go further still—this is the argument we find in certain Digger tracts—and say that any form of power leads to domination ... that there are no historical forms of power, whatever they may be, that cannot be analyzed in terms of the dominion of some over others?. ...Yet the fact remains that you see here the first formulation of the idea that any ... type of power ... has to be analyzed not in terms of natural right and the establishment of sovereignty, but in terms of the unending movement—which has no historical end—of the shifting relations that make some dominant over others. (2003, 109)

Foucault's account of how the Norman Yoke was preceded by the Saxon Yoke echoes Milton's cyclical view of history. The way out of this cycle of violence lies in critical engagement with foreign writings and, by extension, foreign experience. Did Milton share the view that "there are no historical forms of power, whatever they may be, that cannot be analyzed in terms of the dominion of some over others?" In *Paradise Lost* Adam asks, "Among unequals what society / Can sort, what harmony or true delight?" (VIII.383–384), and later praises God for creating equals: "but Man over men / He made not Lord; such title to himself / Reserving, human left from human free" (XII.69–71). This contrasts with Satan, whose "monarchal pride" (II.428) and "God-like imitated State" (II.510–511), as his dominion in Hell is described, reveals the truth that all kings falsely aspire to a heavenly power they are unfit and indeed forbidden to wield. But if we take Foucault's observation to its logical conclusion, Adam's claim that God "gave us only over beast, fish, fowl Dominion absolute; that right we hold By his donation" (XII.67–69) becomes a problematic exercise of sovereignty in itself. When Thomas Jefferson praised English efforts to recover the Saxon Constitution after the Norman Conquest, his literary reference was to Satan's defiant opening speech in *Paradise Lost* (Davies 1995, 257–258). This is ironic since Milton considered the Saxons and Satan well matched.

Milton's anti-Saxonism is strategic. He wished to remind his readers of the ill effects of monarchy and so refused to dwell on inglorious progenitors, whether Britons or Saxons. But there is another twist to the tale insofar as an Anglo-Saxon manuscript—the Caedmonian *Genesis*—may provide a key source for *Paradise Lost* (Lever 1947, 100). Milton gave short shrift to Saxon achievements in his *History*, but his poetry depended upon the pillars laid down by Anglo-Saxon writers. While appearing to undercut the argument presented thus far, it actually supports it insofar as Milton himself is caught up in the process whereby suppressed cultural forms resurface. Just as the rejection of foreign influences by his contemporaries eager to invent an Anglo-Saxon Golden Age proved not just futile but counterproductive in terms of the struggle to establish liberty, so Milton's own anti-Saxonism entailed the deliberate diminishing of Saxon achievements, a rhetorical move compromised by his own dependence on Saxon literary resources.

Paradoxically, Milton's *History of Britain* has the status of a foreign book, marginalized even within Milton's corpus, almost unknown in the English literary canon. Constructed out of sources its author treats with disdain, it has itself been viewed as "an abandoned and unloved gift" (Morrill 1994, 111). I said my first encounter with Milton's *History* came while I was undertaking research on Spenser and Ireland 30 years ago. In the *History*, Milton reproduces a stanza from *The Faerie Queene* (II.x.24) in order to question Spenser's mythmaking (22–23). Spenserians have noted the tension between this gentle rebuke and Milton's praise of his predecessor elsewhere (Gottfried 1937, 317–318). Revisiting Milton's text, I detected another link. In Spenser's *View*, Eudoxus asks Irenius: "Whence commeth it then that the Irish doe so greatly covet to fetch themselves from the Spaniards, since the old Gaules are a more auncient and much more honorable nation?" Irenius's reply is as rich and nuanced as Milton's derivation and denunciation of the Saxons:

> Even of a very desire of new fanglenes and vanity, for they derive themselves from the Spaniards, as seeing them to be a very honorable people, and neere bordering unto them: but all that is most vaine ... for the Spaniard that now is, is come from as rude and savage nations as they, there being, as there may be gathered by course of ages, and view of their owne history ... scarce any drop of the old Spanish blood left in them; for all Spain was first conquered by the Romans, and filled with colonies from them, which were still increased, and the native Spaniard still cut off.
>
> (Spenser 1997, 49–50)

Irenius lists successive colonizers of Spain—Carthaginians, Goths, Huns, Vandals, "and lastly all the nations of Scythia, which, like a mountaine flood, did over-flow all Spaine, and quite drowned and washt away whatsoever reliques there was left of the land-bred people, yea, and of all the

Romans too" (50). Nor does Irenius stop there in his deconstruction of the Irish claim to Spanish provenance:

> And yet after all these the Moores and the Barbarians, breaking over out of Africa, did finally possesse all Spaine, or the most parte thereof, and did tread, under their heathenish feete, whatever little they found yet there standing. The which, though after they were beaten out ... yet they were not so cleansed, but that through the marriages which they had made, and mixture with the people of the land, during their long continuance there, they had left no pure drop of Spanish blood, no more than of Roman or of Scythian. So that of all nations under heaven (I suppose) the Spaniard is the most mingled, and most uncertaine; wherefore most follishly doe the Irish thinke to enoble themselves by wresting their auncientry from the Spaniard, who is unable to derive himselfe from any in certaine.
>
> (Spenser 1997, 50)

This earns a rebuke from Eudoxus—"You speake very sharply, Iren. In dispraise of the Spaniard, whom some others boast to be the onely brave nation under the skie"—which in turn prompts Irenius to elaborate in ways that backlight Milton's own genealogical work:

> I thinke there is no nation now in Christendome, nor much further, but is mingled, and compounded with others: for it was a singular providence of God, and a most admirable purpose of his wisedome, to draw those Northerne Heathen Nations downe into those Christian parts, where they might receive Christianity, and to mingle nations so remote miraculously, to make as it were one blood and kindred of all people, and each to have knowledge of him.
>
> (Spenser 1997, 51)

This passage complicates Spenser's anti-Irish sentiments. Like Milton, Spenser's excavation of English identity uncovered not purity but pollution, and this became a cause for celebration rather than condemnation. Wolfram Schmidgen includes Milton among early modern thinkers arguing against purity, citing his sympathy for Arminianism over Calvinism, free will over predestination (Schmidgen 2013, 79). Milton's Britain, according to his *History*, is not destined to triumph over adversity without foreign implants. Milton offers a version of national history focused on mixed origins and the salutary potential of external influences.

The mingling of nations behind every national narrative, notwithstanding claims of unity and singularity, leads eventually to Daniel Defoe's satire *The True-Born Englishman* (1701), "which mocks those who extolled their own Englishness in order to criticize William of Orange as a foreigner," and "reminds us that, like all peoples, the Anglo-Saxons and the English, in constructing a simple narrative of their origins and of their biological and cultural descent, have chosen to forget much more of their past than they have chosen to remember" (Ward-Perkins 2000, 533). Milton differs from Defoe in his republican refusal of all monarchs as 'foreign' by definition, or at least alien to the commonwealth he wishes to inhabit.

I share Thomas Corns's view of Milton's *History* as a "neglected master-piece of verve, wit, and playfulness [that] spiritedly rehearses Miltonic themes," but cannot concur with Corns's claim that Milton's "perspective on the people who had inhabited Britain before the Norman Conquest sub-ordinates any concern with national identity to his recurrent and pervasive values of anticlericalism and, widely defined, antimonarchism and repub-licanism" (Corns 2008, 211). Conversely, questions of national identity, widely defined, include religion and republicanism. Finally, before we get too carried away by Milton's demolition job on origin myths and debunking of his nation's heroic past, specifically the Saxon inheritance, we should be mindful of the forms nationalism can assume. When Nicholas von Maltzahn says, "[i]t is of course characteristic of humanism so to press rhetoric into patriotic service," excluding Milton's *History* from this urge, he overlooks a different, deeper patriotism that consists in telling the unvarnished truth as a means of improvement (von Maltzahn 1991, 50). Nationalism need not be an exclusionary project. Critical national histories can contribute to a deeper understanding of our shared international history.

In *Areopagitica* Milton warned of "the incredible losse" that would follow from state censorship of literature (1644, 29). Ironically, his most heartfelt plea for the reading of foreign books was made in *The History of Britain*, an unjustly neglected work that is a stranger in its own coun-try, less familiar than tales of triumph that outshine it in the eyes of those for whom national history must be both backward-looking and insular. Milton's vision is forward-looking. Having started out an Anglophile, he finishes an Anglosceptic. That the Restoration of the monarchy in 1660 left the republican Milton "without a country" means his critique of imperial monarchy remains relevant even as its lessons go unlearned (Zagorin 1992, 123). Earlier I cited Milton's letter to his German friend, Peter Heimbach, on his post-Restoration homelessness and hopelessness, but a fuller citation proves salutary:

> For the virtue you call statesmanship (but which I would rather have you call loyalty to my country), after captivating me with her fair sounding name, has, so to speak, almost left me without a country. However, the chorus of the others makes a fine harmony. One's country is wherever it is well with one.
>
> (Milton 1932, 51)

In *The Tenure of Kings and Magistrates* (1649), Milton spoke of "a mutual bond of amity and brotherhood between man and man over all the World"

(Milton 1649, 19). In writing the *History*, a patriotic project that became an appeal for foreign writings—"the chorus of the others"—Milton values this bond above all the yokes of tyranny that beset humanity. The positive impact of foreign writings cuts both ways. The traditional view that Milton's early reception in Germany was hostile has been countered in ways that suggest a sympathetic hearing for his arguments for popular sovereignty (Stackhouse 1974). Milton was not writing a history of Britain. He was mapping out a democratic future for Europe. A comparative national history, a truly European history, would harness the lessons of Milton's deconstructive, postcolonial historiography and its final fervent appeal to foreign literature as essential to native liberty.

Works Cited

All quotations from Milton's *History of Britain* are taken from Graham Parry's facsimile edition (1991), which reproduces the text of the second edition of 1677; references to the poetry are to Gordon Campbell's edition (1980); and allusions to the prose, unless otherwise stated, are to the Yale *Complete Prose Works* (*CPW*), edited by Don Wolfe.

Armitage, David. 1995. "John Milton: Poet Against Empire." In *Milton and Republicanism*, edited by David Armitage, Armand Himy and Quentin Skinner, 206–225. Cambridge: Cambridge University Press.

Baldwin, Leland D. 1943. *God's Englishman: The Evolution of the Anglo-Saxon Spirit*. London: Jonathan Cape.

Binney, Matthew W. 2010. "Milton, Locke, and the Early Modern Framework of Cosmopolitan Right." *The Modern Language Review* 105 (1): 31–52.

Campbell, Gordon, ed. 1980. *John Milton: The Complete Poems*. London: J. M. Dent.

Corns, Thomas N. 2008 "Milton and the Limitations of Englishness." In *Early Modern Nationalism and Milton's England*, edited by David Loewenstein and Paul Stevens, 205–216. Toronto: University of Toronto Press.

Cunningham, J. S., and Eithne Henson, eds. 1998. *Tamburlaine the Great: Christopher Marlowe*. Revels Student Editions. Manchester: Manchester University Press.

Davies, Tony. 1995. "Borrowed Language: Milton, Jefferson, Mirabeau." In *Milton and Republicanism*, edited by David Armitage, Armand Himy and Quentin Skinner, 254–271. Cambridge: Cambridge University Press.

Defoe, Daniel. 1997. *The True-Born Englishman and Other Writings*, edited by P. N. Furbank and W. R. Owens. London: Penguin Books, 1997.

Dzelzainis, Martin. 2008. "Dating and Meaning: *Samson Agonistes* and the 'Digression' to Milton's *History of Britain*." *Milton Studies* 48: 160–177.

Escobedo, Andrew. 2004. "Poetical History: Spenser and Milton Ornament the Nation." In *Nationalism and Historical Loss in Renaissance England: Foxe, Dee, Spenser, Milton*, 141–204. Ithaca, NY: Cornell University Press.

Firth, Charles H. 1938. "Milton as an Historian." In *Essays Historical and Literary*, 61–102. Oxford: Clarendon Press.

Fogle, French. 1965. "Milton as Historian." In *Milton and Clarendon*, edited by French Rowe Fogle and Hugh Trevor-Roper, 1–20. Los Angeles, CA: William Andrews Clark Memorial Library.

Fogle, French, ed. 1971. *Complete Prose Works of John Milton 5: Part 1, "The History of Britain."* In *The Complete Prose Works of John Milton*, edited by Don M. Wolfe, 8 vols., 1953–1982. New Haven, CT: Yale University Press.

Foucault, Michel. 2003. *"Society Must Be Defended": Lectures at the Collège de France, 1975–1976.* Edited by Mauro Bertani and Alessandro Fontana, translated by David Macey. London: Allen Lane.

French, J. Milton. 1935. "Milton as a Historian." *PMLA* 50 (2): 469–479.

Gottfried, Rudolf B. 1937. "Spenser as an Historian in Prose." *Transactions of the Wisconsin Academy of Sciences, Arts, and Letters* 30: 317–329.

Hadfield, Andrew. 1993. "Briton and Scythian: Tudor Representations of Irish Origins." *Irish Historical Studies* 28 (112): 390–408.

Hamilton, Gary D. 1990. *"The History of Britain* and its Restoration Audience." In *Politics, Poetics and Hermeneutics in Milton's Prose*, edited by David Loewenstein and James Grantham Turner, 241–255. Cambridge: Cambridge University Press.

Hill, Christopher. 1958. "The Norman Yoke." In *Puritanism and Revolution: Studies in Interpretation of the English Revolution of the 17th Century*, 50–122. London: Secker & Warburg.

Horsman, Reginald. 1976. "Origins of Racial Anglo-Saxonism in Great Britain before 1850." *Journal of the History of Ideas* 37 (3): 387–410.

Jenkins, Hugh. 1999. "Shrugging off the Norman Yoke: Milton's *History of Britain* and the Levellers." *English Literary Renaissance* 29 (2): 306–325.

Knoppers, Laura Lunger. 2000. *Constructing Cromwell: Ceremony, Portrait, and Print 1645–1661.* Cambridge: Cambridge University Press.

Lever, J. W. 1947. *"Paradise Lost* and the Anglo-Saxon Tradition." *The Review of English Studies* 23 (90): 97–106.

Loewenstein, David. 1990. *"The History of Britain."* In *Milton and the Drama of History: Historical Vision, Iconoclasm, and the Literary Imagination*, 81–88. Cambridge: Cambridge University Press.

McCrady, Matthew. 1999. "Breaking the Norman Yoke: Milton's *History of Britain* and the Construction of the Anglo-Saxon Past." *West Virginia Shakespeare and Renaissance Association Selected Papers (SRASP)* 22: 31–46.

Milton, John. 1641. *Of Reformation Touching Church-Discipline in England.* London: Thomas Underhill.

Milton, John. 1644. *Areopagitica; a speech of Mr. John Milton for the liberty of vnlicens'd printing, to the Parlament of England.* London.

Milton, John. 1649. *The Tenure of Kings and Magistrates.* 2nd ed. London.

Milton, John, 1681. *Mr John Milton's Character of the Long Parliament and Assembly of Divines in 1641.* London.

Milton, John. 1932. *Private Correspondence and Academic Exercises.* Translated by Phyllis Tillyard. Cambridge: Cambridge University Press.

Morrill, John. 1994. "Review of Nicholas von Maltzahn, *Milton's History of Britain: Republican Historiography in the English Revolution* (Oxford: Clarendon Press, 1991)." *Review of English Studies* 45 (177): 110–111.

Parry, Graham. 1991. *Milton's History of Britain: A Facsimile Edition with a Critical Introduction.* Stamford, CT: Paul Watkins.

Parry, Graham. 1996. "Milton's *History of Britain* and the Seventeenth-Century Antiquarian Scene." *Prose Studies* 19 (3): 238–246.

Reynolds, Susan. 1985. "What Do We Mean by 'Anglo-Saxon' and 'Anglo-Saxons'?" *Journal of British Studies* 24 (4): 395–414.

Roots, Ivan. 1994. "Review of Nicholas von Maltzahn, *Milton's History of Britain: Republican Historiography in the English Revolution* (Oxford: Clarendon Press, 1991)." *Literature and History*, 3rd series, 3 (1): 114–116.

Rossi, Paolo. 1990. "Bacon's Idea of Science." In *The Cambridge Companion to Bacon*, edited by Markku Peltonen, 25–46. Cambridge: Cambridge University Press.

Schmidgen, Wolfram. 2013. *Exquisite Mixture: The Virtues of Impurity in Early Modern England*. Philadelphia: University of Pennsylvania Press.

Shawcross, John T. 1974. "A Survey of Milton's Prose Works." In *Achievements of the Left Hand: Essays on the Prose of John Milton*, edited by Michael Lieb and John T. Shawcross, 291–391. Amherst: University of Massachusetts Press.

Sidney, Philip. 1595/2002. *An Apology for Poetry (or A Defence of Poesy)*, edited by R. W. Maslen. Manchester: Manchester University Press.

Spenser, Edmund. 1633/1997. *A View of the State of Ireland (1633): From the First Printed Edition*, edited by Andrew Hadfield and Willy Maley. Oxford: Blackwell.

Spenser, Edmund. 1590–1596/2007. *The Faerie Queene*, edited by A. C. Hamilton. Harlow: Pearson Education. First published 2001.

Stackhouse, Janifer Gerl. 1974. "Early Critical Response to Milton in Germany: The *Dialogi* of Martin Zeiller." *Journal of English and Germanic Philology* 73 (4): 487–496.

Underdown, David. 1994. "Review of Nicholas von Maltzahn, *Milton's History of Britain: Republican Historiography in the English Revolution* (Oxford: Clarendon Press, 1991)." *Renaissance Quarterly* 47 (1): 211–212.

von Maltzahn, Nicholas. 1991. "Culture and Conquest: Milton and the Saxons." In *Milton's History of Britain: Republican Historiography in the English Revolution*, 166–197. Reprinted 2002. Oxford: Clarendon Press.

von Maltzahn, Nicholas. 1993. "Dating the Digression in Milton's *History of Britain*." *Historical Journal* 36 (4): 945–956.

Von Sneidern, Maja-Lisa. 2005. *Savage Indignation: Colonial Discourse from Milton to Swift*. Cranbury, NJ: Associated University Presses.

Ward-Perkins, Bryan. 2000. "Why Did the Anglo-Saxons Not Become More British?" *English Historical Review* 115 (462): 513–533.

Wolfe, Don M., ed. 1953–1982. *The Complete Prose Works of John Milton*. 8 vols. New Haven, CT: Yale University Press.

Woolrych, Austin. 1993. "Dating Milton's *History of Britain*." *Historical Journal* 36 (4): 929–943.

Zagorin, Perez. 1992. *Milton: Aristocrat and Rebel: The Poet and his Politics*. Suffolk: D. S. Brewer.

9 "The Ship of Europe"

The Iconography of John Dee's *General and Rare Memorials*

Eliza Richter

The focus of this chapter is the historical and iconographic context of the sailing ship named "Europe" depicted in the frontispiece of John Dee's *General and Rare Memorials Pertayning to the Perfect Arte of Navigation* (1577, Fig. 9.1). Dee's title page has been variously analysed and interpreted in the last 40 years (e.g., Yates [1975], Corbett and Lightbown [1979], and Lesley B. Cormack [2001]), with an emphasis, by and large, on its use of allegory, personification, and symbolism, as well as on its historical context. The allegory of the 'ship of Europe' itself and the concepts of Europe it entails have, however, not been examined in greater detail. I argue that Dee's 'ship of Europe' articulates a concept of Europe marked by competition for naval power; not only in the symbolism of the title page but also in the text of the *Memorials*. According to Corbett and Lightbown, the iconography of the frontispiece is central to the publication as it "represents the sum of Dee's prophetic hopes" for England (1979, 56). Queen Elizabeth I in the role of helmswoman establishes a discernible link to Dee's national vision, whilst naming the ship 'Europe' gestures beyond a merely national framework.

What lay behind Dee's use of this European allegory in *Memorials*? As I intend to show, the 'ship of Europe' validates a claim for English hegemony over Europe based on Dee's vision of England as the leading naval power. This is reflected in the iconography of the title page, which also indicates a conceptualisation of Europe as a system of (naval) powers competing for dominion at sea. The 'ship of Europe' must, moreover, be read in a context of Christian symbolism and Graeco-Roman imperial iconography, as these represent the central European traditions in which the allegory is embedded. The term 'Europe' is conspicuously absent from the text of the *Memorials* at large; this discrepancy raises the question of how the frontispiece correlates with, or diverges from, its description.

John Dee was cosmographer and counsellor to Queen Elizabeth and interested in matters of science and magic (cf. French 1972; Clulee 1988; Sherman 1997; Clucas 2006; Parry 2011). His many benefactors at court make it more than likely that influential courtiers constituted the intended readership of *Memorials*: one such benefactor was Christopher Hatton, to whom Dee dedicated his book. These courtiers were in a position to realize Dee's vision for England, and as the supposed addressees they could bring about its fruition through financial support or by influencing Elizabeth's

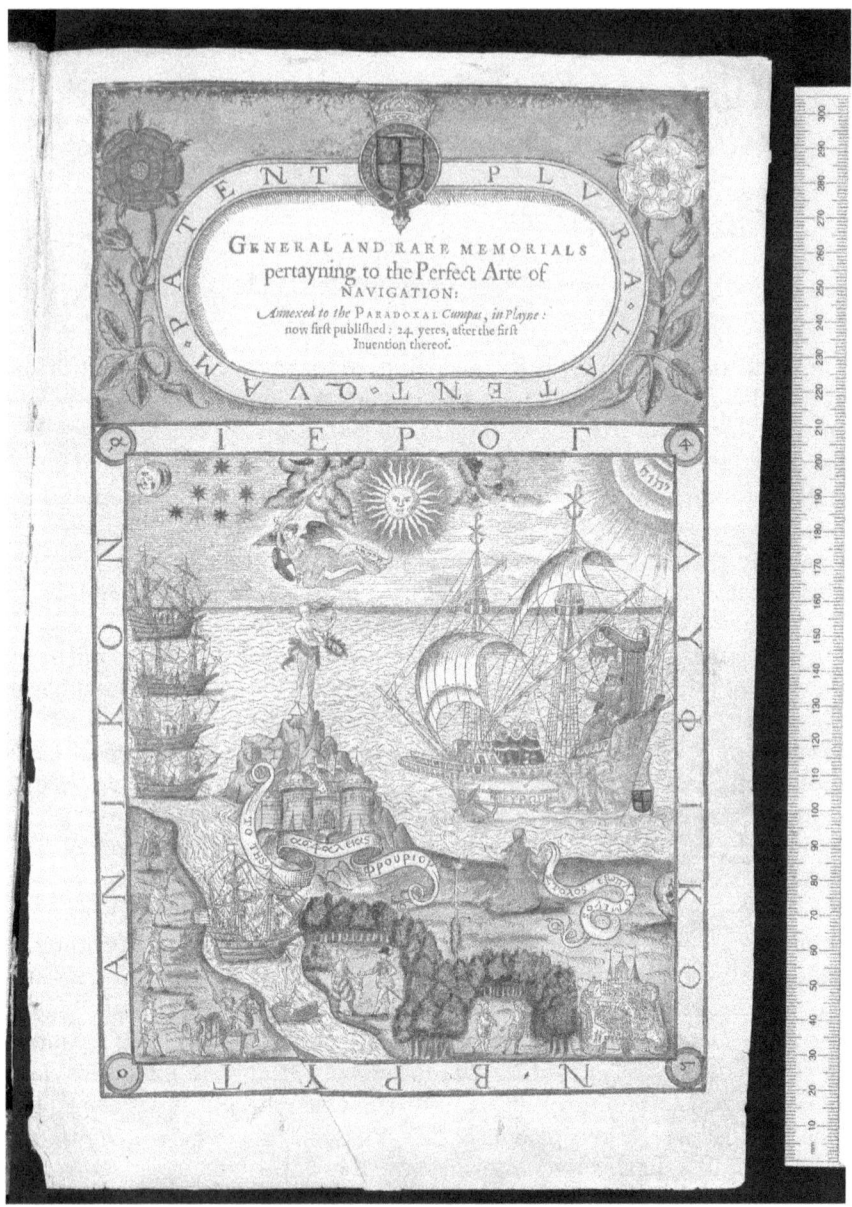

Figure 9.1 John Dee: Title page. *General and Rare Memorials Pertayning to the Perfect Arte of Navigation.* London: 1577. Hand-coloured woodcut with gold and silver. Douce, D. subt. 30. Bodleian Library, Oxford.

policies. Dee's aspirations for England, presented in the *Memorials*, hinged on the country's development as a naval power and on England's engagement in the contemporary European struggle for both overseas expansion and hegemony at sea. Dee envisioned that England would make use of its insularity—its harbours, mariners, and general maritime aptitude—to become an influential naval power. England's ready access to the sea could be a decisive advantage in the struggle for naval sovereignty. When the *Memorials* were published in 1577, England was only a minor player in that struggle. The country's privateering activities represented a "way between piracy and war" and were the most notable undertakings against rival powers at sea (Loades 2009, 137) next to attempts at expanding the English maritime sphere of influence through exploration. Like other European powers, the English sought precious foreign goods by trade or plunder, and they realized that discovery of new sea routes was the key to advantageous overseas trade. Decisive achievements like Sir Francis Drake's circumnavigation of the earth (1577–1580) or the defeat of the Spanish Armada (1588) were yet to come, and Dee's work is an early indicator of the increasing Elizabethan interest in naval matters.

Dee intended his *Memorials* to consist of several volumes, but only the first, subtitled "The Brytish Monarchie," was ever published (Corbett and Lightbown 1979, 51). He had planned them as a "Plat Politicall" to outline political, economic, and other national advantages of overseas imperialism and to highlight the need to increase the country's naval strength (Yates 1975, 48). His repeated references to the realm of Queen Elizabeth as an 'Impire' (Dee 1577, 5, 13) echo Henry VIII's 1533 Act in Restraint of Appeals, and the description of the 'ship of Europe' as an "IMPERIALL SHIP" (Dee 1577, 53) reflect this ambition. As Tristan Marshall remarks: "Dee saw the internal imperium and overseas empire as being fundamentally interconnected" (2000, 30). Considered altogether, the distinct parts of Dee's publication support and justify England's development as a naval, imperial power: the first two consist of the advertisement to the reader and a dedication to Sir Christopher Hatton. In both of these parts, Dee presented his vision of England utilizing a strong navy and drawing on this naval power for protection and expansion. The third and main part of the publication, entitled "The Brytish Monarchie," sets out Dee's plan of establishing a patrolling navy to secure the coast and realize his vision of England as a naval power. Dee identifies several sources for his justification for establishing an English navy. Three of these sources are framed and set apart typographically from the rest of the text. The first is an excerpt from Pliny the Elder's account of Pompey's triumph in 61 BC (in *Naturalis Historia* VII, 98). It begins: "CVM ORAM MARITIMAM PRAEDONIBVS LIBERASSET: ET IMPERIVM MARIS, POPVLO ROMANO RESTITVISSET" ["After having rescued the sea coast from pirates and restored to the Roman People the command of the sea]" (Dee 1577, 39). The term 'IMPERIUM MARIS' is of particular significance in the context of *Memorials* as Dee remarked about the ancient source:

> Oh Note, What was the Actuall Praeface, and politik preparative to all these Triumphes? Was it any other, than, IMPERIVM MARIS,

POPVLO ROMANO RESTITVTVM? God graunt vs (therefore) the verity and frute, of this Sea Souerainty euery way: And that, with all Opportunity. (1577, 39)

The second source to stand out is a section referring to King Edgar (reg. 942–975). Dee praises Edgar by naming him "one of the perfect Imperiall Monarchs of this Brytish Impire" and further remarks that "[h]is Sommer Progresses, and Yerely chief pastymes, were The Sayling rownd this Whole Ile of Albion: Garded with hys Grand Nauy of 4000 Sayle, at the least" (Dee 1577, 56). This glorification of Edgar as an "Imperiall" king is thus closely linked to the establishment of a navy and shows Dee to construct a tradition of English monarchs claiming "Sea Souereignty" over the surrounding waters (Dee 1577, 39). The third prominent source in "The Brytish Monarchie" is a paragraph taken from the philosopher Gemistus Plethon's letter of advice to the final Byzantine emperor, Constantine XI. Dee's Latin quotation, "Cvm in Naui Gubernator," opens with the initial "C" containing an illumination of Elizabeth on her throne (Dee 1577, 69). Frances Yates interprets this combination of a foreign source and the depiction of the queen as follows: "Dee's virgin [Queen Elizabeth] seeks practical advice from the traditions of the Greek empire for the defence and expansion of her realm" (1975, 50). Dee's text thus draws a parallel between England's contemporary struggle to establish and preserve an empire and historical developments in Byzantium that had, by this time, succumbed to the Ottoman empire.

Furthermore, the end of *Memorials* includes a poem written for Christopher Hatton that focusses on the necessity of protecting England (Dee 1577, 81). Dee stresses throughout that only a patrolling navy can "secur[e] the country's maritime defences" against the threat of pirate attacks and invasions by other European powers (Dalton 2000, 188). His declared aim was "[t]hat, henceforward, neither *France, Denmark, Scotland, Spaine,* nor any other Cuntry, or Ayds, any way, Transporting: to annoy the blessed State of our Tranquillitie" (1577, 4).

One reason for producing this "advertisement" for imperialism and naval expansion may have been "Elizabeth's reluctance to play her assigned imperial role" (Parry 2006, 644). The queen's careful avoidance of openly provoking other European princes at the time was well known, and Dee tried to convince Elizabeth and her courtiers to take a more active, leading role within the European system of powers. This system consisted of foreign powers perceived as openly hostile, against whom naval protection was advised, and of competitors for determining the 'course' Europe was to take a whole: As I will discuss in more detail below, the frontispiece's 'ship of Europe' only carries an English crew and excludes all other nations. I argue that the competition between powers for the role of the crew aboard and, more importantly, for the helm of the 'ship of Europe' is a binding element that characterizes Europe as a coherent power structure. Dee envisions the English taking the position of the leading, or rather steering, power aboard the ship, while the other European powers mentioned in the text are an 'absent presence' in the image as obvious competitors for control of the vessel.

Dee's Vision of England as a European Naval Power

The frontispiece is divided into two parts: a woodcut image with a frame and, above it, a cartouche containing the title of the book. Two roses flank the cartouche, referring to the rise of the Tudor dynasty out of the Wars of the Roses. The book's title is literally crowned with the royal arms and the Garter, which highlights the author's proximity to the queen and her courtiers. The cartouche framing the title contains the motto "Plura latent quam patent," meaning: "More things are concealed than revealed" (Corbett and Lightbown 1979, 49). On the one hand, this hints that the frontispiece contains various layers of information for the competent 'reader.' Dee's well-known inclination to hermeticism and use of cryptic symbols underline this interpretation (cf. Whitby 1988; Harkness 1999; Szonyi 2004). On the other hand, the motto also alludes to the discoveries that can be made through maritime voyages of exploration.

A woodcut image forms the centre of the frontispiece. This image is divided into three areas: coast, sea, and sky. The focus is on the sea, or, to be more precise, on the huge sailing-ship named 'Europe.' In an elevated position on the poop deck Queen Elizabeth is pictured, identified by a scroll above her head ("ELIZABETH"). She is not only taller than the other people aboard—a use of perspective in which persons are scaled according to their importance—but also in the crucial position of the helmswoman. In her left hand she appears to hold a sceptre, which is in fact the tiller attached to the rudder. Furthermore, there are three men in red robes on the deck of the ship. John Cooper suggests that they might be the dedicatee Sir Christopher Hatton, one of Elizabeth's favourites and "Capitain of her Maiesties Garde" (Dee 1577, 1); Sir Francis Walsingham, the principal secretary to the queen and a supporter of Martin Frobisher's attempts to find the Northwest Passage; and William Cecil, baron of Burghley, chief advisor of Queen Elizabeth, lord high treasurer from 1572, and twice secretary of state (1550–1553; 1558–1572) (Cooper 2011, 235). Their red robes indicate that they are courtiers in the queen's service and members of the Order of the Garter. They are the deckhands or officers under the helmswoman's command. Consequently, the queen sets the ship's course while the officers execute royal commands and function as decision makers on behalf of the monarch. These officers are vital to Dee's plans for the development of England as a naval and imperial power in Europe, for example, as supporters of voyages of exploration (Cooper 2011, 314). Dee stresses not only the importance of naval ventures for some of the courtiers or the queen herself, but for the whole country: "for the State Publik of this BRYTISH MONARCHIE, to become florishing, in HONOR, WEALTH, and STRENGTH" (1577, viii). This prospect of a strong and flourishing state is bound to the extension of English sea power, and the opportunities for doing so have never been better:

> NO KINGDOM, in these Dayes, hath more nede of a PETY-NAVY-ROYALL, and to be Continually at Sea maintayned, for the Respects aboue rehearsed: No Kingdome, hath apter TYMBER for Shipping: And therof (YET) store enough: No Kingdome, hath Skilfuller, and more SHIP-WRIGHTS: No Kingdome, hath Subiects better HABLE, and which more willingly will be Contributary for the sufficient Setting forth, and mayntenace of such a PETY-NAVY-ROYALL, continually, at Sea (and that, for the former Respects:) No Kingdome, hath better store of APT and willing MEN: as well couragious Ientlemen, as other: very manfully disposed, to furnish the foresayd Nauy with, for all kynde of purposes: No Kingdome, hath better, or more Hauens, and HARBOROVGHS, (and those, round about it) to Succour a Navy in, from Dangers, or Distres of Sea: No King, nor Kingdome, hath, by Nature and Humayn Industry (to be vsed) any, more LAWFULL, and more Peaceable Means (made evident) wherby, to become, In wealth far passing all other: in Strength, and Force, INVINCIBLE: and in Honorable estimation, Triumphantly Famous ouer all, and aboue all other. (1577, 63)

Dee elevates England's naval aptitude above those of others. He urges the increase in England's naval power in order to become "[t]riumphantly Famous ouer all." Even though the protective purpose of the navy is apparent, the prospects of wealth and invincibility hint at objectives that clearly transcend mere defence. The various smaller ships depicted in the frontispiece give an impression of generally busy maritime activity that pressures the English to keep up with the naval progress of other nations. The name of the large sailing ship establishes Europe as the wider framework for Dee's vision, even though the name 'Europe' is not elsewhere employed in Dee's description of the frontispiece.

The courtiers' and the queen's presence on the ship represent England as the leading (and thus 'steering') power in the European system of powers, a fact corroborated by the royal coat of arms on the ship's rudder, which represents the primary means of controlling the ship's course. Lesley B. Cormack has identified these details as support for "Dee's prophesy (and present claim) of England's supremacy and leadership of Europe" (2001, 48). The English appear to have taken control of the vessel, and only the name on the hull and the figure of Europa distinguish it from an English 'ship of state.' The crew and helmswoman determine the ship's course and use their 'Sea Souerainty' to exert power on a European scale (Dee 1577, 39). At the same time, the ship also represents the means to gain this power: the navy that Dee suggests be built and the 'expeditionary force' that the personification of Res Publica Brytanica asks for in the title page of *Memorials* (1577, 53). The officers support this aim and hold the ship on course, for example, as benefactors of explorers and their voyages of discovery. Europe appears as a hierarchical system in which the most powerful nation occupies the helm and thus controls the others. Dee's depiction of Queen Elizabeth and her court-iers on the ship indicates the enormous influence and power that England could gain over other "King[s] [or] Kingdome[s]" by his plan (1577, 63).

Symbolism in the Frontispiece

The symbolism employed in Dee's frontispiece is a complex combination of various traditions. In the text of the *Memorials*, Dee (partly) explains the scene depicted in the frontispiece and sheds light on some of the per-sonifications and symbols employed in it. His textual description is linked to the title page by the term "hieroglyph of Britain" ("ΙΕΡΟΓΛΥΦΙΚΟΝ ΒΡΥΤΑΝΙΚΟΝ") that frames the woodcut and also reappears in the book itself, also in the margin, next to a discussion of the frontispiece (1577, 53). The inscription in the frontispiece renders the framed scene itself the hiero-glyph, a "figure, device, or sign having some hidden meaning; a secret or enigmatical symbol; an emblem" (*OED* 2015). The description of the scene in the woodcut in the text of *Memorials* concludes with an appeal to God to protect the nation from foreign enemies:

> Why should not we HOPE, that, RES-PVBL. BRYTANICA, on her knees, very Humbly, and ernestly Soliciting the most Excellent Royall Maiesty, of our ELIZABETH, (Sitting at the HELM of the IMPERIALL SHIP, of the most parte of Christendome: if so, it be her Graces Pleasure) shall obteyn, (or Perfect Policie, may perswade her Highnes,) that, which is the Pyth, or Intent of RES-PVBL. BRYTANICA, Her Supplication? Which is, That, [a fully equipped expeditionary force], may helpe vs, not onley, to [a fortress of safety]: But make vs, also, Partakers of Publik Commodities Innumerable, and (as yet) Incredible. Vnto which, the HEAVENLY KING, for these many yeres last past, hath, by MANIFEST OCCASION, most Graciously, not only inuited vs: but also, hath made, EVEN NOW, the Way and Means, most evident, easie, and Compendious: In-asmuch as, (besides all our own sufficient Furniture, Hability, Industry, Skill, and Courage) our Freends are become strong: and our Enemies, sufficiently weake, and nothing Royally furnished, or of Hability, for Open Violence Vsing: Though their accustomed Confidence, in Treason, Trechery, and Disloyall Dealings, be very great. Wherin, we besche our HEAVENLY PROTECTOR, with his GOOD ANGELL to Garde vs, with SHIELD AND SWORD, now, and euer. Amen. (1577, 53)

Dee emphasizes that, in contrast to her competitors, Queen Elizabeth is divinely ordained and can therefore rely on God's support as he invites her people to make use of this opportunity. The frontispiece reflects this characterisation: in the upper right-hand corner a source of light containing the Tetragrammaton, the Hebrew word for God, illuminates Elizabeth, enthroned on the sailing-ship below. A further indication that the queen should take this chance is the woman depicted as standing above the city. She is holding a wreath of laurel and waving in the queen's direction. This is a personification of Lady Occasion, the female version of Caerus from Greek mythology or Occasio/Tempus from Roman mythology. Her long lock of hair, to be grasped only when the occasion arises, and her invitational gesture certify her identity. Dee's statement that "the HEAVENLY KING, for these many yeres last past, hath, by MANIFEST OCCASION, most Graciously, … inuited vs" (1577, 53) clearly refers to her. Hence, (pagan) Lady Occasion here represents a divinely sanctioned opportunity for the nation, underlining the righteousness of the venture. Furthermore, Res Publica Brytanica is depicted as a woman kneeling on the shore, her body turned towards the queen with a scroll next to her head. It bears her supplication for "Στολος εξωπλισμενος [a fully equipped expeditionary force]" in Greek letters (Corbett and Lightbown 1979, 50). Dee's description of the frontispiece suggests that Elizabeth is "[s]itting at the HELM of the IMPERIALL SHIP, of the most parte of Christendome" in response to the plea of her realm (albeit by the queen's own pleasure). These personifications place the desired development of English sea power in the ancient Graeco-Roman and Judaeo-Christian lines of tradition, both of which are marked as 'European': for example, Dee describes the vessel as representing "the most parte of Christendome," thus rendering that phrase synonymous with the ship's Greek name "ΕΥΡΩΠΗ." The significance of Christian belief for 'the ship of Europe' is obvious, as the masts of the ship are crowned with the Chi-Ro, the symbol of Christ. Moreover, the ship itself stands for the church as an entity in Christian iconography (*Oxford Dictionary of Christian Art and Architecture* 2013, s.v. "Ship of the Church"). This identification of 'Europe' with "the most parte of Christendome" is clearly based in the widespread acceptance that geographical Europe was largely united by the Christian faith (Adam 2006, 25). Dee also hints at the existence of Christians outside Europe, for example, due to overseas colonialism: as a crucial characteristic of Europe, Christianity was one of the ideas 'exported' to overseas regions by means of navigation (Smith 1993, v). Hence, the 'ship of Europe/Christendom' also signifies a means of cultural export, spreading the Christian faith. According to Dee, the English enjoy God's particular favour within this Christian community, as the source of light containing the Tetragrammaton indicates, which seems to be blessing the crew of the giant sailing-ship. Besides, the archangel Michael, identified by an adjacent scroll and carrying a sword in one hand and a shield embossed with a Saint George's Cross in the other, also seems to be guarding the large sailing ship. His presence again stresses that active divine support for and protection of the ship sought in Dee's prayer: "[W]e beseche our HEAVENLY

PROTECTOR, with his GOOD ANGELL to Garde vs, with SHIELD AND SWORD" (1577, 53).

The mythological aspects in the frontispiece are especially conspicuous in the image painted on the side of the ship. In a clear allusion to Ovid's *Metamorphoses*, it shows a woman riding a bull alongside the Greek word for 'Europe.' Establishing a line of tradition stretching from Graeco-Roman mythology to the Elizabethan present, Dee yokes the myth of Europa to the English queen steering the 'ship of Europe.' The course of the ship is likened to Zeus's flight with the princess towards her destined land, and this carries a double connotation: on the one hand, the sea functions as a border in the Greek myth and prevents Europa from returning to her home in Tyre; it had equally restricted Europeans from long-distance overseas travel in the past. It also signifies a cultural export of ideas and values across the waters to overseas regions, just like Europa herself was brought to Crete from foreign shores in Tyre. Translating the Greek myth to the depiction of the 'ship of Europe,' the crossing of the sea stands for an unprecedented expansion of the sphere of influence to overseas regions.

While the immediate reason for writing the *Memorials* appears to have been the need for a navy patrolling the coasts, Dee's vision of England as an imperial power exceeds this objective. His reference to the ship as imperial underscores that the *Memorials* were "part of a larger scheme which [Dee] was anxious to promote for the restoration of a 'British Empire', covering England, Wales, Scotland, Ireland, the Hebrides, the Orkneys, and (hopefully) some outposts in the New World" (Loades 2009, 130). David Armitage remarks that Dee "was the first to theorise the maritime conception of the British Empire," and he adds that Dee elaborated this idea "over two decades, until it became the defining feature of the empire itself" (2000, 105–106). Dee justifies the English claim to certain overseas territories dynastically through the mythical ancestor of the Tudors, King Arthur, who had reigned over a vast empire (Yates, 1975, 50). The *Memorials* casually allude to entitlements to territories beyond the British Isles. Dee had elaborated on these claims in his previous work, *Brytanici Imperii Limites*, published in 1576 and promoting an "Arthurian British Empire, stretching from Florida through north-east America to Scandinavia and France" (Parry 2006, 645). In *Memorials*, Dee referred to "the lawfull and very honourable Entitling of our most gratious and Soueraigne Lady, QUEENE ELIZABETH, (and so, this BRYTISH SCEPTRE ROYALL) *to very large Forrein Dominions*" (1577, xvi). The "IMPERIALL SHIP" in the frontispiece does not directly indicate the English claim to these territories, but it does represent a means of conquest and overseas travel. Elizabeth in the role of helmswoman controls the extension of her sphere of influence and an English 'Sea Soueraignty' (1577, 39). While Dee's reference to further foreign territories of a British empire remains vague in the *Memorials*, the sovereignty over the sea adjacent to the British Isles is, in contrast, clearly stated: his historical reference to King Edgar and his navy gives prominence to this statement (1577, 39). Sea power and sovereignty over Europe are closely linked (Armitage 2000, 102), as the leading power steers the vessel while other nations are dismissed from the 'ship of Europe' entirely. The woodcut pleads to make its vision a reality.

'Ship of State' and 'Ship of Europe': Contesting Allegories

The representation of the English court on board the ship and the depiction of the royal coat of arms on the rudder seem to suggest a primarily national context. John Cooper, for example, ignores the writing and the figure of Europa on the side of the ship and simply refers to it as a "ship of state" (Cooper 2011, 313). According to Stephan Leibfried, use of the 'ship of Europe' allegory represented a novelty, whereas the 'ship of state' allegory originated from an ancient figure of speech (2010, 6). Leibfried points out the currency of this allegory since the fifth century BC in Aristophanes's *The Wasps*, with other prominent occurrences in Plato's *Republic* and in Horace's poem *O Navis Referent* (Leibfried 2010, 5). Ship and state both represent governable entities, as the Latin root of 'govern,' 'gubernare,' meaning "to con a ship" (*OED*, s.v. "govern"), indicates. Dietmar Peil observes that the allegory of the 'ship of state' is a complex construct with blurred contours in several respects: like the state, the ship represents an entity of compound parts that make it difficult to pinpoint an exact counterpart (1983, 863). Generally, the ship functions as a vehicle and the state is the tenor: there is a helmsman who steers the ship and sets the direction of the vessel, in the same way that a monarch rules the country. The ability to steer a ship is thus transferable to the ability to rule (Wolff 2011, 327). The officers are either the courtiers or, more generally, subjects executing certain tasks and acting on behalf of the monarch. Both ship and state are finite in extent and governed by certain rules and hierarchies.

While still finite in extent, the tenor of Dee's 'ship of Europe' is expanded from a single state to an entire continent. Like a ship, Europe is framed (in the south, west, and north, at least) by the sea, which functions as a border, but also as a space to be explored and expanded into. Of course, such expansion worked primarily on a national level as countries and their monarchs, courtiers, or trading companies sent ships overseas. However, as a whole, the ships that were sent out represented a peculiarly European domain of activity and competition. From today's perspective, this phenomenon is underlined by a phrase like 'Age of Discovery,' which indicates that "mastery of the sea became the basis for the eventual extension of European influence into every inhabited continent" (Arnold 2002, xi). It is evident that only those who took an active part in seafaring could become influential powers in Europe. Naval power equalled political power in early modern Europe due to the significance of overseas trade and colonialism. In that sense, the ship represents 'Europe,' even though there is clearly no individual who might be identified as the institutional 'helmsman' of Europe. It is remarkable that Dee's frontispiece constructs this office as a position of power and honour: through the image of the ship, Europe becomes conceivable as a unit to be (literally) governed by a single leader "[i]n wealth far passing all other: in Strength, and Force, INVINCIBLE: and in Honorable estimation, Triumphantly Famous ouer all, and aboue all other" (1577, 63).

Conclusion

My reading of Dee's frontispiece and its gloss in the *Memorials* has revealed a number of European contexts for the allegory of the 'ship of Europe': the first is closely linked to the image of the ship itself, as it denotes naval and political power, overseas expansion, and the struggle for hegemony at sea that were central to contemporary European powers. Consequently, the depiction of Elizabeth and her courtiers on board can be interpreted as Dee's vision for the English joining this struggle for naval supremacy at a time he presents as particularly promising. The power that gains the position of the helmsman will 'steer' Europe into the future. Europe emerges as a system of powers marked by hierarchy and internal competition, not least with respect to seafaring: the powers competing with one another for the rule of the seas—the position of helmsman and crew of the 'ship of Europe'—form a distinct group of rivalling countries bound by antagonistic relations. The allegorical 'ship of Europe' symbolizes not only the means to gain supremacy, but more poignantly, it marks the hegemonic struggle, the present sphere of influence that the victors stand to gain, and the future 'foreign' destiny of that entity, Europe, across the sea. That destiny is framed in an imperial tradition that the English ought to preserve, as Dee pleads.

The Judaeo-Christian and Graeco-Roman symbolism employed in the frontispiece implies cultural and religious lines of tradition that are taken up by the English as form of legacy. The reference to the myth of Europa, like the precedent Dee evokes from Pliny, provides a classical legitimation for England's projected rise as a leading naval power. Dee's use of this type of symbolism is national rather than European, however: England partakes of this tradition, but it must play its own part within it. The Judaeo-Christian symbols in the frontispiece stress the sense of Europe as *Christianitas*. "Europe" and "the most parte of Christendome" appear interchangeable, and the allegorical 'ship of Europe' thus comprises a community in Christian belief. Both lines of tradition, the use of Graeco-Roman and Judaeo-Christian symbolism, are combined in the woodcut to emphasize and legitimize the opportunity that Dee saw for the English to become the leading power in Europe. Dee claimed that this opportunity constituted a divine invitation, represented through Lady Occasion. The multiplicity of dimensions to the frontispiece—*plura latent quam patent*—makes it difficult to guess what ultimately prompted Dee to label the ship 'Europe'; however, I hope to have shown that he perceived a distinctly and multifariously 'European' dimension to the contemporary struggle for naval supremacy and the rivalry it entailed.

Works Cited

Adam, Armin. 2006. "Res Publica Christiana? Die Bedeutung des Christentums für die Idee 'Europa'." In *Politik und Religion in der europäischen Union. Zwischen nationalen Traditionen und Europäisierung*, edited by Hartmut Behr and Mathias Hildebrandt, 21–32. Wiesbaden: VS Verlag für Sozialwissenschaften.

Armitage, David. 2000. *The Ideological Origins of the British Empire*. Cambridge: Cambridge University Press.

Arnold, David. 2002. *The Age of Discovery, 1400–1600*. 2nd ed. London: Routledge.

Clucas, Stephen. 2006. *John Dee: Interdisciplinary Studies in English Renaissance Thought*. Dordrecht: Springer.

Clulee, Nicholas H. 1988. *John Dee's Natural Philosophy: Between Science and Religion*. London: Routledge.

Cooper, John. 2011. *The Queen's Agent: Francis Walsingham and the Court of Elizabeth I*. London: Faber & Faber.

Corbett, Margery, and Ronald Lightbown. 1979. *The Comely Frontispiece: The Emblematic Title-Page in England 1550–1660*. London: Routledge & Paul.

Cormack, Lesley B. 2001. "Britannia Rules the Waves?: Images of Empire in Elizabethan England." In *Literature, Mapping, and the Politics of Space in Early Modern Britain*, edited by Andrew Gordon and Bernhard Klein, 45–68. Cambridge: Cambridge University Press.

Dalton, Karen C. C. 2000. "Art for the Sake of Dynasty." In *Early Modern Visual Culture: Representation, Race, and Empire in Renaissance England*, edited by Peter Erickson and Clark Hulse, 178–214. Philadelphia: University of Pennsylvania Press.

Dee, John. 1577. *General and Rare Memorials Pertayning to the Perfect Arte of Navigation*. London.

Dee, John. 1577. Title page. *General and Rare Memorials Pertayning to the Perfect Arte of Navigation*. London. Hand-coloured woodcut with gold and silver. Douce, D. subt. 30. Bodleian Library, Oxford University.

French, Peter J. 1972. *John Dee: The World of an Elizabethan Magus*. London: Routledge & Kegan Paul.

"govern, v." *OED Online*. March 2014. Oxford University Press.

Harkness, Deborah E. 1999. *John Dee's Conversations with Angels: Cabala, Alchemy, and the End of Nature*. Cambridge: Cambridge University Press.

"hieroglyph, n." *OED Online*. March 2015. Oxford University Press.

Leibfried, Stephan. 2010. "Das Staatsschiff Europa: Eine kleine Bildgeschichte." SFB 597 "Staatlichkeit im Wandel"—*Transformations of the State*. TranState Working Papers 118. Bremen: Universität, Sonderforschungsbereich 597.

Loades, David. 2009. *The Making of the Elizabethan Navy 1540–1590: From the Solent to the Armada*. Woodbridge: Boydell.

Marshall, Tristan. 2000. *Theatre and Empire: Great Britain on the London Stage under James VI and I*. Manchester: Manchester University Press.

Oxford Dictionary of Christian Art and Architecture. 2013. Edited by Tom Devonshire Jones, Linda Murray and Peter Murray. Oxford: Oxford University Press.

Parry, Glyn. 2006. "John Dee and the Elizabethan British Empire in Its European Context." *The Historical Journal* 49 (3): 643–675.

Parry, Glyn. 2011. *The Arch Conjuror of England: John Dee*. New Haven, CT: Yale University Press.

Peil, Dietmar. 1983. *Untersuchungen zur Staats- und Herrschaftsmetaphorik in literarischen Zeugnissen von der Antike bis zur Gegenwart.* Munich: Fink.

Sherman, William Howard. 1997. *John Dee: The Politics of Reading and Writing in the English Renaissance.* Amherst: University of Massachusetts Press.

Smith, Roger C. 1993. *Vanguard of Empire: Ships of Exploration in the Age of Columbus.* New York: Oxford University Press.

Szonyi, Gyorgy E. 2004. *John Dee's Occultism: Magical Exaltation Through Powerful Signs.* Albany: State University of New York Press.

Whitby, Christopher. 1988. *John Dee's Actions with Spirits.* Vols. 1 & 2. New York: Garland.

Wolff, Vera. 2011. "Schiff." In *Handbuch der politischen Ikonographie,* Vol. 2, edited by Uwe Fleckner, Martin Warnke und Hendrik Ziegler, 325–331. Munich: C. H. Beck.

Yates, Frances A. 1975. *Astraea: The Imperial Theme in the Sixteenth Century.* London: Routledge and Kegan Paul.

10 The European Imaginary in the Discourse on Peace

Paul Michael Lützeler

Theories on the Foundational Components of European Culture

Whenever discourses concerning national and continental cultural developments are discussed, theories of identity, ideology, and the imaginary come into play. First, it is necessary to speak about identity formation at the individual and collective level, which means that the theories of Erik Erikson (1968) and Benedict Anderson (2003) have to be considered. Furthermore one has to explain what the imaginary is all about, referring to the theories of Maurice Halbwachs (1952), Cornelius Castoriadis (1975), and Jan Assmann (2011) and Aleida Assmann (2007) as well as Michael Rothberg (2009)—in other words, one needs to speak of memory as an imagined past. Yet there is also the imagined future, an aspect dealt with by Karl Marx (1969), Karl Mannheim (1929), and Paul Ricoeur (1997) in their reflections on utopia and ideology. Memories and utopias have a special function within identity constructs. Memory provides contours for past experiences, while the utopian element, with its creative, critical, and potentially subversive characteristics, prepares the way for future identity changes. The imaginary, with its plasticity, processual quality, and openness, can prevent the ideologization of memory and utopia. The imaginary moment allows collective identities to adapt to new social and historical realities. In addition, the imaginary ensures that, on the one hand, memory will not be understood as a neutral container or storehouse for fixed data, while on the other hand, utopian ideas will be saved from becoming stagnant and dogmatic. The imaginary keeps both past and future dimensions dynamic and changing, thereby working against taboos and calling conventional ideas into question. By contrast, ideology—because it is determined by power interests—is constantly striving to reduce dominant aspects of a collective identity to a system of creedal principles that may be used as a social or political tool. The imaginary and the ideological are in a constant state of negative tension. While the imaginary tends towards expanding the boundaries of collective identities, ideology seeks to represent those boundaries as closed and the collective identity as final and usable in a power struggle.

Here we want to achieve insight into the European imaginary as a vision of peace. It is not our ambition to come up with a theory about European identity as such or with a model that tries to explain European cultural developments in general. Castoriadis has described the social imaginary as a set of values, institutions, laws, and symbols to a particular group. The imaginary is not necessarily 'real' as it is contingent on the imagination of a social subject. Castoriadis is interested in the effect the imaginary has on institutions and the effect the institutions have on the imaginary. In the case of the discourse on Europe, the discourse on peace is of particular relevance. Different from specialized discourses on Europe concerned exclusively with political, economic, or educational topics, the discourse on peace encompasses the realm of politics, economics, and culture in the broadest sense. The discourse on peace, time and again, produced a European imaginary (a social imaginary in the words of Cornelius Castoriadis), that suggested alternatives to the bellicose nationalist politics of domination and destruction. The discourse on European peace had and has both a historical and a future-oriented dimension. These dimensions are, on an abstract level, reflected in the theories of collective memory by Halbwachs and cultural memory by Jan Assmann and in the theories on utopia by Karl Mannheim and Paul Ricoeur. According to Halbwachs, human memory can only function within a collective context, and Assmann describes how cultural memory of a social group is activated by education and rituals. This is what the European imaginary is about: keeping the positive and negative experiences of the past alive, extrapolating utopian visions of the future that could continue the best traditions of the past (like the struggle for human rights), and avoiding the self-destructive clashes of the past. While the discourse on peace is only one segment of a larger European imaginary, it is of particular relevance since it never confined itself to glorifying or condemning the past but always had a strong utopian and future-oriented component. While the discourse on European peace is primarily concerned with a continental imaginary, there is nothing exclusionary or essentialist about it. Victor Hugo and Coudenhove-Kalergi showed that the function of a Europe that maintains a domestic peace would have a pacifying effect on the world in general. After the catastrophes of World War II and the Holocaust, the cosmopolitan and global aspects within the European imaginary have been strengthened, especially—but certainly not exclusively—by the contributors to the discourse on Europe in the German-speaking countries (see Lützeler 1994).

It makes sense to have a critical look at two contemporary theories of European culture and see whether they can be helpful in our endeavor. Two books by the French intellectuals Edgar Morin and Rémi Brague about the cultural foundations of Europe have to be mentioned here. Morin speaks in *Penser l'Europe* (1987) about the dialogic relationship that exists between the Greek, the Roman, the Jewish, and the Christian basic elements of European civilization. Morin picks up the idea of the dialogical as developed by Michail Bakhtin in his study on 'the dialogic imagination' (1981). Unlike Hegel and Marx, the proponents of 'dialectics,' Bakhtin discusses the concept of 'dialogics.' Morin does not view the European cultural mix either as a synthesis or as the result of a dialectic process, but rather as a combination of elements that have kept their original 'logics.' These different logics of the Greeks, the Romans and the Jewish and the Christian cultures are now combined in an antagonistic, competitive, or complementary manner. In other words: these building blocks have kept their peculiarities within the cultural mix that has developed over the centuries. This survival of the different logics gives the European culture its specific and productive tension and allows for the different renaissances or revivals of its Greek, Roman, Jewish, and Christian parts. This is a plausible theory, and one could add that each of these four foundational elements is in turn structured internally in a dialogic manner. Greek culture encompasses the very different, if not contradictory, value systems of Sparta and Athens. Rome under republican rule stood for other values and goals than Rome governed by the Caesars. Jewish life is, on the one hand, regulated by Mosaic law, and on the other hand, it has a strong messianic dimension. Christianity is based on the Torah, but also on the belief that the Messiah has introduced new ethical rules. What Morin also does not consider is the fact that in addition to the four elements mentioned, Celtic, Germanic, and Slavic cultures became important parts of the European mix.

Rémi Brague developed his theory of the eccentric structure of the four elements of European culture in his book *Europe. La voie romaine* (1992). Like Morin (whose insights he ignores), Brague considers the building blocks of European culture, that is, the Greek, Roman, Jewish, and Christian heritage. He does not discuss them in terms of a dialogic relationship, but instead focuses on the eccentric constellation between them as segments of the cultural foundation. Rome is the center of a Mediterranean empire of antiquity as well as the center of a Christian west-European culture. Yet neither the Rome of the Caesars nor that of the popes can, according to Brague, claim originality since, as far as goals and aspirations are concerned, they are dependent on Athens on the one hand and on Jerusalem on the other. The Rome of antiquity as well as that of the Christian era are called 'eccentric' because their centers are located outside of their realms in the original cultures of Athens and Jerusalem. Roman culture during the era of the Caesars supposedly was an imitation of Athenian civilization, while the Rome of the popes remained dependent on the religion of Mosaic law and the Jewish prophecies regarding the Messiah. Athens and Jerusalem are considered primary and authentic cultures, while the Rome of antiquity as well as that of Christianity are seen as secondary and imitative. Secondary cultures do not see themselves as complete. The lack of originality and authenticity is, according to Brague, compensated by a dynamic openness that enables the secondary cultures to adjust to ever-new historical developments. Brague's theory provokes a number of questions: can the Rome of the Caesars really be seen in a dependent and secondary situation vis-à-vis Athens? Rome had developed its own myths of origin, in which Athens plays no role. When telling the story about Aeneas as the founder of a new empire in Latium,

Virgil rehabilitated the Trojan dynasty that had been defeated by the Hellenic coalition. It was one of the virtues of Rome that it was able to tolerate and (at least in part) imitate other cultures, that it did not outright reject them as barbarian in principle. Rome had conquered Greece and integrated it into its empire. It was not inclined to look at Hellenic culture from a point of view of inferiority in general. Its own Roman legal system, its political structure, its architectural art, and its military organization were superior to that of the so-called *Graeculi*. When the Romans took lessons in Greek art, mathematics, philosophy, and literature, they did this with the intention to reach Athens' level of learnedness and sophistication. During the age of Augustus, they were rapidly approaching this goal with writers such as Virgil, Horace, and Ovid, with historians like Livius, and with architects like Vitruvius. Rome's superiority was also expressed in its idea of Pax Romana (see Petit 1976), as one can tell from the writings of Pliny the Elder in his *Naturalis Historia*, from Virgil in his *Aeneid*, and from Ovid in his *Fasti*. According to Pliny, Rome spreads *humanitas* all over the world (*Naturalis Historia* III.39); in Virgil's epic, Jupiter lets Aeneas know that he is going to lay the foundations to an "empire without limits" (*Aeneid* I.279), and Ovid has the vision that the space of the city of Rome is identical with that of the earth (*Fasti*, II.684). There is nothing in these statements about a feeling of 'secondarity.' Turning to Christianity: did Paulinian Christianity, which spread through the entire Roman empire, really see itself as dependent on Judaism? Paul saw the future of the new religion more in the conversion of the so-called pagan world than in preaching the gospel to the Jewish communities. He first sought to convert the Greek-speaking population of the eastern part of the Roman empire, and then he turned to the Latin-speaking western part, with the city of Rome as its center. And one can observe an emancipation process of the Ecclesia from the synagogue in the teachings of Paul himself and later in the dogmas of the church fathers and popes in Rome as well as those of the patriarchs in Constantinople. (A weak point in Brague's book is that Europe is only seen on the way to 'Romanity' but that he does not manage to integrate the thousand years of a Christian European development in the Eastern Roman Empire of Byzantium.) It is difficult to accept the hierarchy between the Torah ('original') and the New Testament ('secondary') when studying the history of Christianity. Both the authors of the four canonic gospels and the church fathers try to show that the prophecies of the Old Testament regarding the Messiah find their fulfillment in Jesus Christ. Fulfillment implies both an ending and a new beginning (see Dahlheim 2013).

One should also note that neither Morin nor Brague integrates more recent theories of hybridity and cultural transfer into their studies.[1] During the 1990s, a number of cultural critics and philosophers reflected on inter-cultural constellations, on migration, exile, postcolonialism, and globalization. One thinks of names such as Edward Said (1978, 1993, and 2000), Édouard Glissant (1996), Zygmunt Bauman (2000), Homi Bhabha (1994), Michael

Werner (Werner and Lackner 1999), Stephen Greenblatt and Catherine Gallagher (2001), and Gayatri Chakravorty Spivak (1990 and 2012). Since then, at least, the 'authentic' nature of cultures has been called into question by new theoretical models, in field- and case studies regarding cultural fluidity, subversion, mimesis, adaption, métissage, and creolization. In respect to the Mediterranean region Fernand Braudel has done groundbreaking work (2001, see also Seznec 1940). How interrelated were the cultures in this part of the world? How 'original' was the Hellenic civilization? How much did it owe to earlier cultures like those of the Phoenicians and the Egyptians?

The Discourse on Peace from the Fourteenth to the Seventeenth Century

In connection with the discourse on Europe as a discourse on peace, it seems preferable to focus on the interrelation of its imaginary memorial as well as utopian and ideological aspects than to develop yet another theory about the mechanism and impact of the relation between the foundational components of European identity. The visions of peace summarized here show that this continental imaginary has a subsidiary structure. The discourse on European peace has hardly ever tried to promote European identity as a totalizing concept that would supersede all other identities. On the contrary, it has not simply allowed for, but has actually sought to reinforce, other collective identities, including familial, religious, professional, local, regional, national, or, for that matter, cosmopolitan, global ones. Thus, one can speak of the subsidiary structure of a collective identity in terms of ever-widening concentric circles, from the local to the regional, the national, the continental, and finally the global. At the same time, the relationship among these collective identities is dialogic, with inevitable internal frictions. Whenever a certain identity formation, such as that of nationality, developed dogmatic, dominating, and militaristic ideologies, the European imaginary served to relativize and attack such ambitions. The discourse on European peace reminded the representatives of other collective groups that the continent shared a multifaceted culture that was worth protecting against destructive forces from within and without.

Over the centuries, representatives from all layers of society and from nearly all European countries have contributed to the Europe discourse: writers, politicians, philosophers, church leaders, and scholars from all branches of the social sciences and the humanities. Interestingly, the particular discourse on continental peace was carried forward almost exclusively by writers, thinkers, and intellectuals. At its very core, the discourse on Europe is a discourse on peace. It developed in response to a succession of great continental wars, as an expression of trauma, of pain and shock; and it created imaginaries that, as memory, harked back to peaceful times in the past, or, as utopia, articulated visions of a united Europe that would cultivate attitudes or build institutions designed to prevent a recurrence of war. From medieval times to the present, various writers have attempted to add to the continental discourse on peace. It is a dialogue that continues through the ages, for these authors were aware of the contributions of their predecessors.

Just as the national discourse started long before the invention of the printing press, the continental discourse was already part of medieval thought. Pierre Dubois (1250–1320), who nowadays would be described as a publicist, was trained in philosophical and legal studies. A prolific writer, he eventually became a royal advisor at the Court of Philip the Fair in Paris. In 1306 Dubois published *De recuperatione Terrae Sanctae* [The Recovery of the Holy Land], in which he suggested—and this was revolutionary for the time—a federation of European states. This federation would guarantee peace between the different European states by creating a permanent court of arbitration, where all major conflicts between different dynasties and nations could be discussed and peacefully resolved. The arbitration committee would consist of leading politicians from the member states, along with Church representatives, and would be chaired by the pope. At the time, a conflict was brewing between England and France that, less than 30 years later, would develop into the Hundred Years' War. In order to prevent Europe's self-destruction, Dubois wanted to see a continental peace guarded by a supranational institution. Still, he was anything but a pacifist, nor was his argument informed by the ethics of Christian love for humanity as such. What Dubois proposed was that, instead of destroying itself, a united Europe should combine its forces and fight against the so-called infidels in the Holy Land. His plea was in vain, as the Crusades were over; and so, European unity remained a dream for the time (see Terminski 2011).

At about the same time, in 1308, Dante Alighieri (1265–1321) began work on his *Commedia*, and during the same year, he wrote the treatise *De Monarchia* [On Monarchy].[2] Like Dubois before him, Dante advocated both a European federation of states and a court of arbitration to secure peace between the states of the continent. However, this court was to be headed not by the pope, but by the emperor of the Holy Roman Empire. Dante envisioned a European universal monarchy as it had existed under Charlemagne some 500 years earlier. He foresaw a further disintegration of the Holy Roman Empire, which, along with the growing power of nation-states like Spain and France, would lead to territorial wars in the future. Unlike Dubois, however, Dante did not propose to exchange internal European wars for military campaigns against external adversaries.

It took another 150 years for a historic constellation to emerge that would again give rise to a plan for a federation of European states. In 1453, the Ottoman empire had conquered Constantinople, and this victory raised the alarm throughout the Continent. Anton Marini of Grenoble, a diplomat specialized in international law, was much sought after as an advisor by a number of European courts. The plan he came up with in 1464 was more detailed than those of Dubois and Dante: Marini not only proposed that a federal court of arbitration be set up, but he also favored the creation of other institutions, such as a federal council, a federal assembly, and a corps of federal officials. The original purpose of the plan was to create a united European military force that would combat the Ottoman empire's ongoing expansion into the southeastern parts of the Continent. Marini, however, had to scale down his ambitions, as the only king who showed any enthusiasm for these ideas was Georg Podiebrad (1420–1471) of Bohemia, who adopted Marini's treatise as his own (it has been called the Podiebrad Plan ever since). The plan centered on a combined military effort by Bohemia, France, and the Republic of Venice against the Turks. The pope in Rome, who should have been happy about this Bohemian initiative, in fact did not like it at all, as Podiebrad had meanwhile become a follower of Jan Hus (1369–1415). Podiebrad was declared a heretic, and Marini's federation plan was shelved (see Heymann 1965).

Still, the ideas remained out there, and another 170 years later, Europe was confronted with renewed catastrophe in the form of the Thirty Years' War, a continent-wide orgy of destruction that prompted renewed reflections on European unity and peace. At the beginning of the 1630s, Maximilien de Béthune, better known as the Duc de Sully, wrote his memoirs. He had been the friend and right-hand man of Henri IV, and at the center of his autobiography he included "Le Grand Dessein" [The Great Plan] of his revered king (see Heater 1992, 22–38). Historians have since determined that this very detailed plan was in large part a product of Sully's own political imagination. Had it not been for the looming disaster of the continental war, Sully quite possibly might never have disclosed his grand design for a European federation. In any case, none of his predecessors had formulated a more differentiated and action-oriented plan for a continental political union than Sully had. His 'Great Plan' developed the vision of a federated continental union in which each member state would be represented and would have an impact on insuring peaceful developments in Europe. Sully called this union a 'General Council of Europe,' or a 'Confederation of Princes.' The major goals of this union would be religious tolerance in order to prevent civil wars, a balance of power on the Continent, and a common defence system against the Ottoman empire as well as against Russia.

Sully argued that the old idea of a universal monarchy could not work for the many powerful, independent nations that had since arisen in Europe. He counted 15 major Christian states which he intended to form into a federation to replace the Holy Roman Empire as the dominant continental power. Sully—like Richelieu at the time (see Blanchard 2011)—firmly opposed the European dominance of the House of Habsburg; he wanted the House of Bourbon to be placed in charge of the great continental changes. He believed that, far from preventing wars, Habsburg had instigated them, and instead of preserving the peace, the Habsburgs had broken it. The new instrument of power for securing continental peace would be a European

Senate with 66 members. Depending on the power and size of each country, it would send two to four representatives, with a new delegation to be chosen every three years. The decisions made and the laws passed in the Senate would be binding for all member states.

Reasonable and forward looking as its provisions were, there remained one major problem with this Grand Design. As Sully explains, Henri IV wanted to start the great European war against the house of Habsburg—one of those infamous wars "to end all wars." Specifically, the king's plan was to expand the War of the Jülich Succession into a continental war against Habsburg supremacy. However, in 1610, just as he was about to join his waiting army and enter the war, Henri IV was assassinated. This meant the end also of his—or rather, Sully's—Great Plan, although it did retain a life of its own during the centuries that followed, becoming a blueprint for several other peace plans in Europe. Indeed, a number of the federal institutions described by Sully are recognizable to this day in the administrative, political, and legal structures of the European Union. The idea of basing the federal institutions of the Council of Europe in different European cities was Sully's; among other locations, he had suggested the cities of Luxembourg and Strasbourg as centers of European federalism. (Interestingly enough, among the peace strategists who contributed to the discourse on Europe, Sully remains the only politician—although he penned his memoirs as a retired politician-turned-author.)

Fifty years later, in 1693, William Penn (1644–1718) drafted another plan for establishing peace in Europe. Penn was a British citizen who had founded the English colony of Pennsylvania in North America in 1681, with Philadelphia ('the city of brotherly love') as its capital, and who in all likelihood never would have left England for America, had he not suffered persecution, including incarceration, in London because of his religious beliefs. As a young man, Penn had joined the Society of Friends, a move that immediately landed him in deep trouble in England under Charles II (1630–1685). The visionary and charismatic Penn spent more time in England than in America, travelled back and forth, and considered himself a European. Having previously drafted a plan for the unification of the British colonies in North America, Penn drew up a similar proposal for the European nations. An active citizen and politician, Penn was equally productive as a writer. His farsighted "Essay towards the Present and Future Peace of Europe by the Establishment of an European Dyet, Parliament of Estates" (1693) proposed a European union that would secure continental peace, as well as an increase in trade and economic productivity. He even suggested the creation of a European passport that would permit its holders free movement across the Continent. The European assembly Penn envisioned would have representatives from all states, and their number would depend on the economic strength of the individual country. As was the case with earlier, similar drafts, the decisions of the Assembly would be binding for all member states (see Dunn 1967).

The Discourse on Peace from the Eighteenth to the Twentieth Century

Only a few years later, from 1712 onwards, the French writer and philosopher Charles-Irénée Castel (1658–1743), better known under his pseudonym, Abbé de Saint-Pierre, published his "Projet pour rendre la paix perpétuelle" [Project on Perpetual Peace]. Saint-Pierre had lived through the War of Spanish Succession (1701–1714), subsequently becoming an advisor to the French delegation during the peace negotiations in Utrecht in 1713. The House of Bourbon under Louis XIV and the House of Habsburg under Charles VI were once again involved in a major conflict, this time over the succession to the throne in Madrid (see Lynn 2002). A number of leading powers in Europe, including England, became involved in this conflict both on the European Continent and in North America, and after a dozen years the war had cost the lives of close to half a million people. In the end—and this had been England's goal—the balance of power had been restored on the Continent, ending the dominance of France for at least a century. Saint-Pierre wrote one of the most detailed and, in the long run, most influential treatises on European peace. He discussed the suggestions Sully had made and built on them. His federation would also consist of a European Council or Senate, a European Secretariat, and a court of arbitration. The Senate would be charged primarily with the task of securing the peace and would determine troop contingents of each country, but it would also deal with economic relations. Once the union had 14 members, countries not joining the league would be considered enemies of European peace, and the union could enforce membership. Like Sully, Saint-Pierre saw in the power of the emperor in Vienna the major reason for the never-ending succession of wars in Europe. According to Saint-Pierre, the Habsburg dynasty used its dominance in Germany to enrich itself illegally. The end of the Holy Roman Empire and the reduction of Austria to a 'normal' nation were seen as the preconditions of continental peace. Saint-Pierre consulted leading European minds on this issue, among them Gottfried Wilhelm Leibniz (1646–1716). Leibniz did not agree with Saint-Pierre's suggestions, since they were directly opposed to his own vision of peaceful relations between the European nations. Those who knew his publications on the role of the Holy Roman Empire could hardly believe that he would suggest anything that would bring harm to the integrity of this political body. Leibniz brought it to Saint-Pierre's attention that the Empire left a maximum of autonomy to its German states but that, at the same time, the emperor made sure that the glue that kept them together was strong enough to guarantee peace among its members. For him, the 'Reich' represented an ideal model of peace and a symbol of European unity. He argued against Saint-Pierre in pointing out that the emperors had not usurped their power but that they had restrained the leaders of individual German states and principalities from fighting each other over territories and influence. Furthermore, it was the emperor and his 'Reich' that—with increasing success—protected Europe against the assaults of the Ottoman empire. Saint-Pierre's vision also conflicted with his utopian idea of the reunification of the Christian denominations in Europe. Leibniz saw this as the precondition for forming a global cultural community. Without the support of the emperor as the protector of the Christian world, this goal seemed unattainable to him (see Tielker 1998, 121ff.).

It was Jean-Jacques Rousseau (1712–1778) who, between 1754 and 1761, rediscovered Saint Pierre's plan. Rousseau edited a popular version that included his own comments, and he wrote a separate piece in which he assessed the plan, at the same time reminding his readers of the older, similar proposals developed by Sully. His different comments on Saint-Pierre's book were published posthumously under the title "Jugement sur le projet de la paix perpétuelle de l'Abbé de Saint-Pierre" [Judgement of Monsieur l'Abbé de Saint-Pierre's 'Plan for Perpetual Peace'] (see Stelling-Michaud 1964). Rousseau criticized Saint-Pierre, dismissing a number of his assumptions and ideas as illusory. Yet, in the end, he too supported the idea of a federal European community and a court of arbitration along with other viable institutions designed to secure peace on the Continent. Where Saint-Pierre had argued that preserving peace would serve the cause of justice, Rousseau pointed out that peace would also be in the interest of the rulers of the European states, monarchs who tended to think exclusively in terms of war when reflecting on their relations with other powers. War was again raging as Rousseau began a new discussion of Saint-Pierre's project: France was now heavily involved in the Seven Years' War in Europe, which in turn was connected with the French and Indian War in North America, with France and England fighting to secure spheres of influence in Europe as well as dominance on the North American continent. As Churchill once observed, this conflict was truly the first World War in human history, and by the time it ended, some one million people had lost their lives. Rousseau had been right in stating that peace would be in the interest of the kings, at least as far as France was concerned at that particular moment in history. Having lost the war, France was now no longer the dominant continental state in Europe, and was finished as a power in the Americas, where it lost all its colonial territories except for a handful of Caribbean islands (see Anderson [2000]).

Forty years went by before another writer, Immanuel Kant (1724–1804), presented a treatise on the topic of Europe, which he called "Zum ewigen Frieden" [Towards Perpetual Peace] (published 1795). At the time, Prussia had made peace with the French, ending its participation in the First Coalition War against revolutionary France. As a Prussian, Kant reflected on the conditions that would be necessary to secure this peace treaty. His essay differs from those of his predecessors in many ways. While also suggesting the formation of a "federation of free states" in Europe, Kant did not go into any detail regarding its institutional structure. In his view, legal foundations and political actions in each European nation were of greater relevance with regard to preventing wars and guaranteeing peace between states. Kant's advice to political leaders is contained in the following postulations: no independent nation may be taken over by another nation; standing armies are to be abolished; no nation shall forcibly interfere with the constitution and government of another country; and the civil constitution of every nation is to be republican. Kant's suggestions are based on the idea of natural law developed by Hugo Grotius and Samuel von Pufendorf in the seventeenth century, including the right to life, to the integrity of one's body, and to liberty. In his treatise, Kant sought to apply the principles of natural law to the relations between states. However, Kant himself was well aware of the utopian character of the idea of perpetual peace, something he made clear in his opening statement, which alludes to the fact that "eternal peace" is commonly associated with the buried dead in churchyards (see Vohra [2007]).

Four years later, in 1799, during the Second Coalition War against France, the young Romantic Novalis (1772–1801) wrote his essay "Europa" (later called "Die Christenheit oder Europa" [Christendom or Europe]). Unlike Saint-Pierre, Novalis was not concerned with political structures, and unlike Kant, he did not place his trust in legal arrangements. For him, the unity of Europe and continental peace could only be guaranteed by a revival of Christian culture, by rediscovering the religious basis of the Continent. It may well be that Novalis had been influenced by Erasmus's plea for peace in the name of Christianity, in a treatise appealing to the Christian rulers of his time published in 1517 (the same year that Luther pinned his reform theses to the entrance door of the church in Wittenberg; see Huizinga 1957). Erasmus's message articulates an unshakeable conviction that Christ, as the Prince of Peace, must be a model for all European monarchs. He must have known that his plea would be in vain, however, since the ruling dynasties of Europe had never been influenced by Christian charity in making decisions about war and peace. In spite of this, and possibly due to the influence of writings such as those of Erasmus, Novalis projected the idea of cultural unity, harmony and peace onto medieval Europe. And while he did not plead for a return to medieval conditions, Novalis did in fact think of the cultural 'Golden Age' of the Middle Ages as a model for a future united Europe, centered upon a revitalized Christianity, that would serve as a guarantee for perpetual peace (see Lützeler 1992, 33ff.). Novalis's ideas touched the Romantic generation. A point in case is the *Lukasbund* of young painters, the so-called "Nazarenes," who in 1808 travelled from Vienna to Rome to dedicate their talent to the revival of a Christian art that would be rooted in the works of late medieval and early modern painters such as the Van Eyck brothers, Raphael, Michelangelo and Dürer (see Frank 2001).

Novalis had written his essay on Europe in 1799, at the very beginning of Bonaparte's rule in France. In 1814, immediately after Napoleon's resignation, we find ourselves back in Paris, where the philosopher Claude-Henri de Saint-Simon (1760–1825), together with the historian Augustin Thierry (1769–1825), published a most remarkable plan with the title "De la réorganization de la société Européenne" [On the Reconstruction of the European State System]. After nearly 25 years of Napoleonic wars, including the horrors of the disastrously failed campaign against Russia, the time was ripe for another peace plan. Saint-Simon builds on the ideas of Sully and Saint-Pierre. In a different way than Novalis, he is both highly pragmatic and very utopian at the same time. He proposes the unification of the Continent under a European monarch, a European Parliament (with a House of Commons and a House of Lords), and a common European legal system. Britain's constitutional monarchy served as the state model for a unified Continent. Saint-Simon believed that the unification process would take place in different phases, starting with a nucleus consisting of France and England, later to be joined by Germany. Once this triad was cooperating, the remaining countries would join, one after the other. Saint-Simon had no illusions about the length of the process: he considered that it would take about 200 years—a good estimate, as it turned out (see Pétré-Grenouilleau 2001).

Another three decades later, the Romantic novelist Victor Hugo (1802–1885), following the smashing success of *The Hunchback of Notre Dame*, became one of the most active participants in the discourse on Europe. In 1849, after Europe had experienced civil wars in a number of countries, Hugo delivered a speech titled "Les états unis d'Europe" [The United States of Europe] as his presidential address to the International Peace Congress in Paris. As president of the Congress, Hugo advocated universal peace, but as the title of his lecture indicates, he was primarily interested in creating political structures that would guarantee peace in Europe. Though not a Eurocentrist, Hugo understood clearly that, for the foreseeable future at least, peace on the Continent could well lead to peace on earth more generally. He predicted that European unity would come and that the European nations would one day become provinces within a 'United States of Europe'—just as, over the centuries, Burgundy, Normandy, and Brittany became regions within the state of France. Hugo gave a detailed report on the enormous financial burdens Europe's citizens must shoulder in order to support their countries' war machineries. If that money were instead invested in science, art, agriculture, industry, trade, and navigation, poverty would disappear—not only in Europe but probably globally. Later in his life, following the Franco-German War of 1870/1871, Hugo proposed the unification of France and Germany as the nucleus of a united Europe of the future (see Metzidakis 1994/1995). He was joined by an admirer and ally, Bertha von Suttner, author of the bestselling *Down with Arms* and a leading supporter of international peace movements who had experienced at first hand the horrors of recent wars between Italy and Austria and between Austria and Prussia. In 1882, during the Fourth World Peace Congress in Berne, von Suttner proposed the establishment of a Federation of European States that would make peacekeeping its first priority and that would also work to improve conditions for free trade on the continent. She published her ideas about European and international peace in the volume *Der Menschheit Hochgedanken* [High Aspirations of Mankind] in 1910 (see Hoock-Demarle 2013).

In the short run, all of the peace efforts articulated by writers and philosophers in the European discourse were in vain. The First World War seemed to demonstrate that Europe was destined to destroy itself. During that war, the French government even forced the writer Romain Rolland (1866–1944) into exile in Geneva for his pacifist activities (see Fisher 1988). Rolland had been a tireless proponent of European cooperation and peace, as he had shown before the war with his novel *Jean-Christophe* (see Lützeler 2007, 162–185). He inspired a group of writers including Annette Kolb, Stefan Zweig, René Schickele, and Heinrich Mann, all of whom supported peace efforts in their writings.

A few years after the First World War, the intellectual Richard Coudenhove-Kalergi (1894–1972) demonstrated that he had closely studied the ideas of Sully, Saint-Pierre, Rousseau, Saint-Simon, Victor Hugo, and Bertha von Suttner when, in 1922, he drafted a visionary plan for a united Europe (Pan-Europa, as he called it) with the aim of preventing another catastrophe like the one that had engulfed the continent between 1914 and 1918. Despite support from many writers, among them Thomas Mann, as well as from such leading politicians as Aristide Briand, the Pan Europe group was far from a grassroots movement; in terms of public support, it lagged far behind the right-wing nationalist parties. And in spite of all of Coudenhove-Kalergi's great efforts on behalf of peace, the German National Socialists soon started a war in Europe that quickly turned into another world war (see Ziegenhofer-Prettenthaler 2004 and Saint-Gille 2003).

The first person to come up with a peace plan for Europe after World War II was, once again, a writer. Beginning in 1945, numerous copies of Ernst Jünger's essay "Der Friede" ["The Peace"] circulated throughout Germany. A historian by training, Jünger was certain that the continent's longing for unity had started centuries before Charlemagne had founded his Christian empire. "The Peace" is a document that combines French pragmatism and German Romanticism in an interesting manner. Much like his French predecessors, Jünger proposed a unified Europe with its own constitution, one that would guarantee peace in the future. He believed that both the nations and their regions would profit from such a federation, in which the national borders would disappear. Federal systems like the United States or Switzerland could serve as models for a united Europe. However, as Novalis too had argued, Jünger insisted that rationally constructed institutions alone would not lead to continental peace. He believed that religion would have to play a central role in the reconstruction process, and he demanded that the best European minds study theology in order to better understand the continent's cultural foundation and its cultural mission, with peace at its very center (see Lützeler 1992, 402–408).

It is not surprising that, during the Cold War, the most prominent contribution to the European peace discourse came from a country located behind the so-called Iron Curtain. The Hungarian novelist and essayist György Konrád (1933–) published his book *Antipolitik* (Anti-Politics) in 1985, at a time when the political classes in the West and the East still believed the division of Europe would continue forever. Konrád defines an antipolitical attitude as a position from which one thinks about political issues in terms that are alien to politicians. Only such a nonprofessional point of view, with its possibility of thinking beyond the status quo, would guarantee new questions and bring about new solutions. Konrád's proposal was that the Yalta Agreement be dissolved, that the Russians withdraw their armies and their bureaucrats behind their own national borders, that the Americans in turn leave western Europe, and that Europe be left to the Europeans. This would bring about new debates over political organization, leading ultimately to the unification of Europe, which would guarantee peace on a continent that, for some 40 years, had been on the verge of nuclear war between NATO and the Warsaw Pact.

These were mere dreams in 1985; at the time, Konrád himself spoke of "my dream of Europe" (Lützeler 1997, 177–194). Meanwhile, of course, much of Konrád's vision has become a reality, although no one seems to have foreseen the civil war in former Yugoslavia, nor the territorial conflicts between Ukraine and Russia. The ensuing flood of political statements from writers and public intellectuals around these conflicts has so far produced no document comparable to the farsighted "Grand Designs" of thinkers from Sully to Saint-Simon, or from Kant to Konrád. Rather, Konrád's understanding of "antipolitics" can be seen as having been a hallmark of the writers' peace-oriented Europe discourse from the very beginning. All had in common a capacity for "thinking outside the box" of routine politics, and this is what saved their imaginaries from becoming ideologically petrified.

In the end, we have to ask ourselves whether these contributions to the European peace discourse had any effect at all; one ought, perhaps, neither to overestimate nor underestimate them. What seems clear, however, is that, in these writings, fundamental ideas about and designs for the institutions of a unified Europe were developed. Only in the wake of the catastrophe of World War II, after Europe had lost its independence—that is, its status as subject, as a major player in world history—did the time appear to be ripe for building, on the ruins of a continent, a new edifice that would have unity and peace as its goal. And at that very moment in time, the vocabulary and grammar for a new political language, for a new common discourse on European unity and peace were available, thanks to the centuries-old efforts of European writers and intellectuals. Their language was adopted by the founding fathers of Europe, the Adenauers and de Gasperis, the Schumanns and Monnets, the Spaacks and Hallsteins. It is not by chance that most of these politicians, signatories of the Treaty of Rome in 1957, were students of Coudenhove-Kalergi; and Couldenhove-Kalergi in turn is unthinkable without the earlier Great Plans of Sully, Saint-Pierre, Saint-Simon, and Victor Hugo. In other words, their intellectual efforts surely were not in vain. An idea destined to change the course of history must have deep roots in discourses that are themselves centuries old. Or, as Nietzsche put it in

Beyond Good and Evil: "It takes a great thought to make a cause or action great" (1886/2002, 132).

Notes

1. Instead of many, see the perspectives presented in Brah and Coombes, ed. (2000).
2. The plans on peace discussed in the following are listed by title and year of publication only, since they all were published widely and in numerous languages.

Works Cited

Anderson, Benedict. 2003. *Imagined Communities. Reflections on the Origin and Spread of Nationalism*. 2nd ed. London: Verso.

Anderson, Fred. 2000. *Crucible of War. The Seven Years' War and the Fate of the Empire in British North America, 1754–1766*. New York: Knopf.

Assmann, Aleida. 2007. *Geschichte im Gedächtnis. Von der individuellen Erfahrung zur öffentlichen Inszenierung*. Munich: Beck.

Assmann, Jan. 2011. *Cultural Memory and Early Civilization: Writing, Remembrance, and Political Imagination* [1992]. Cambridge: Cambridge University Press.

Bakhtin, Mikhail M. 1981. *The Dialogic Imagination. Four Essays*. Edited by Michael Holquist. Austin: University of Texas Press.

Bauman, Zygmunt. 2000. *Liquid Modernity*. Malden, MA: Blackwell.

Bhabha, Homi K. 1994. *The Location of Culture*. New York: Routledge.

Blanchard, Jean-Vincent. 2011. *Eminence. Cardinal Richelieu and the Rise of France*. New York: Walker & Co.

Brague, Rémi. 1992. *Europe. La voie romaine*. Paris: Gallimard.

Brah, Avtar, and Annie E. Coombes, eds. 2000. *Hybridity and Its Discontents. Politics, Science, Culture*. London: Routledge.

Braudel, Fernand. 2001. *The Mediterranean in the Ancient World*. Edited by Roselyne de Ayala and Paule Braudel, translated by Siân Reynolds. New York: Allen Lane.

Castoriadis, Cornelius. 1975. *L'institution imaginaire de la société*. Paris: Éditions du Seuil.

Dahlheim, Werner. 2013. *Die Welt zur Zeit Jesu*. Munich: Beck.

Dunn, Mary Maples. 1967. *William Penn: Politics and Conscience*. Princeton, NJ: Princeton University Press.

Erikson, Erik. 1968. *Identity, Youth, and Crisis*. New York: Norton.

Fisher, David James. 1988. *Romain Rolland and the Politics of the Intellectual Engagement*. Berkeley: University of California Press.

Frank, Mitchell Benjamin. 2001. *Romantic Painting Redefined: Nazarene Tradition and the Narratives of Romanticism*. Aldershot: Ashgate.

Glissant, Édouard. 1996. *Introduction à une poétique du divers*. Paris: Gallimard.

Greenblatt, Stephen, and Catherine Gallagher. 2001. *Practicing New Historicism*. Chicago, IL: University of Chicago Press.

Halbwachs, Maurice. 1952. *Les cadres sociaux de la mémoire*. Paris: Presses Universitaires de France.

Heater, Derek. 1992. *The Idea of European Unity*. New York: St. Martin's Press.

Heymann, Frederick G. 1965. *George of Bohemia. King of Heretics*. Princeton, NJ: Princeton University Press.

Hoock-Demarle, Marie Claire. 2013. "Der Europa-Diskurs Bertha von Suttners im Umfeld des internationalen Pazifismus der Jahrhundertwende." In *Der literarische Europa-Diskurs. Festschrift für Paul Michael Lützeler*, edited by Peter Hanenberg and Isabel Capeloa Gil, 75–84. Würzburg: Königshausen & Neumann.

Huizinga, Johann. 1957. *Erasmus and the Age of Reformation. With a Selection from the Letters of Erasmus* [1924]. Translated by F. Hopman. New York: Harper & Row.

Lützeler, Paul Michael, ed. 1994. *Hoffnung Europa. Deutsche Essays von Novalis bis Enzensberger*. Frankfurt am Main: S. Fischer.

Lützeler, Paul Michael. 1992. *Die Schriftsteller und Europa. Von der Romantik bis zur Gegenwart*. Munich: Piper.

Lützeler, Paul Michael. 1997. *Europäische Identität und Multikultur*. Tübingen: Stauffenburg.

Lützeler, Paul Michael. 2007. *Kontinentalisierung. Das Europa der Schriftsteller*. Bielefeld: Aisthesis.

Lynn, John A. 2002. *The French Wars 1667–1714. The Sun King at War*. Oxford: Osprey.

Mannheim, Karl. 1929. *Ideologie und Utopie*. Bonn: F. Cohen.

Marx, Karl, and Friedrich Engels. 1969. *Die deutsche Ideologie*. Vol. 3 of *Werke*. Berlin: Dietz.

Metzidakis, Angelo. 1994/5. "Victor Hugo and the Idea of the United States of Europe." *Nineteenth-Century French Studies* 23 (1–2): 72–84.

Morin, Edgar. 1987. *Penser l'Europe*. Paris: Gallimard.

Nietzsche, Friedrich. 1886/2002. *Beyond Good and Evil. Prelude to a Philosophy of the Future*. Edited by Rolf-Peter Horstmann and Judith Norman, translated by Judith Norman. Cambridge: Cambridge University Press.

Petit, Paul. 1976. *Pax Romana*. Berkeley: University of California Press.

Pétré-Grenouilleau, Olivier. 2001. *Saint-Simon: l'utopie ou la raison en actes*. Paris: Editions Payot.

Ricoeur, Paul. 1997. *L'idéologie et l'utopie*. Paris: Éditions du Seuil.

Rothberg, Michael. 2009. *Multidirectional Memory. Remembering the Holocaust in the Age of Decolonization*. Stanford, CA: Stanford University Press.

Said, Edward W. 1978. *Orientalism*. New York: Pantheon Books.

Said, Edward W. 1993. *Culture and Imperialism*. New York: Knopf.

Said, Edward W. 2000. *Reflections on Exile and Other Essays*. Cambridge, MA: Harvard University Press.

Saint-Gille, Anne-Marie. 2003. *La 'Paneurope': un débat d'idées dans l'entre-deux-guerres*. Paris: Presses de l'Université de Paris-Sorbonne.

Seznec, Jean Joseph. 1940. *La survivance des dieux antiques: essai sur le rôle de la tradition mythologique dans l'humanisme et dans l'art de la Renaissance*. London: Warburg Institute.

Spivak, Gayatri Chakravorty. 1990. *The Post-Colonial Critic. Interviews, Strategies, Dialogues*. New York: Routledge.

Spivak, Gayatri Chakravorty. 2012. *An Aesthetic Education in the Era of Globalization*. Cambridge, MA: Harvard University Press.

Stelling-Michaud, Sven. 1964. "Ce que Rousseau doit à l'Abbé de Saint-Pierre." In *Études sur le 'Contrat social' de Jean-Jacques Rousseau*, 35–45. Paris: Les Belles Lettres.

Terminski, Bogumil. 2011. "The Evolution of the Concept of Perpetual Peace in the History of Political-Legal Thought," *Revista Escuela de Historia* 10 (1): 277–290.

Tielker, Wilhelm. 1998. *Europa—Die Genese einer politischen Idee. Von der Antike bis zur Gegenwart*. Münster: LIT.

Vohra, Ashok. 2007. "Perpetual Peace and Just War." In *Terror, Peace, and Universalism: Essays on the Philosophy of Immanuel Kant*, edited by Bindu Puri and Heiko Sievers, 32–45. New Delhi: Oxford University Press.

Werner, Michael, and Michael Lackner. 1999. *Der ‚cultural turn' in den Humanwissenschaften*. Bad Homburg v.d.H.: Werner-Reimers-Stiftung.

Ziegenhofer-Prettenthaler, Anita. 2004. *Botschafter Europas: Richard Nikolaus Coudenhove-Kalergi und die Paneuropa-Bewegung in den zwanziger und dreißiger Jahren*. Vienna: Böhlau.

List of Contributors

Gerd Bayer is a tenured faculty member (Akademischer Oberrat & Privatdozent) in the English Department at the University of Erlangen, having held teaching positions at Canadian and American universities. The author of a book on nature in John Fowles's writing (2004) and the (co-)editor of seven books, including *Narrative Developments from Chaucer to Defoe* (2011), he has also published articles on postmodern and postcolonial literature, early modern fiction, Holocaust studies, and mockumentary film.

Nina Berman is Professor of Comparative Studies at Ohio State University. She has published widely on German orientalism and colonialism, humanitarianism, transnationalism, multiculturalism, disability in Kenya, and travel literature. Her most recent book publications are *German Literature on the Middle East: Discourses and Practices, 1000–1989* (2011) and a co-edited anthology (with Klaus Mühlhahn and Patrice Nganang), *German Colonialism Revisited: African, Asian, and Oceanic Experiences* (2014).

David Blanks is Professor of History and Political Science and head of department at Arkansas Tech. A previous faculty member and department chair at The American University in Cairo, he has written widely on world history and European-Islam exchanges. His authored and edited books include *Images of the Other: Europe and the Muslim World before 1700* (1997), *Western Views of Islam in Medieval and Early Modern Europe* (1999), and *Humanist Perspectives on Sacred Space* (2011).

Nicolas Detering (M. St. Oxford 2010, M.A. Freiburg 2011) is a Research Assistant at Freiburg University's Department of German Literature. He has edited a book on the poetry of the First World War and published a number of articles on German literature of the seventeenth and eighteenth centuries. His PhD thesis examines concepts of 'Europe' in early modern German literature.

Florian Kläger is Assistant Professor (Akademischer Oberrat & Privatdozent) of British Studies at the University of Münster, where he also co-heads a research project on constructions of Europe in British literature. He is the author of a book on Elizabethan negotiations of Irish history and has also edited books and published articles on diaspora studies, ideas of Europe in literary and historiographical writing, the contemporary novel, and Irish drama.

Paul Michael Lützeler is Rosa May Distinguished University Professor in the Humanities at Washington University, St Louis. He is the founder of Washington University's European Studies Programme and founder and chair of the *Max Kade Center for Contemporary German Literature*. The author of *Die Schriftsteller und Europa* (1992) and *Kontinentalisierung: Das Europa der Schriftsteller* (2007), Lützeler has published widely on the contributions of literary authors to the discourse on Europe.

Willy Maley is Professor of Renaissance Studies at the University of Glasgow. He is the author of *Salvaging Spenser: Colonialism, Culture and Identity* (1997) and *Nation, State and Empire in English Renaissance Literature: Shakespeare to Milton* (2003). Among his many publications are several co-edited collections on national identity, including *British Identities and English Renaissance Literature* (2002), *Shakespeare and Scotland* (2004), *Shakespeare and Wales* (2010), *This England, That Shakespeare* (2010), and *Celtic Shakespeare* (2013).

Nabil Matar is Presidential Professor in the English Department at the University of Minnesota. His most recent publications include *Henry Stubbe and the Beginnings of Islam* (2013) and *British Captives in the Mediterranean and the Atlantic, 1563–1760* (2014). He is currently working on a book about religious encounters in the Euro-Arab Mediterranean, 1598–1798. In 2011, he was chosen Scholar of the College in the College of Liberal Arts, University of Minnesota, and on 28 March 2012, he received the "Building Bridges" award at the University of Cambridge.

Ladan Niayesh is Professor of English Studies at Université Paris Diderot Paris 7. Her publications include *Aux Frontières de l'humain: figures du cannibalisme dans le théâtre anglais de la Renaissance* (2009) and the edited volume *A Knight's Legacy: Mandeville and Mandevillian Lore in Early Modern England* (2011). Her edition of *Alphonsus, King of Aragon* will appear in *Three Romances of Eastern Conquest*.

Clara Pascual-Argente is Assistant Professor of Spanish at Rhodes College, Memphis. She specializes in medieval and early modern Castilian literature and culture, with an emphasis on its relationships with other European literatures. She has published on thirteenth-century narrative poems such as the *Libro de Alexandre* and the *Poema de mio Cid*, as well as on two fifteenth-century Castilian translations from European vernaculars, Alain Chartier's *Quadrilogue invectif* and John Gower's *Confessio Amantis*.

Eliza Richter studied English and History at the University of Paderborn and the University of Sheffield with a focus on early modern history and English literature. She is a fellow of the University of Münster's *Europa-Kolleg*, which focuses on literary constructions of European identities. She is currently preparing a monograph on maritime constructions of collective identities in early modern English travel writing (1570–1642).

Goran Stanivukovic is Professor of English at Saint Mary's University, Canada, and most recently the author of *Knights in Arms: Prose Romance, Masculinity, and Eastern Mediterranean Trade in Early Modern England, 1565–1655* (2015). He has published on early modern prose fiction, the Mediterranean, Shakespeare and the drama and poetry of his contemporaries.

Index

Lightning Source UK Ltd.
Milton Keynes UK
UKHW022156060521
383286UK00005B/87